Developing Countries and Global Trade Negotiations

The Doha round of WTO negotiations commenced in November 2001 to further liberalise international trade and to specifically seek to remove trade barriers so developing countries might compete in major markets. This book analyzes the development of Doha round negotiations, the emergence of regional or bilateral trade negotiations and their implications.

Developing Countries and Global Trade Negotiations brings together an international team of leading academics and researchers to explore the main issues of the Doha round trade negotiations, such as agriculture, pharmaceuticals and services trade. In particular, it looks at how the formation of the G20 has complicated negotiations and made it harder to balance the competing interests of developed and developing countries, despite rhetorical assertion that outcomes of this Round would reflect the interests of developing countries. The authors both examine how developing countries form alliances (such as the G20) to negotiate in the WTO meetings and also explore specific issues affecting developing countries including trade in services; investment, competition policy, trade facilitation and transparency in government procurement; TRIPS and public health; and agricultural tariffs and subsidies.

Contributing to an understanding of the dynamics of trade negotiations and the future of multilateralism, this book will appeal to students and scholars in the fields of international trade, international negiotiations, IPE and International Relations.

Larry Crump is Senior Lecturer in the Department of International Business and Asian Studies, Griffith University, Australia.

S. Javed Maswood is an Associate Professor in the Department of International Business and Asian Studies at Griffith University, Australia.

Routledge Advances in International Relations and Global Politics

Developing Countries and Global Trade Negotiations

Edited by
Larry Crump
and S. Javed Maswood

Routledge
Taylor & Francis Group

LONDON AND NEW YORK

First published 2007
by Routledge
2 Park Square, Milton Park, Abingdon, Oxon OX14 4RN

Simultaneously published in the USA and Canada
by Routledge
270 Madison Ave, New York, NY 10016

*Routledge is an imprint of the Taylor & Francis Group,
an informa business*

Typeset in Sabon by
GreenGate Publishing Services, Tonbridge, Kent
Printed and bound in Great Britain by
MPG Books Ltd, Bodmin

British Library Cataloguing in Publication Data
A catalogue record for this book is available from the British Library

Library of Congress Cataloging in Publication Data
A catalog record for this book has been requested

ISBN10: 0-415-41734-1 (hbk)
ISBN10: 0-203-96283-4 (ebk)

ISBN13: 978-0-415-41734-1 (hbk)
ISBN13: 978-0-203-96283-1 (ebk)

Contents

Figures

Tables

Contributors

Kym Anderson, Lead Economist, The World Bank, Washington DC, USA.

Larry Crump, Senior Lecturer, Griffith University, Brisbane, Australia.

Peter Drahos, Professor, The Australian National University, Canberra, Australia.

Christopher Findlay, Professor, University of Adelaide, Australia.

Will Martin, Lead Economist, The World Bank, Washington DC, USA.

Javed Maswood, Associate Professor, Griffith University, Brisbane, Australia.

Pradeep S. Mehta, Secretary General, CUTS International, Jaipur, India.

Nitya Nanda, Policy Analyst, CUTS International, Jaipur, India.

John S. Odell, Professor, University of Southern California, Los Angeles, California, USA.

Alexandra Sidorenko, Research Fellow, The Australian National University, Canberra, Australia.

Introduction

Javed Maswood and Larry Crump

Developing countries have been a part of the global trade policy development process since the inception of the General Agreement on Tariffs and Trade (GATT) – Brazil and India were two of the 23 GATT founding members – although they have not played a significant role in establishing international trade policy. The United States and Europe have always played an important role in determining international trade policy although during the latter GATT years it was the Quad (Canada, the European Union, Japan and the United States) that established the treaties that were eventually signed by all GATT members. For example, GATT Director-General Peter Sutherland succeeded in bringing the Uruguay round to an end in 1993 by forcing the EU and US to reach an agreement that was basically presented to other GATT member nations for adoption.

As developing countries did not play a significant role in GATT proceedings the fundamental interests of developing countries did not receive substantial consideration during the GATT negotiation process and outcome. This realization served as a primary force for establishing the first World Trade Organization (WTO) round, the Doha Development Agenda in November 2001, as the WTO Doha round formally sought to focus on the needs and interests of developing countries. As the Doha round evolved, developing nations became more involved in these negotiations. The power of developing countries first became evident at the fifth WTO Ministerial conference held in Cancun, Mexico in September 2003. At this meeting the EU insisted that the so-called "Singapore issues" (trade facilitation, rules on investment, transparency in government procurement and competition policy – see Chapter 6) be included as a part of the Doha Development Agenda, but developing countries believed that inclusion of such issues would come with substantial costs. An impasse occurred, negotiations broke down and the meeting came to an abrupt end. Many observers interpreted events at Cancun as a fiasco and a multilateral failure, but when we look a bit deeper we see developing countries forming an alliance (often referred to as the G20 – see Chapter 2) that effectively represented their interests. Delays and disruption to negotiations are to be expected in any setting with emerging and shifting power relations.

After Cancun the power held by the Quad diminished, as other groups have evolved to provide WTO negotiations with guidance – and these groups include developing countries. For example, WTO Director-General Pascal Lamy formally suspended Doha negotiations in July 2006 after spending two days in intense negotiations with representatives of six nations: Australia, Brazil, the EU, India, Japan and the US. What role might developing countries play in global trade negotiations? What opportunities and constraints do developing countries face currently and in the future? How can developing countries utilize their strengths and manage their weaknesses to achieve their trade policy goals? This book has been written to seek answers to the many questions that are relevant to an enhanced understanding of developing countries in global trade negotiations. While the primary focus of this book is on multilateral process we give some consideration to regional and bilateral trade policy process as well.

The chapters collected together in this volume were first presented at a workshop in Brisbane sponsored by Griffith University and funded by the Griffith Asia Institute in August 2005. We are grateful to all the workshop participants and chapter authors for their timely revisions and submission to ensure that there were no lengthy delays in publication. In Chapter 1, John Odell (University of Southern California), provides a foundation for the chapters that follow by examining recent facts and forces that shape developing country involvement in multilateral trade negotiations. Odell begins by recognizing that there will be no WTO Doha agreement as long as a substantial set of governments from developing nations prefer no deal. Then Odell identifies the major opportunities and problems for developing countries within the WTO Doha round, while presenting evidence that suggests that despite their relative political weakness developing countries do have some space in which to negotiate. Odell documents the limited gains and deadlocks that exist on major issues and draws some provisional lessons including the importance of coalition formation for developing countries, framing negotiation issues so that they favor the positions of developing countries, identifying fallback positions that would be better than no deal at all and focusing on a nation's alternative to a new WTO agreement.

This analysis is followed by a chapter prepared by Javed Maswood (Griffith University) that examines the G20 in the Doha round. Informally led by Brazil and India, the G20 is a coalition of developing countries that emerged during WTO Doha negotiation. Maswood charts the development of the G20, their initial actions in Cancun and their unambiguous demand for trade liberalization in agriculture, while also arguing that multilateral rules are unfair and discriminate against the interests of developing countries. Maswood observes that the G20 has succeeded in questioning, for the first time, the duopoly of the EU and the US within the WTO system and then examines how this development has shaped WTO Doha negotiations since Cancun. Maswood concludes Chapter 2 by considering likely WTO Doha outcomes and the future of the G20.

It is only fitting that Maswood's analysis of the G20 be followed by an examination of agriculture trade policy within the Doha round. Prepared by Kym Anderson and Will Martin (The World Bank), Chapter 3 considers the extent to which various regions, and the world as a whole, could gain from multilateral trade reform over the next decade. Anderson and Martin first examine the impact of current trade barriers and agricultural subsidies and then consider possible WTO Doha round outcomes. Results suggest that moving to free global merchandise trade would boost real incomes in Sub-Saharan Africa and Southeast Asia proportionately more than in other developing countries. Real returns to farmland and unskilled labor, and real net farm incomes, would rise substantially in those developing country regions, thereby helping to reduce poverty. Anderson and Martin conclude by observing that major gains are possible if only the political will to reform protectionist policies, especially in agriculture, can be mustered.

In addition to reforming international agricultural trade policy, developing countries are also concerned about access to medicines. This, together with issues of intellectual property rights, is explored by Peter Drahos (the Australian National University) in Chapter 4. Drahos begins by providing some background on the agreement on the Trade-Related Aspects of Intellectual Property Rights (TRIPS) that came into effect in January 1995, and the Doha Declaration on the TRIPS Agreement and Public Health adopted by WTO members in November 2001. Among other things, the Doha Declaration affirmed the right of states to use, under certain conditions, patents without the permission of the patent owner. TRIPS 1995 is considered a win for the US and the pharmaceutical industry they represent, while the 2001 Doha Declaration is considered a win for developing countries. Drahos then looks at how hard-won negotiating gains can be eroded or lost in subsequent negotiations by examining bilateral and multilateral negotiations involving access to medicines. Through this analysis Drahos derives a number of lessons for developing countries such as the importance of having a strategy to actually realize a negotiation gain once this gain is achieved, and the need for a strategy to counter forum shifting by powerful losing states that seek to recapture that gain.

Christopher Findlay (University of Adelaide) and Alexandra Sidorenko (The Australian National University) focus on trade in services in Chapter 5 and argue that developing countries have considerable interest in export markets for services and that they stand to gain significantly from reform of their own services sector. Findlay and Sidorenko provide a brief overview to world trade in services and review the links between trade and development, with special attention to studies of the effects of services liberalization. They also consider the effects of restrictions on specific sectors such as banking and financial services, telecommunications and transport, and health services. Findlay and Sidorenko conclude by observing that significant gains for developing countries are associated with domestic reform of the impediments to competition and that commitments made within the WTO process have much to offer in support of such reform. However, with the Doha round suspended, attention may now shift to bilateral trade negotiations.

It was the so-called "Singapore issues" (trade facilitation, rules on investment, transparency in government procurement and competition policy) that brought the developed world into direct and open conflict with the developing world at Cancun in September 2003. Pradeep S. Mehta and Nitya Nanda (CUTS International) examine in Chapter 6 how the four Singapore issues evolved from being a WTO study program to a proposed negotiating project. They consider the strategy behind the EU push to include the Singapore issues and the reasons developing countries were adamantly opposed to their inclusion within the WTO Doha round. Then Mehta and Nanda conduct an analysis of each of the four Singapore issues from the perspective of developing countries. The chapter concludes by recognizing that the future of the Singapore issues within the WTO Doha round will largely depend upon what happens in agriculture, as liberalization of agriculture would likely see renewed demands for an agreement on some or all of the Singapore issues. However, inclusion of these issues in bilateral and regional trade agreements may gradually make these issues more acceptable to developing countries.

The final chapter takes a step back from the primary focus of this book to consider broader issues that are relevant to developing and developed countries. Prepared by Larry Crump (Griffith University), Chapter 7 examines and seeks to understand the nature of bilateral and regional trade policy negotiations, as nearly 40 percent of total global trade now occurs through such treaties. Crump begins by examining the three primary arguments against bilateral trade agreements (often called preferential trade agreements or free trade agreements) and then compares this system of bilateral and regional trade negotiations to WTO-sponsored multilateral negotiations. In so doing, we can observe how these two systems naturally interact, thus enabling us to consider how that interaction may be better designed to enhance the international trade policy system. Developed and developing countries benefit through such analysis, as higher quality international trade policy can emerge as a result.

In concluding our introduction we wish to express our gratitude to Professor Michael Wesley, Director of the Griffith Asia Institute (GAI) for his generous funding and continuing support, which made the workshop and subsequent publication of this volume possible. Meegan Thorley, Cassandra Van Wyk and Pearl Lee looked after all the administrative detail and we are grateful to them for ensuring that the workshop was properly organized and successfully managed. Robyn White did an excellent job in formatting the chapters for publication and we thank her for her efficient and cheerful service. Finally, we wish to thank Professor Iyantul Islam, Convenor of the International Political Economy Program within the GAI, for his initial financial support and for bringing us together to work on this project. Convening the workshop and editing this book has been rewarding and intellectually stimulating.

1 Growing power meets frustration in the Doha round's first four years

John S. Odell

Developing country governments obviously face a highly skewed power structure in multilateral trade negotiations, but they greatly increased their preparation, organization, and active participation after the Uruguay round (UR) and creation of the World Trade Organization (WTO) in 1995. More governments reinforced or established missions in Geneva. In 1999, during preparations for the WTO's ministerial conference in Seattle, developing countries voiced concerns and injected dozens of formal proposals into the negotiation process. This participation explosion drew in many small trading countries that had been passive or not signatories at all prior to 1994. The European Union was attempting to convince others to launch another major round of liberalizing negotiations. Seattle was a debacle, however, and some developing country ministers publicly denounced the United States and the WTO for the way they had been treated.

At their next conference in Doha, Qatar on 14 November 2001 the ministers did agree to launch a new round, the "Doha Development Agenda." They pledged to "place [developing countries'] needs and interests at the heart of the Work Programme adopted in this declaration" (WT/MIN(01)/DEC/W/1). To add credibility to their commitment, they used the expressions "least developed" countries 29 times, "developing" countries 24 times, and "LDC" 19 times (Panagariya 2002).

The work program was daunting. It encompassed no fewer than 19 technical issues, each reflecting major differences between states that would have to be bridged. In addition, the ministers adopted a separate decision on 12 implementation-related issues and a special declaration interpreting the TRIPS agreement on questions of public health, both in response to developing country demands. Ministers set themselves the deadline of 1 January 2005 for completing the round, and they set interim deadlines for steps along the way: a plan for WTO technical assistance was due by December 2001; a solution for legal problems of developing countries that lacked capacity for making medicines was to be reached by the end of 2002; modalities for agricultural commitments were to be agreed by March 2003; in services, initial requests were due by June 2002 and initial offers by March 2003; and improvements to the Dispute Settlement Understanding were to be finished by May 2003.

At the end of the planned three years, however, member states had agreed to almost nothing on the Doha agenda. Delegations and chairs of negotiating bodies had made many proposals to one another, but they missed one interim deadline after another, as some held one issue hostage until seeing greater concessions on another issue. There was significant movement from opening positions, and elements of a provisional deal were set provisionally. But after major players deadlocked over remaining key elements, the Doha round was suspended indefinitely in July 2006. Several parties expressed a preference to revive the talks, but the future was unclear. Everyone remained frustrated and the WTO's credibility as negotiating forum was widely questioned.

This chapter offers some thoughts that might help us understand recent facts and grasp forces that will shape future negotiations. The main points will be that on the one hand, WTO member states have significant opportunities to create joint gains through new agreements, as judged by many independent analysts. Many developing countries (DCs) have also improved their negotiation capacity and have shown they can influence this process to some extent if they negotiate shrewdly. As long as a substantial set of these governments prefers no deal, there will be no deal. On the other hand, the Quad countries still hold disproportionate power to shape the process and the outcome. The EU, Japan, and the US adapted slowly to the long-term power shift, especially on high-priority issues for DC governments such as agriculture, implementation of past agreements, special and differential treatment, and the so-called Singapore issues (a high defensive priority). Groups of DCs responded by refusing to make concessions demanded by the North on other issues.

The first section will summarize the round's setting, highlighting major opportunities and problems for developing countries. A second section will present evidence suggesting that despite their relative political weakness, they do have some space in which to negotiate, and that their strategy choices have made a difference. A third section will document the limited gains and deadlocks on major issues after four years, and a concluding section will draw provisional lessons from recent experience.

The negotiation setting for developing countries

Developing countries face a mix of opportunities and obstacles to achieving their goals in WTO negotiations. This setting gives low and middle income countries some space for negotiating, and that space has been growing slowly at the expense of traditional industrial states.

The pull of market opportunities

World market conditions, given present policies, offer WTO members the opportunity to create significant new joint economic gains through new WTO agreements, according to many analysts. Present policies are blocking trade that would otherwise flow in response to differences in comparative advantage. Exchanges of concessions on remaining goods tariffs and barriers to services trade would allow those differences to expand trade and improve economic efficiency in many countries. This could include substantially greater flows among developing countries and China as well as in the traditional North–South channel. Cline (2005) offers the optimistic estimate that if all world trade barriers were eliminated, developing countries would gain approximately \$200 billion a year in income, half of which would come from industrial countries removing barriers to their exports. He claims that 500 million people could be lifted out of poverty over 15 years. A World Bank simulation of a different outcome put the gains for developing countries at \$350 billion and 140 million people lifted out of poverty by 2015 (World Bank 2003: xxix).[1] Even if these figures prove exaggerated, these opportunities are pulling governments toward negotiation and encouraging them to consider compromises to achieve gains.

At the same time, all negotiated joint gains must be distributed among the parties, and within the zone of agreement, the more one player grabs the less is left for the others. If players anticipate this and believe that all others will do so too, negotiators can be expected to use distributive tactics during the process to establish the credibility of their respective commitments to claim their shares in the end.[2] When these players' demands are inconsistent with one another, they generate an impasse to be resolved or not. And in distributive bargaining especially, we would expect differences in power to set boundaries on the likely process and outcome.

The skewed power structure

Quickly we come to the most obvious obstacle to developing countries' efforts to achieve their goals, at least their distributive ones. They still face a highly skewed international distribution of power, one skewed spectacularly against the many small states. Few insiders speaking privately would quarrel with Richard Steinberg when he observes that the WTO actually makes decisions with "invisible weighted voting" (Steinberg 2002). By power I have in mind one of the two traditional meanings in political science – the presence or absence of assets that give a state the capacity to achieve influence abroad and resist influence attempts from abroad on the issue in question. Power refers here to a potential, not realized, influence, the second traditional meaning. One useful indicator for the structure most relevant for global trade negotiations is the share of world goods imports each member buys. One prominent objective of each negotiating government is to increase its country's exports. If so, the larger the import market a government commands, the more it has to offer or threaten to withhold, as a way to induce concessions from others in market access talks. This is only one indicator. Governments have other objectives, including increasing their own imports of goods and services, improving various rules such as property rights and dumping, and protecting the intangible value of the WTO as an institution. Governments have other power assets and weaknesses. In principle some governments could deploy financial or other assets to influence trade negotiations, and some small states are weakened by severe political instability. What affects state behavior most directly is the governments' perceptions of their relative alternatives to agreement in a particular situation, which can vary from this measure. But this indicator gives us one reasonable first approximation.

Table 1.1 shows that this distribution is still extremely skewed, as it always has been. Even though we are aware of this in general, looking at current data leaves a striking impression. Tables in this chapter treat the European Community as a single player because that is how it negotiates in the WTO, delegating standing authority to the European Commission to speak for the members. EC imports are defined as imports from outside the Community. By this indicator the median WTO member states are Uruguay and Zimbabwe, each buying 0.04 percent of world imports. The hierarchy consists of two superpowers (the US and the EU) at the top, followed far below by two major powers (China and Japan), then by 13 others (including five DCs) whose individual shares of world imports ranged from 1 to 4 percent each,

Table 1.1 WTO members' trade power, 2004 (shares of world merchandise imports)

Serial no.	Member nations of WTO	Share in world imports (%)	GDP in 2004 (US$ billions)
1	USA	21.95	11,750.41
2	European Communities (EU)	18.40	12,481.83
3	China	8.07	1,601.02
4	Japan	6.54	4,621.20
5	Canada	3.97	970.34
6	China, Hong Kong SAR	3.93	164.03
7	Korea, Republic of	3.23	667.38
8	Mexico	2.97	663.06
9	Chinese Taipei	2.41	307.48
10	Singapore	2.36	103.62
11	Switzerland	1.60	351.89
12	Australia	1.55	602.75
13	Malaysia	1.51	112.52
14	Turkey	1.40	312.60
15	Thailand	1.37	165.72
16	India	1.37	654.82
17	Brazil	0.95	558.42
18	South Africa	0.79	174.46
19	Norway	0.69	242.82
20	United Arab Emirates	0.68	93.08
21	Indonesia	0.66	222.04
22	Israel	0.62	1,130.03
23	Philippines	0.61	84.21
24	Romania	0.47	67.00
25	Chile	0.36	89.31
26	New Zealand	0.33	92.89
27	Argentina	0.32	144.84
28	Pakistan	0.26	81.85
29	Morocco	0.25	49.29
30	Venezuela (Bolivarian Republic of)	0.25	104.12
31	Croatia	0.24	33.01
32	Colombia	0.24	92.20
33	Bulgaria	0.21	23.80
34	Nigeria	0.20	70.73
35	Egypt	0.18	74.28
36	Tunisia	0.18	28.83
37	Bangladesh	0.17	58.75
38	Kuwait	0.17	51.62
39	Peru	0.14	66.16
40	Costa Rica	0.12	18.28
41	Sri Lanka	0.11	20.00
42	Jordan	0.11	10.71
43	Oman	0.11	24.35
44	Ecuador	0.11	29.00

Serial no.	Member nations of WTO	Share in world imports (%)	GDP in 2004 (US$ billions)
45	Dominican Republic	0.11	16.18
46	Guatemala	0.11	26.12
47	El Salvador	0.09	13.59
48	Qatar	0.09	26.45
49	Bahrain	0.09	10.43
50	Trinidad and Tobago	0.08	12.29
51	Angola	0.07	20.19
52	Cuba	0.07	n.a.
53	Kenya	0.07	15.09
54	Ghana	0.06	8.65
55	Honduras	0.06	7.36
56	Iceland	0.05	12.28
57	Côte d'Ivoire	0.05	15.62
58	Jamaica	0.05	8.03
59	China, Macao SAR	0.05	10.31
60	Panama	0.05	14.07
61	Uruguay	0.04	11.86
62	Zimbabwe	0.04	5.76
63	Cambodia	0.04	4.51
64	Paraguay	0.04	7.00
65	TFYR of Macedonia	0.04	4.94
66	Mauritius	0.04	5.92
67	Senegal	0.04	7.44
68	Botswana	0.04	8.75
69	Tanzania	0.04	10.63
70	Namibia	0.04	4.64
71	Myanmar	0.03	7.73
72	Albania	0.03	7.86
73	Cameroon	0.03	14.44
74	Swaziland	0.03	1.96
75	Democratic Republic of the Congo	0.03	6.75
76	Nicaragua	0.03	4.38
77	Nepal	0.03	6.31
78	Georgia	0.03	4.45
79	Republic of Moldova	0.03	2.29
80	Bolivia	0.03	9.30
81	Mozambique	0.03	5.28
82	Papua New Guinea	0.02	3.95
83	Zambia	0.02	5.14
84	Congo	0.02	4.33
85	Uganda	0.02	7.43
86	Armenia	0.02	3.03
87	Haiti	0.02	4.78
88	Barbados	0.02	2.84
89	Gabon	0.02	6.84
90	Madagascar	0.02	4.21
91	Lesotho	0.02	1.31

Serial no.	Member nations of WTO	Share in world imports (%)	GDP in 2004 (US$ billion)
92	Fiji	0.02	1.86
93	Brunei Darussalam	0.02	5.25
94	Mali	0.02	5.03
95	Burkina Faso	0.02	5.04
96	Mongolia	0.01	1.29
97	Kyrgyz Republic	0.01	1.95
98	Togo	0.01	1.92
99	Chad	0.01	4.18
100	Suriname	0.01	1.27
101	Benin	0.01	4.05
102	Malawi	0.01	1.85
103	Guinea	0.01	3.54
104	Maldives	0.01	0.73
105	Guyana	0.01	0.78
106	Niger	0.01	3.22
107	Belize	0.01	1.05
108	Antigua and Barbuda	0.01	0.78
109	Mauritania	0.01	1.26
110	Djibouti	0.01	0.66
111	Sierra Leone	0.00	1.03
112	Rwanda	0.00	1.72
113	Grenada	0.00	0.45
114	St. Vincent and the Grenadines	0.00	0.39
115	St. Kitts and Nevis	0.00	0.40
116	Gambia	0.00	0.40
117	Burundi	0.00	0.67
118	St. Lucia	0.00	0.71
119	Central African Republic	0.00	1.36
120	Dominica	0.00	0.26
121	Solomon Islands	0.00	0.24
122	Guinea Bissau	0.00	0.27
	TOTAL SUM	94.48	

Serial no.	Non-member nations of WTO	Share in world imports (0.4%)	GDP in 2004 (US$ billion)
1	Russian Federation	1.30	571.92
2	Saudi Arabia	0.62	251.955
3	Vietnam	0.45	40.414
4	Ukraine	0.42	61.737
	TOTAL	2.84	

Sources: Imports, WTO Trade Statistics; GDP, International Monetary Fund, World Economic Outlook Database, September 2004.

Notes: Imports of the EC and world imports are after subtracting trade between EC members. Data are missing for Liechtenstein and Malta imports and Cuba GDP. Four selected non-member countries are also shown.

followed by another 43 countries that each accounted for 0.05 percent to 1.0 percent, and finally another 62 (roughly half the membership) whose world trade power ranged from tiny to imperceptible. The shares of 12 members even failed to reach 0.01 percent that year. Thus if we considered individual trade power alone – before introducing bargaining coalitions and the existence of the WTO as an institution – most DCs would have virtually no position at all from which to negotiate globally.

Over the long term, though, the trade power structure has been shifting slowly in favor of developing countries and China, at the expense of traditional industrial states. Table 1.2, upper panel, shows the shares of world imports of five groups of countries over two decades, classifying countries according to their World Bank status in 1984 and holding category membership constant. The EC figure adds new entrants when they joined, subtracting them from other rows. The 2004 column represents the EU 25. The traditional high-income countries' power, as measured by this indicator, slipped from 63 to 57 percent. The market power of DCs in the aggregate, not counting China, expanded from 24 to 30 percent of the world market. More attention has rightly fallen on China's dramatic rise in trade – so rapid that China surpassed Japan in 2004 to become the third largest importing power in the world. The lower panel of Table 1.2 uses the World Bank's 2004 classification of countries in all columns, which moves Hong Kong, Republic of Korea, Singapore, and Chinese Taipei from the developing to the high-income row. It shows how much of the DC expansion in the upper panel was due to expansion by these four countries. This gradual shift in the power structure will almost certainly continue into the long-term future.

The institutional context and the coalition option

Developing states, notwithstanding the weakness of most, do have their numbers, their legal equality, and the WTO consensus norm. In this institutional setting there is a strong norm that decisions are made by consensus, defined as the absence of expressed dissent. This norm gives the smallest member the authority, at least, to block the whole. A threat to do so from a tiny member by itself would not be highly credible, in view of the costs that could fall on that player.

But credibility increases if the member is part of a coalition of states.[3] Starting in the 1950s, developing country leaders began to form groups in an attempt to combine their weight in global negotiations. Formal regional organizations have often been justified partly

Table 1.2 Changes in trade power, 1984 to 2004

A. Using 1984 country classifications

	1984 (%)	1994 (%)	2004 (%)
Developing countries	23.69	29.20	30.12
China	1.59	3.20	8.07
Centrally planned and transition countries except China	9.93	3.87	3.76
European Community	17.95	19.48	18.40
High income countries except EC	45.27	40.77	38.29
Subtotal	98.44	96.51	98.64
Territories not classified by the World Bank	1.52	2.27	1.31
Total	99.96	98.78	99.95

B. Using 2004 country classifications

	1984 (%)	1994 (%)	2004 (%)
Developing countries	18.34	17.41	19.30
China	1.59	3.20	8.07
Centrally planned and transition countries except China	8.94	4.50	3.69
European Community	17.95	19.48	18.40
High income countries except EC	51.31	54.01	50.48
Subtotal	98.13	98.60	99.95
Territories not classified by the World Bank	1.83	0.17	0.00
Total	99.96	98.78	99.95

Source: WTO Trade statistics (1984)

Notes
The upper panel classifies countries into rows according to the World Bank list for 1984. Developing countries are defined as all except European Community, other high income, China, and other centrally planned or transition countries. The World Bank did not classify certain countries in 1984. Among those, Chinese Taipei is included here with developing countries, and Cuba, Kampuchea, Vietnam, North Korea, and former Soviet states are included with centrally planned and transition countries, or as EU members when appropriate in 2004. For comparison, the lower panel uses the World Bank's 2004 classification of countries in all columns, except that the centrally planned and transition countries are grouped together to match the upper panel, rather than scattered among the middle or low income groups.

on these grounds. Bargaining coalitions have become common in the WTO, though they vary on several dimensions. Many select members according not to geography but to a common interest in a trade sector or specific product, or a common concern about the international trade rules. Some cover a narrower scope of issues while others range more widely. Some operate for a short time and do not become institutionalized. Others develop a regular schedule of meetings, issue statements and proposals in the coalition's name, establish a website, and even a secretariat.

We could get a first impression of different groups' capacities for influence, if they stay unified, by summing the respective trade weights of the members. Table 1.3 compares the 2004 power of a diverse sample of relatively established WTO coalitions. Each has defended a common position at least on occasion. The Quad countries clearly would carry the largest sway of the groups listed if they unified behind the same position. Together the US, the EC, Japan, and Canada alone command half the trade power in the system by this measure. The four met occasionally during the UR and after, but they have also lined up on opposite sides of a variety of commercial issues, which opens space for weaker countries.

The Textile and Clothing Bureau, formed in 1984, consists of 25 developing countries that fund a secretariat in Geneva and cooperate to oppose restrictions against their exports. Australia led the formation

Table 1.3 Coalition trade power (combined shares of world merchandise imports 2004)[a]

Coalitions	Share in world imports (%)
Quad Countries (US, EC, Japan, Canada	50.86
ITCB (International Textiles and Clothing Bureau)[b]	30.05
Group of 20	18.70
Cairns Group	13.01
ASEAN (Association of South East Asian Nations) [c]	7.07
ACP (Africa, Caribbean and Pacific Countries) [c]	2.49
AFR (African Union) [d]	2.36
MERCOSUR (Southern Common Market)	1.35
LDC (Least Developed Countries) [c]	0.99

Notes
a World imports and EC imports exclude intra-EC trade.
b Includes Vietnam, a non-member of WTO; data not available for Democratic People's Republic of Korea.
c Includes some countries not members of the WTO.
d Data not available for 13 countries (non-members of WTO).

of the Cairns Group of agricultural trading countries during the UR. It consists of 18 developed and developing members, continues to meet at the ministerial level and below, and has issued joint proposals on agriculture in the Doha round. In August 2003 Brazil, a Cairns member, took the initiative to form a new Group of 20, limited to DCs including China and India, to block a joint agriculture proposal from the EU and US and offer an alternative.[4] As a result, the unified superpowers, to their consternation, did not get what they wanted in Cancún. The Association of Southeast Asian Nations (ASEAN) operated jointly during the 1980s and would carry serious weight if its members did so today. But in recent years Singapore, now a high-income country, has gone its own way through bilateral free trade agreements with New Zealand, Japan, Australia, the US, and others. Thailand has also chosen to negotiate its own network of bilateral arrangements. Thus ASEAN is much less cohesive in the WTO today.[5] Later in this chapter the African Group and the Least Developed Countries will appear briefly.

WTO membership also gives a state or coalition an additional potential distributive negotiation tactic: filing a legal complaint against an adversary under the Dispute Settlement Understanding. This tactic has been used most often to bring a respondent country to the table and influence settlement negotiations among the parties to the dispute, by worsening the respondent's alternative to settlement. But recent complaints by Brazil, India, Thailand, and others against the EU and US Generalized System of Preferences (GSP) and agricultural programs seemed partly aimed at leveraging earlier or greater concessions from Brussels and Washington in the Doha talks (Davey 2005: 25, Petersmann 2005; 127–44).

Developing country negotiation choices make a difference

This negotiating setting, then, gives developing countries tangible incentives to negotiate for improvements in the world trading system, and some legal and institutional assets to mobilize, either effectively or poorly. There is good evidence that developing countries' past choices made a difference to whether agreement was reached and the distribution of gains. What follows is a brief sampling from recent research.[6]

Coalition design

Developing countries including the least developed are now better organized and more willing to threaten to block consensus to shift the distribution of gain. Yet what results from coalition activity depends on the coalition's design and how coalition members negotiate. A coalition designer faces several choices: Will the coalition address a wide or narrow range of issues? Which countries and how many should be invited to join and how much trade power will they bring? Some leaders have favored the most inclusive possible coalition of developing countries, to unify the most voices possible and capture the legitimacy to speak for the entire developing world. The Group of 77 and the Informal Group of Developing Countries in the GATT during the 1970s and 1980s are examples. Shukla (2002) has advocated resuscitating the G77. This group has not been a significant factor in the Doha round to date, but a very large coalition of 90 DCs did hold firm against the Singapore issues, and at the Hong Kong ministerial in December 2005, coalitions representing some 110 members met for the first time and jointly demanded a date for ending farm export subsidies and other gains for development (*Bridges Daily Update,* 17 December 2005).[7]

A contrary hypothesis holds that in general, narrower issue-specific coalitions are likely to gain more for any country than coalitions spanning a wide set of issues, other things being equal. If the goal is to influence the round's final outcome by negotiating as a unit, then the group must be able to agree, during the end game, on how and how much to fall back from their opening positions, unless their counterparts should decide to accept their maximum demand. The wider the scope of issues and the greater the number and heterogeneity of members, the wider the range of specific demands the group will need to add to its wish list to hold its members' support, and the more difficult it will be to secure agreement among them to lower demands at the end. Great heterogeneity may limit a coalition's strategy of rigid adherence to its high opener and a blocking function, which may in turn open the coalition to splitting tactics by others and fragmentation, discussed below. A set of countries that have similar preferences on an issue and that all give it similar priority has higher credibility with others and better odds of holding together during the final bargaining (Hamilton and Whalley 1989).[8]

Two recent studies give examples consistent with this narrow-scope idea. Several DC coalitions worked intensively in 2001 to influence the proposed round's agenda. The Like Minded Group (LMG) was broad in scope and its 14 DC members were heterogeneous as to chief exports and levels of development. Its defining property was agreement on the principle that the Uruguay round agreements as implemented by the industrial countries had been unbalanced against DCs. The LMG, led by India, demanded changes in a wide range of those agreements as pre-conditions for engaging in any new round. This coalition's delegations invested a remarkable amount of time and energy coordinating common positions, meeting weekly in Geneva that year, yet they fragmented in the last weeks. Members dropped out until in Doha, India was left alone trying to defend against the launch of a new round. The coalition gained relatively little on its signature demand – implementation – and sustained a major loss in its eyes, the launch of a new round without prior compensation for the UR deals (Narlikar and Odell 2006).

At the same time another coalition was designed to concentrate on a single issue, the meaning of the TRIPS agreement for public health policy. Initiated by the WTO African Group in 2001, this coalition grew to 60 members including Brazil and India. They proposed that WTO ministers in Doha adopt a special declaration clarifying that nothing in the TRIPS agreement should prevent members from taking measures to protect public health. They hoped that this form of soft law would influence dispute settlement panels, should their governments be sued in Geneva. The US tried to tempt African states to accept less than they were demanding, but some members of the coalition made vigorous efforts to persuade others not to defect, and this coalition held together. The US, facing this unity in Doha, agreed to negotiate on the basis of the coalition's proposal. Despite opposition from the global pharmaceutical industry, the ministers adopted a declaration similar to the coalition's proposal, which was a significant gain over the status quo. These two cases differed on dimensions besides coalition composition, and some of the other factors are added below (Odell and Sell 2006).

Some qualifications to the narrow-scope idea may also be valid. A broad coalition need not face the disadvantages of scope and heterogeneity if its ambition is limited to drafting or blocking a specific proposal, rather than completing negotiations (Hamilton and Whalley 1989). And if issue-specific coalitions are short-lived and new ones must be formed frequently on different issues, the transaction costs can be prohibitive for many small low-income players (Narlikar 2003: 51–2, Ch. 5 and Ch. 9.2). These costs may force them to rely on larger traders among developing or developed countries or region-based groups to form and lead coalitions covering their interests. If such groups do not form and work effectively, the weakest players may feel their best option is to settle for bilateral deals with superpowers, inside or outside the WTO.

A second obvious hypothesis is that among issue-specific coalitions, those with larger combined trade power, and especially those including a Quad member, will gain more than coalitions with smaller clout. This was the logic behind Uruguay round crossover coalitions combining countries from North and South such as the Cairns Group in agriculture. Also, in intellectual property rights, India found the EC, Japan, and Canada to be allies on gaining authority for compulsory licensing (TRIPS article 31). In telecommunication services, the EC supported developing countries to oppose a US demand for cost-based pricing. Yet in the clash over the audio-visual exemption India sided with the US, and Brazil with the EC (Singh 2006). Following this model in 2001, Peru and the Philippines joined a WTO group called the Friends of Fish that included the US, Australia, New Zealand, and Norway. Their agenda item was included in the Doha declaration. Japan led a different coalition to demand tighter disciplines on anti-dumping measures. Joining were Korea, Chinese Taipei, Hong Kong China, Thailand, Brazil, Chile, Colombia, Costa Rica, Mexico, Norway, Switzerland, and Turkey (*Bridges,* 26 March 2003). This item was also added to the Doha agenda, despite strong opposition from the US delegation.

Choice of strategy and tactics

States and coalitions also must choose a strategy and tactics to follow.[9] Another plausible hypothesis in recent research is that what I call a mixed strategy will gain more for developing countries in most conditions than a strictly distributive strategy (Walton *et al.* 1994; Odell 2000: Ch. 7; Odell 2006: Ch. 1). A strictly distributive strategy is a set of tactics that are functional only for claiming value from others and defending against such claiming, when one party's goals are partly in conflict with those of others. These tactics include opening with high demands, refusing all concessions, exaggerating one's minimum needs and true priorities, manipulating information to others' disadvantage, taking others' issues hostage, worsening their alternative to agreement, making threats, and actually imposing penalties. A purely integrative strategy would be a set of tactics instrumental to the attainment of goals that are not in fundamental conflict and hence can be integrated for mutual gain to some degree. One subset of these tactics involves sharing information relatively openly to explore common problems or threats in a search for mutual gain solutions. Another well-known integrative move is proposing an exchange of concessions or fallbacks that might benefit more than one party (as opposed to demanding a concession without compensation). In WTO talks, proposing a formula for cutting all tariffs, including those of the speaker's state, can embody such an exchange of concessions. A third subset of integrative tactics involves reframing the issue space itself in a way that eases impasses.[10] Another possibility is bringing in a mediator. These are behaviors for gaining (through cooperation with others), not ways of giving up value to others.[11]

A mixed strategy combines elements from both ends of this spectrum, either in sequence – say distributive first then integrative – or simultaneously. The mixed strategy allows other delegations some gains to show their constituents, moving the deal above the others' reservation values, and hence is less likely to produce a breakdown. It may also permit discovery of ways to craft joint gains that would not be discovered if all held strictly to distributive behavior. Evidence from the Dillon and Kennedy rounds indicates that developing countries that offered concessions on their imports gained far more for their exports than passive countries (Finger 1974 and 1976). Brazil, defending itself in a bilateral dispute with the US over instant coffee in 1969, began strictly distributive and gained nothing at first, but after adding an integrative move, escaped without much damage to its trade interests (Odell 2000: Ch. 7). Likewise Mexico in NAFTA talks in the early 1990s and the 2001 WTO coalition for TRIPS and public health (Odell 2006: Chs 6 and 3) opened with distributive tactics, later mixed in some integrative moves, and captured some gains as a result. The Like Minded Group held to the strictly distributive strategy throughout 2001. The superpowers offered separate deals to members, who then achieved little as a group. Many developing countries feel too weak to turn down such lesser offers.

Strictly distributive tactics may be effective temporarily for some developing country coalitions, if the goal is only to block inferior proposals and force discussion on their own proposals. The initial G20 agriculture proposal in August 2003, while not purely distributive, was tilted strongly in favor of developing countries,[12] and had these effects in Cancún. The risks of refusing to blend in integrative tactics eventually, however, are that the coalition will gain little either because the coalition breaks down, or because it deadlocks the entire round permanently, reducing the WTO's credibility and pushing other states to seek alternatives to the WTO.

Reframing issues

Part of the negotiation process takes place at the subjective level, where partisans contend to establish the dominant subject frame in which the issues will be understood. Interests defined objectively do not account for all the variation; cognitive psychologists have shown that when the psychological frame changes, behavior also changes, including on economic issues. Thus negotiators routinely attempt to frame options under discussion and expectations about what is possible. The case of the declaration of TRIPS and public health also illustrates the possibility that a campaign to reframe an issue will increase gains for developing countries, at least in some circumstances. The agreement's original advocates had framed TRIPS as an alternative to allowing piracy of private property. Opponents beginning in 1999 attempted to reframe TRIPS using a different reference point: as a barrier to treating AIDS and other dire threats to public health. Their campaign through the mass media encouraged political pressure on US and other Northern negotiators from within their own politics toward compromise in the WTO talks. Other reframing attempts have not had as great an effect, and more research is needed to clarify the boundaries of this distributive tactic.[13]

Some movement at a glacial pace, deadlock after four years

From the beginning the Doha "development" round was troubled by an ambiguity regarding its central objectives. The apparently new emphasis on development as a goal was a classic example of using ambiguity to promote a negotiated agreement (in Doha on the agenda). One school believed that trade liberalization is always an effective means to development and the more liberalization the better. Affirming development as a goal, interpreted this way, added nothing to the traditional GATT/WTO agenda and required no special treatment for the poor. A second school believed that more trade liberalization can damage or distort existing human development, at least in some circumstances, or that undertaking it quickly in a poor country without adequate domestic institutions and preparations can produce excessive adjustment costs. For this school, gearing WTO negotiations toward "development" meant slowing liberalization, granting exceptions from obligations and preferences for the less developed, concentrating on products they export, and increasing aid from North to South. From the beginning the "push on" school and the "hold back" school fought with one another. Negotiating under the WTO umbrella rather than elsewhere gives the advantage to trade liberalization, this institution's central norm, at the expense of competing norms.

In 2002 the Director General and members established eight negotiating groups to work simultaneously on the main agenda items:

agriculture, trade and development, non-agricultural market access, WTO rules, services, dispute settlement, intellectual property rights, and trade and environment. The heavy meeting schedule meant that many small countries were unable to participate seriously in many sessions. Many could afford only one or two professional diplomats in their Geneva missions, and some 30 members had no mission in Geneva at all.

TRIPS/health, implementation and special and differential treatment

Many proposals were defined to benefit developing countries alone. Donor countries did deliver a promised increase in technical assistance to train officials of poor countries to participate at a somewhat higher level of expertise. Additionally, in August 2003 the members decided, at the request of developing countries, to authorize a waiver of Article 31(f) of the TRIPS agreement for any member that lacked sufficient medicine-manufacturing capacity to import needed medicines from any other member. This authority was not restricted to any list of diseases or set of countries, as the US had sought, but it did carry a set of procedural requirements, justified as needed to prevent diversion of low-cost medicines to more lucrative markets. Critics complained that the procedural requirements were deterring countries from using this new authority. In 2005 the General Council also decided to propose a formal amendment to the TRIPS agreement to make this waiver permanent. The amendment would take effect if ratified by member governments (*Bridges*, 7 December 2005).[14]

Many DC Geneva delegations had insisted more generally on improved implementation of earlier WTO agreements. These matters, along with agriculture, dominated the contentious 1999 talks. In Doha, however, ministers scattered implementation issues across other negotiating bodies rather than dedicating a group to them. These issues then dropped below the radar and developing countries achieved little on them. In one paragraph in their July 2004 framework agreement the members urged themselves to "redouble their efforts" and asked the Director General to consult them about implementation matters. Similar lip-service was buried at the end of the Hong Kong ministerial declaration in December 2005 (WT/GC/W/535, *Inside US Trade (IUST)*, 6 August 2004: 9, WT/MIN(05)/DEC).

DCs also had long complained that language according them special and differential treatment was loose and not enforceable on the rich countries, while obligations imposed on the poor countries were binding and legally enforceable. The ministers in Doha fulfilled one condition for DC acceptance of other agenda items by mandating that "all special and differential treatment provisions shall be reviewed with a view to strengthening them and making them more precise, effective, and operational." These issues were assigned to a negotiating group on Trade and Development.

DC delegations then submitted 88 proposals in this group. Some were specific to a particular WTO agreement; others were general. In December 2002 the chair proposed a deal that would accept 22 of the demands. But poorer countries especially from Africa did not accept, saying much of the language was non-mandatory and added little to existing rules (*Bridges,* 20 December 2002: 2–4 and 17 February 2003: 4–5). Some of the other proposals were opposed even by larger DCs, who saw them as cutting into South-South trade (*IUST,* 24 June 2005: 9).[15] These talks have been blocked in part by a consensus among Northern economists that traditional preferences as implemented have had little value for development (Hoekman 2005: 223–44).[16] Agreements have also been blocked by a divide between rich country delegations that have resisted schemes that would benefit competitive middle-income exporters, and DC delegations that have resisted any effort to introduce concepts of differentiation among developing countries (*IUST,* 15 April 2005: 19).[17] The US has argued that the emphasis should be on the talks in other groups on market access for agriculture, industrial goods, and services, where many members are willing to grant developing countries special treatment.

One item in the Doha agenda promised special attention to the needs of least developed countries. This was a response to credible demands by their large coalition, meeting separately at ministerial level for instance in Zanzibar in July 2001. In Hong Kong ministers adopted several decisions in favor of least developed countries (conditional on agreement on the rest of the Doha package). One would allow them to maintain or add new measures inconsistent with the Trade-Related Investment agreement, until 2020. The most notable was a decision that all developed members, joined by any developing members who felt able, will grant duty-free and quota-free access to their markets for LDC exports in 97 percent of tariff categories – a major demand of this group. It had also been agreed that the least developed could be exempt from new obligations of their own to liberalize in agricultural and services trade, and in non-agricultural market access (NAMA) they would be obliged only to increase substantially the number of tariffs they bind.

Agriculture

Border barriers against farm exports remain far higher than those facing industrial goods, in developing as well as industrial countries. The EU, Japan, and the US spend huge sums to subsidize their farmers, something developing countries cannot match. This sector is still not integrated like others under the main WTO rules. In 2002 the US took a major step backward by increasing its domestic farm supports by 80 percent. The Cairns Group declared that they will not approve a final Doha deal without substantial export gains in agriculture. Many developing states attached a high priority to this general issue or a particular commodity within in it.

In August 2003 the EU and US crafted a joint proposal for greater liberalization. Immediately a new G20 coalition rejected it and advanced a rival proposal tilting the negotiation gains far more toward developing countries, and there was no convergence for months. To add credibility, Brazil and India withheld serious offers in services and took a hard line on industrial market access, explicitly linking concessions on these issues to gains in agriculture (*IUST,* 8 April 2005: 3). A different Group of 33 developing countries, led by Indonesia, also formed to advocate a right for DCs to list certain special products as exempt from liberalization, as well as a special safeguard mechanism for emergency protection against imports of any farm product.

Intense discussions in July 2004 resulted in what was called the July framework for saving the Doha talks from collapse (WT/GC/W/535, 31 July 2004). Several sections of the document merely reaffirmed their commitments to original goals and moved interim deadlines forward once again. Agriculture was the area in which they had the most news to report. Some compromises had been hammered out informally in a grouping called the Five Interested Parties (EU, US, Australia, Brazil, and India), and the results included several concessions to DCs. In 2001 the EU had agreed to negotiate toward "reductions of, with a view to phasing out, all export subsidies." This language had been silent about the pace of reduction and the number of years before it reached zero. In 2004 the EU agreed that export subsidies, now for all products and not just those of particular interest to developing countries, would be eliminated by some "credible end date," and agreed to negotiate such a date as part of the single undertaking. The end date and the schedule of reductions were left for later talks. The US will have to phase out its export credit programs in parallel.

The members affirmed their intention to negotiate some formula for reducing trade-distorting domestic support that will require members providing higher total levels of support (the EU) to cut more than those with lower levels, but they still failed to agree on the formula itself. It would cut *de minimis* programs for the first time, but an exemption was accepted for countries that allocate almost all such programs for subsistence farmers (India). Subsidizers agreed to cut trade-distorting domestic support by at least 20 percent during the first year of an eventual new agreement. At the same time the US sought and others agreed to authorize a "blue box" category to justify certain domestic supports. Soon the United States Trade Representative (USTR) was explaining to US farmers and legislators that the 20 percent cut, calculated from the higher combined bound level, would actually mean no cut at all below amounts currently paid to US farmers (*IUST*, 6 August 2004: 3).

Improvements in market access were the most difficult to come by, and the July framework left most gaps still unclosed. Delegations agreed only that subsequent talks will aim for a tiered formula that would require tariff reductions, greater cuts for higher tariffs than lower ones, and "flexibilities" for "an appropriate number" of sensitive or special products. Every member other than the least developed will make a contribution, and "substantial improvement" is to be achieved somehow on every product. Exporters also accepted the G33 demand that DCs be able to designate special products needing protection on grounds of food security, livelihood security, and development needs, as well as their demand for some safeguard mechanism.

Meanwhile several middle-income countries found that after expiry of the "peace clause," they could achieve significant results through dispute settlement without a Doha deal. Panels and the Appellate Body ruled in favor of their complaints against the US cotton program and the EC sugar program. The legal problems at issue in those cases are not confined to these commodities. Having this legal option as an alternative could only have hardened the bottom lines of Brazil and its allies in the multilateral talks.

Non-governmental organizations (NGOs) and Benin, Burkina Faso, Chad, and Mali had mounted a global campaign against subsidies for cotton in particular, demanding a special deal implemented early. In Hong Kong it was agreed that all export subsidies on cotton would be eliminated by the end of 2006, that cotton imports from least developed countries would be free of duty and quota at the beginning of the implementation period, and that domestic subsidies would be reduced faster and more than the agriculture formula would require.

In Hong Kong, the top headline was that the members settled on 2013 as the date for eliminating all other farm export subsidies, as well as discounted food aid that displaces commercial production, except for emergency situations. But regarding domestic subsidies, they remained divided over the numbers in the general formula that would determine the size of cuts in bound ceilings. In market access, they completed technical work on how to convert specific tariffs into ad valorem equivalents. But here too members continued to insist on inconsistent demands regarding the key numbers determining how much tariffs would be cut by whom, and regarding how many and which products could be exempted from the formulas.

Non-agricultural market access (NAMA)

Manufactures now account for more than two-thirds of the exports of developing countries in the aggregate, with over 40 percent of those exports now going to other developing countries. The larger traders among them are increasingly concerned about South–South as well as North–South trade. Average tariffs in rich countries are already quite low. But four months after Doha the Bush administration took a step backward here too, temporarily increasing protection against steel imports. Later, governments advanced more than 25 proposals with differing general formulas for cutting industrial barriers globally. The EU offered the least developed countries zero-duty treatment for all their exports except arms. In December 2002 Washington tabled a radical opening proposal that all members cut all duties to zero by 2015.

The July 2004 framework recorded agreements on some principles to guide a final NAMA deal, though it was vaguer than the agriculture text. Moving off its opening position, the US along with all others endorsed several principles for developing countries: less-than-full reciprocity; credit in some form for unilateral liberalizations since the Uruguay round; and special provisions for newly acceded members (like China) to credit commitments undertaken upon joining. DCs would be able to take longer periods to implement tariff cuts and have a limited option to exempt a few tariff lines from cuts. Members committed to cut industrial tariffs by applying some non-linear formula on a line-by-line basis. Tariff reductions would begin from bound rates (which for several major developing country industries could mean little immediate effect because they had already dropped their applied rates well below their bound rates), except that countries that have not bound many rates would be expected to bind many rather than apply the formula. A sectoral tariff component could be a key element.

In Hong Kong, members further agreed to adopt a so-called Swiss formula that would cut higher industrial tariffs more than lower ones. This formula would address tariff peaks and tariff escalation in developed countries, a demand of DCs for years. But they remained divided over the magnitudes of the coefficients in the formula and the treatment of exceptions that would determine how much each was obliged to liberalize.

Services

Talks on liberalizing services trade, a top priority for the Quad, lagged behind those on agriculture and industrial goods. In 2002 some 30 mostly developed and larger developing countries presented requests for new commitments to other members bilaterally and confidentially. Members were to circulate initial offers of new commitments bilaterally by 31 March 2003. Only a handful of industrial states had done so by then. Brazil later made an offer of little economic significance, saying it was holding back in protest against failure in agriculture. In 2004 members moved the deadline forward once again.

India emphasized its interest in mode 4, temporary movements of labor. But despite economists' calculations of huge potential welfare gains for developing countries from freer trade in this mode, coalition activity was almost entirely absent.[18] Undoubtedly many governments were discouraged by the strength of social resistance to immigrants inside developing countries as well as elsewhere. Hardly any of them made significant offers in mode 4, even though most would be unlikely to experience much inflow. Furthermore, India's emphasis was on exporting skilled labor, while many poor countries suffer severe shortages of skilled professionals and may fear brain drain (Winters 2005: 147–65).[19]

In 2005 developed countries promoted the idea of plurilateral request-offer talks to gain a more ambitious result in services, but developing countries resisted. In early 2006 reports indicated that little more was being accomplished on this basis, and that a Doha services deal would be limited to commitments to bind current levels of market access, rather than significant new increases in liberalization.[20]

Singapore issues and summary

The EU, supported by Japan and with less enthusiasm the US, spent years beginning in 1996 campaigning to add new issues to the WTO agenda, attempting to use the WTO to regulate more behind-the-border policies on international investment, competition, transparency in government procurement, and trade facilitation. The advocates framed these proposals as pro-development, but the World Bank's staff estimated that the proposed agreements would do little to promote development (World Bank 2003: xxv–xxvi). Many poor members were still struggling to comply with resource-intensive obligations they had accepted in the last round. They had watched the Quad add a seemingly modest item to the UR agenda and later expand it into a costly agreement on intellectual property rights, which made them suspicious of the Quad's intentions now. Large coalitions of poor countries repeatedly refused to add any Singapore issues to the already daunting agenda. After a second ministerial breakdown in Cancún the European Commission finally bowed to reality. In July 2004 developing countries, after they saw a bit more on the table for agriculture, agreed to add trade facilitation, one Singapore issue, to the agenda. The main effect of this long campaign on the round had been to inject conflict and divert work away from other issues.[21]

In summary, after four and a half years developing countries managed to keep three of the proposed Singapore issues off the agenda. On the other issues, members had settled on crucial design elements that would be needed for final deals in agriculture and NAMA, and there was movement on other issues, including a number of concessions to developing country demands.

But the members remained divided over key numbers required to seal the deal. Celso Amorim, the Brazilian foreign minister who led the G20, identified what he called the

> 'basic triangle' of trade-offs: the European Union and the G20 get the US to cut domestic farm subsidies; the G20 and the US get the EU (and to some extent India) to lower agricultural tariffs, and the US and EU get more access to the goods and services markets of the developing world.
>
> (*Financial Times*, 18 April 2006: 6)

In June 2006 Director-General Lamy floated a possible settlement revolving around the number 20: the G20 position on farm market access (an average 54 percent cut in tariffs for rich countries, falling between the most extreme demands); "Swiss 20" on NAMA (a coefficient and maximum tariff of 20 percent for developing countries); and less than $20 billion for US domestic subsidies (*Financial Times*, 29 June 2006).[22] Before a Geneva meeting at the end of June, several key negotiators said they had a few chips left in their pockets that they could play if others were willing to compromise.

Yet at that conference, the leading players still reached no settlement. Reportedly the US rejected any greater cuts in its maximum domestic subsidies and refused to fall back from demands for more ambitious increases in market access for its exports; the EU offered no new compromises; developing countries insisted on exemptions to farm market access greater than the US would accept; and Brazil and other developing countries rejected industrial tariff cuts this deep. Each blamed the others. Lamy declared, "We are now in a crisis" (WTO 2006). After three more weeks of deadlock, Lamy on 24 July 2006 suspended the Doha talks indefinitely. If they are not resumed, all the partial negotiated gains will be lost.

Conclusions

Why was the pace of this round so slow, despite the universal commitment to promote development through trade? Several underlying conditions help to explain it. First, the constant background includes several obstacles to collective action in any large international negotiation. With so many parties with diverse concerns participating, they face a huge information problem: ascertaining which technical solutions would be favorable for which parties economically and which are negotiable politically. They face the general free-rider problem and the suspicion that arises from vast inequalities of power and wealth. In the WTO in particular, the consensus rule coupled with the absence of formal mechanisms that could facilitate more efficient consensus building add to the difficulty.

Second, in this round the fundamental disagreement about what will promote development has been mentioned. Third, the superpowers demonstrated weak leadership for the first two years. The US undermined the credibility of its own commitment to liberalization by moving initially in the opposite direction in both agriculture and NAMA. The EU doggedly insisted on adding new behind-the-border regulations to the WTO regime, in the teeth of widespread opposition among members. These moves surely discouraged DC leaders from taking domestic political risks for trade liberalization until it was clear the giants were not going to kill the round themselves. This explanation may help account for the slow pace of especially the first two years. After that the superpowers changed their strategies to become more forthcoming.

Beyond these conditions, market conditions during the first three years were generating fairly impressive export growth for many countries without any new WTO deal. Table 1.4 shows the compound average growth rate over the five years from 1999 through 2004 for each member. All the 20 largest traders except the US were expanding by more than 6 percent per year. Ten of them and many smaller traders were growing at double-digit rates. Prominent leaders Brazil and India were enjoying export growth averaging 15 percent every year. Perhaps an attractive short-term alternative hardened many governments' bottom lines and reduced enthusiasm for taking political risks for any except the most valuable new WTO deal. But there is no guarantee that such growth rates will continue indefinitely under current policies.

What lessons can be drawn from this analysis provisionally, while the round stands suspended? (See Odell and Ortiz Mena 2004.)[23] One is that to claim value for themselves, developing countries need to continue forming coalitions. We saw their effects in the areas of technical assistance, TRIPS and health, and agriculture. Even the least developed, despite their tiny trade share, have won the principle that they should have special flexibility to escape new market-access disciplines. Equally, coalition members must cultivate their coalition's credibility and take steps to counter splitting tactics by their adversaries.

Developing countries are obviously a diverse lot, and selecting a heterogeneous coalition makes this challenge more difficult. Narrower coalitions designed around common preferences on a specific issue probably have a better chance of exercising influence through the final stage. Including larger traders with similar preferences will improve the odds.

As for negotiation strategy, governments and coalitions can continue to attempt to frame negotiations in public opinion by reference to principles that favor their positions and counter the campaigns of their adversaries, calling on NGOs and the media for help. But the player who seeks agreement will often want to consider shifting off purely distributive tactics and blending in some integrative tactics, at least by the final stage. To focus exclusively on defending and claiming value to the very end, waiting for the other side to blink first, risks losing whatever gains are available for harvest. Governments and coalitions need to identify possible exchanges of fallbacks that would be better than no deal for their side. They should also identify lower-priority positions, defensive as well as offensive, and prepare to trade them for concessions from others that are worth more. Of course no constituency

Table 1.4 WTO members' compound annual export growth rates, 1999–2004

Serial no	Member state	Share in world imports (%)	Growth (%)
1	USA	21.95	3.40
2	European Communities (EU)	18.40	10.36
3	China	8.07	24.94
4	Japan	6.54	6.25
5	Canada	3.97	6.19
6	China, Hong Kong SAR	3.93	8.78
7	Korea, Republic of	3.23	12.06
8	Mexico	2.97	6.70
9	Chinese Taipei	2.41	7.99
10	Singapore	2.36	9.38
11	Switzerland	1.60	8.07
12	Australia	1.55	9.07
13	Malaysia	1.51	8.42
14	Turkey	1.40	18.75
15	Thailand	1.37	10.83
16	India	1.37	15.25
17	Brazil	0.95	14.98
18	South Africa	0.79	11.45
19	Norway	0.69	12.52
20	United Arab Emirates	0.68	16.86
21	Indonesia	0.66	7.45
22	Israel	0.62	7.41
23	Philippines	0.61	1.60
24	Romania	0.47	22.60
25	Chile	0.36	13.27
26	New Zealand	0.33	10.33
27	Argentina	0.32	8.02
28	Pakistan	0.26	9.61
29	Morocco	0.25	5.57
30	Venezuela (Bolivarian Republic of)	0.25	9.21
31	Croatia	0.24	13.27
32	Colombia	0.24	6.81
33	Bulgaria	0.21	20.06
34	Nigeria	0.20	17.59
35	Egypt	0.18	16.64
36	Tunisia	0.18	10.53
37	Bangladesh	0.17	8.19
38	Kuwait	0.17	17.63
39	Peru	0.14	15.32
40	Costa Rica	0.12	−0.85
41	Sri Lanka	0.11	4.77
42	Jordan	0.11	16.73
43	Oman	0.11	14.49
44	Ecuador	0.11	11.11

Serial no	Member state	Share in world imports (%)	Growth (%)
45	Dominican Republic	0.11	1.96
46	Guatemala	0.11	3.09
47	El Salvador	0.09	5.59
48	Qatar	0.09	18.10
49	Bahrain	0.09	11.31
50	Trinidad and Tobago	0.08	17.97
51	Angola	0.07	22.87
52	Cuba	0.07	0.66
53	Kenya	0.07	8.69
54	Ghana	0.06	10.47
55	Honduras	0.06	6.03
56	Iceland	0.05	7.60
57	Côte d'Ivoire	0.05	3.37
58	Jamaica	0.05	2.24
59	China, Macao SAR	0.05	5.03
60	Panama	0.05	2.94
61	Uruguay	0.04	5.36
62	Zimbabwe	0.04	−7.91
63	Cambodia	0.04	16.81
64	Paraguay	0.04	17.02
65	TFYR of Macedonia	0.04	6.55
66	Mauritius	0.04	5.70
67	Senegal	0.04	8.30
68	Botswana	0.04	5.47
69	Tanzania	0.04	21.54
70	Namibia	0.04	8.20
71	Myanmar	0.03	21.27
72	Albania	0.03	17.05
73	Cameroon	0.03	10.44
74	Swaziland	0.03	14.20
75	Democratic Republic of the Congo	0.03	11.39
76	Nicaragua	0.03	7.18
77	Nepal	0.03	4.66
78	Georgia	0.03	22.22
79	Republic of Moldova	0.03	16.22
80	Bolivia	0.03	14.76
81	Mozambique	0.03	39.51
82	Papua New Guinea	0.02	5.04
83	Zambia	0.02	5.81
84	Congo	0.02	15.09
85	Uganda	0.02	6.32
86	Armenia	0.02	25.25
87	Haiti	0.02	1.62
88	Barbados	0.02	−3.85
89	Gabon	0.02	7.83
90	Madagascar	0.02	11.13

Serial no	Member state	Share in world imports (%)	Growth (%)
91	Lesotho	0.02	27.74
92	Fiji	0.02	2.68
93	Brunei Darussalam	0.02	12.07
94	Mali	0.02	14.83
95	Burkina Faso	0.02	8.31
96	Mongolia	0.01	13.58
97	Kyrgyz Republic	0.01	9.63
98	Togo	0.01	12.99
99	Chad	0.01	49.59
100	Suriname	0.01	15.40
101	Benin	0.01	7.29
102	Malawi	0.01	0.74
103	Guinea	0.01	0.13
104	Maldives	0.01	12.64
105	Guyana	0.01	2.85
106	Niger	0.01	8.42
107	Belize	0.01	3.20
108	Antigua and Barbuda	0.01	−1.63
109	Mauritania	0.01	−0.43
110	Djibouti	0.01	5.46
111	Sierra Leone	0.00	87.76
112	Rwanda	0.00	5.92
113	Grenada	0.00	−4.23
114	St. Vincent and the Grenadines	0.00	−5.46
115	St. Kitts and Nevis	0.00	10.91
116	Gambia	0.00	12.89
117	Burundi	0.00	−4.90
118	St. Lucia	0.00	3.65
119	Central African Republic	0.00	−4.66
120	Dominica	0.00	−5.83
121	Solomon Islands	0.00	−2.68
122	Guinea Bissau	0.00	10.76

Source: WTO Trade Statistics

Note
Rates computed by author.

believes its interests should be traded away, but without some trading, little will be gained for any constituency. Exchanges might take place within or across WTO issues. The shrewd delegation or coalition will initiate confidential discussions with others about possible exchanges, naming an acceptable price for their concession. As an illustration in this round, India, Brazil, and others could offer specified concessions on NAMA and services to the EU if the EU would make specified moves on agriculture, making the deal as ambitious or cautious as they like. Of course the EU and the US can also take the initiative in this dance. Parties can reduce the risk of discussing conditional exchanges by suggesting ideas privately to a chair serving as a mediator who will explore them with others.

Perhaps the most fundamental analytical point is to focus as clearly as possible on the country's alternative to a new WTO deal, at all times. What is our best alternative and how attractive or unattractive is it to us? Without any estimate of how well one could do without a deal, there is no way to make a confident private estimate of the negotiator's resistance point, the worst deal he or she should accept. Officials may often find it unpleasant to concentrate on their minimum – how far down they can be pushed. It is also common to feel partner countries are to blame for impasses and insist that they make the compromise. These feelings may cause negotiators to delay facing the question even when rational choice requires it.

But obviously if any government delays thinking carefully about the value of its best alternative to agreement (its benefits minus costs, intangible as well as tangible), it runs two risks. One is that it will accept a deal that is worse than no deal. The opposite is that it will accept deadlock when an available deal is actually better for the country and thus will lose gains that were available. But if such an estimate can be made even roughly, then the government can confidently accept any final WTO package that exceeds that minimum, even if the gain seems disappointing and unfair. Such estimates will necessarily have some imprecision and uncertainty. Some effects are intangible. One intangible effect of a final deadlock in a WTO round is damage to the institution's reputation and credibility, which has some value for many governments. But a careful rough estimate is better than none.

Analogously, as a member of a coalition a government will attempt to weigh the probable value of continuing to adhere to the coalition's position, against the likely value of defecting and settling for a separate deal. This decision will depend of course on what is offered to the group and to the country separately, and on the odds that the coalition will fragment in any case. Most coalitions split after the formulas to guide specific negotiations have been set, as each government concentrates on its own highest specific priorities.

Meanwhile, improving the country's outside alternative is a way both to strengthen its bargaining position inside talks and to protect the country's interests in case they fail. Many developing countries have been looking to regional and bilateral trade agreements for this purpose, especially since the WTO's train wreck in Seattle. Deals with other countries at similar levels of development are means for capturing some of the benefits of liberalization for the home economy without opening it to competition from the most advanced producers in the world. Filing complaints under the dispute settlement system may also be a way to worsen a defending country's alternative to agreement and move their negotiating position in one's favor, if the legal complaint rests on clear law and clear facts.

But some policy objectives cannot be attained without the WTO. Only a WTO deal is capable of cutting back agricultural subsidies and barriers in the Quad countries, disciplining US anti-dumping practice, opening export markets in countries outside the regional network, and restoring the WTO's credibility as a forum and a system of rules that give investors and traders certainty for the future.

These points will probably be valid in future multilateral and regional negotiations regardless of the Doha round's outcome. In any case, developing countries are now better prepared and organized than in earlier rounds, and their underlying capacity to influence trade negotiations will only continue to grow. Even though the greatest power is concentrated elsewhere, how developing countries use their capacity will also help determine the future value of the WTO as a negotiating forum and will thus be of interest to all the world's peoples.

Acknowledgments

I am grateful to several participants in these negotiations for discussing these events with me off the record, and to Rubina Verma and Rebecca Rivera for able research assistance. I am pleased to acknowledge the USC School of International Relations and the Center for International Studies for supporting my research.

Notes

1 Anderson and Martin (2005) agree that the world and developing countries would reap huge economic gains from agricultural trade liberalization. A substantial discount must be applied to any gains projections that make no allowance for adjustment costs, and any that gloss over the domestic political barriers to converting a country's net gains from trade into benefits for its most vulnerable citizens. For developing countries Charlton and Stiglitz (2005) would put the highest priorities on liberalizing certain services, industrial goods, and unskilled labor mobility.

2 In this chapter gain and loss will refer to negotiation gains, which may be different from welfare improvements. As is well known, negotiators in reciprocal trade bargaining often define concessions that will open their own markets as losses to be minimized. Here gains are defined according to the expressed values of the governments. They gain more to the extent that they receive what they are demanding, and less to the extent they give up what they say they want to keep. Distributive tactics will be defined later.

3 A coalition is defined here as a set of governments that defend a common position in a negotiation by explicit coordination. Not included in this category is a set of states that happen to act in parallel without explicit coordination, or a set of delegations that exchange information and meet to seek compromises but do not defend a common position.

4 See Chapter 2 in this book by Javed Maswood.

5 Interview with a Geneva delegate of an ASEAN state, Geneva (2002); Narlikar (2003: Ch. 8). See Chapter 7 in this book on bilateral negotiations by Larry Crump.

6 Social science knowledge of these phenomena is fairly rudimentary at present. Lacking space for a thorough review of literature, suffice it to say that most theorizing aiming to explain international negotiation – both formal and non-formal – has concentrated on bilateral interactions; little theory has been able to simplify and generalize about the far more complex multilateral and multiparty variety. For reviews see Powell (2002); Jönsson (2002: 212–34); Odell (2000, 2006 introduction); Crump and Glendon (2003). Regarding WTO coalitions, the cutting edge today comprises qualitative descriptions of experience, a few studies attempting to identify and recommend potential coalitions, and a set of hypotheses for further investigation and improvement, supported by limited case studies.

7 Celso Amorim, one of their leaders, believed that this show of unity helped achieve the agreement on a date for eliminating export subsidies. Press conference, Geneva, 30 June 2006, viewed by WTO webcast.

8 This is the earliest work on this subject to my knowledge.

9 Here *strategy* means a set of behaviors or tactics that are observable in principle and associated with a plan to achieve some objective through negotiation. This behavioral meaning differs from the meaning in earlier international cooperation research and in game theory.

10 This typology is elaborated further in Odell 2000, with mixed and integrative strategy the focus of Ch. 7. In the negotiation analysis tradition Zartman's conception of the "deductive" process for overcoming impasses has been influential (Zartman and Berman 1982). Recent empirical studies by Elms 2003), Farrell 2003) and Ives 2003) shed new light on effects of integrative tactics in trade.

11 This typology carries several caveats. It refers to only one party's behavior; it does not assume other parties will necessarily match its strategy. To describe a party's strategy is also not to make a claim about whether it succeeded; it describes an attempt. Nor does it amount to a judgment that the strategy was good or bad. The typology aims only to describe the observed negotiating behavior. Making evaluative judgments is more complex; it requires specifying the standard by which to judge and considering alternative courses of action. The same general strategy could be judged preferable in some circumstances and inferior in others.

12 'Proposal of a Framework Document', Joint Proposal by Argentina, Brazil, Bolivia, Chile, Colombia, Costa Rica, Ecuador, Guatemala, India, Mexico, Paraguay, Peru, Philippines, Thailand, and South Africa, 20 August 2003.

13 Reframing can also be part of a more integrative strategy. Negotiators, mediators, and consensus builders like WTO council chairs sometimes attempt to reframe a contentious set of issues, carving up the issue space itself along different dimensions, in an attempt to break an impasse and broker a mutual-gains deal.

14 The 2003 decision of the TRIPS Council to provide the waiver is at IP/C/W/405. See Matthews (2004) for commentary.

15 Also a telephone interview with a developed country delegate, 6 July 2005.

16 Hoekman reviews this literature.

17 Actually, DC delegations have accepted some differentiation among themselves in talks on agriculture and NAMA. And according to a secretariat leader, the opposition was strongest to any rule that would name particular countries as ineligible, in contrast to a rule that would specify a development threshold such that any country that passed it would lose eligibility (telephone interview, 6 July 2005).

18 A group of 14 middle-income states including India and China issued a joint discussion paper in July 2003 (TN/S/W/14).

19 Also see the companion paper by Alexandra Sidorenko on services.

20 Interviews with two participants, Geneva, 12 and 13 June 2006.

21 Also see Chapter 6 by Pradeep Mehta and Nitya Nanda on Singapore issues in this book. To provide descriptions of the state of play on all other Doha issues as well would make this long chapter too long.

22 Pascal Lamy, press conference, Geneva, 1 July 2006, viewed by WTO webcast.

23 See Odell and Ortiz Mena (2004) for a summary of practical lessons for developing countries from a recent set of case studies. See the website of the Economic Negotiation Network for access to much more recent research on that subject (www.usc.edu/enn).

References

Anderson, Kym and Martin, Will (2005) *Agricultural Trade Reform and the Doha Development Agenda,* World Bank Policy Research Working Paper 3607, *The World Economy,* September 2005.

Charlton, Andrew and Stiglitz, Joseph (2005) 'A development-friendly prioritisation of Doha round proposals', *The World Economy,* March, 28 (3): 293–312.

Cline, William R. (2005) 'Doha can achieve much more than skeptics expect', *Finance and Development,* 42 (1): 22–4.

Crump, Larry and Glendon, Ian A. (2003) 'Towards a Paradigm of Multiparty Negotiation', *International Negotiation,* 8: 197–234.

Davey, William J. (2005) 'The WTO dispute settlement system: the first ten years', *Journal of International Economic Law,* 8 (1): 17–50.

Elms, Deborah Kay (2003) 'When the status quo is not acceptable: resolving US bilateral trade disputes', dissertation, Department of Political Science, University of Washington.

Farrell, Henry (2003) 'Constructing the international foundations of e-commerce – the EU–US Safe Harbor Arrangement', *International Organization*, 57 (2): 277–306.

Finger, J. Michael (1974) 'GATT tariff concessions and the exports of developing countries: United States concessions at the Dillon Round', *Economic Journal*, 84 (335): 566–75.

—— (1976) 'Effects of the Kennedy Round Tariff Concessions on the exports of developing countries', *Economic Journal*, 86 (341): 87–95.

Hamilton, Colleen and Whalley, John (1989) 'Coalitions in the Uruguay Round', *Weltwirtschaftliches Archiv*, 125 (3): 547–62.

Hoekman, Bernard (2005) 'Operationalizing the concept of policy space in the WTO: beyond special and differential treatment', in Ernst-Ulrich Petersmann (ed.) *Reforming the World Trading System: Legitimacy, Efficiency, and Democratic Governance*, Oxford: Oxford University Press.

Ives, Paula Murphy (2003) 'Negotiating global change: progressive multilateralism in trade in telecommunication talks', *International Negotiation*, 8: 43–78.

Jönsson, Christer (2002) 'Diplomacy, bargaining, and negotiation', in Walter Carlsnaes, Thomas Risse and Beth Simmons (eds) *Handbook of International Relations*, Thousand Oaks, CA: Sage.

Matthews, Duncan (2004) 'WTO decision on implementation of paragraph 6 of the Doha Declaration on the TRIPS Agreement and Public Health: a solution to the access to essential medicines problem?', *Journal of International Economic Law*, 7 (1): 73–92.

Narlikar, Amrita (2003) *International Trade and Developing Countries: Coalitions in the GATT and WTO*, London: Routledge.

—— and Odell, John S. (2006) 'The strict distributive strategy for a bargaining coalition: the like minded group in the WTO', in J.S. Odell (ed.) *Negotiating Trade: Developing Countries in the WTO and NAFTA*, Cambridge: Cambridge University Press.

Odell, John S. (2000) *Negotiating the World Economy*, Ithaca, NY: Cornell University Press.

—— (ed.) (2006) *Negotiating Trade: Developing Countries in the WTO and NAFTA*, Cambridge: Cambridge University Press.

—— and Ortiz Mena, Antonio L.N. (2004) *How to Negotiate Over Trade: A Summary of New Research for Developing Countries*. Available at: <www.usc.edu/enn/>, under members, Odell or Ortiz.

—— and Sell, Susan K. (2006) 'Reframing the issue: the WTO coalition on TRIPS and Public Health, 2001', in J.S. Odell (ed.) *Negotiating Trade: Developing Countries in the WTO and NAFTA*, Cambridge: Cambridge University Press.

Panagariya, Arvind (2002) 'Developing countries at Doha: a political economy analysis', *World Economy*, 25 (9): 1205–33.

Petersmann, Ernst-Ulrich (2005) 'Strategic use of WTO dispute settlement proceedings for advancing WTO negotiations on agriculture', in E.-U. Petersmann (ed.) *Reforming the World Trading System: Legitimacy, Efficiency, and Democratic Governance,* Oxford: Oxford University Press.

Powell, Robert (2002) 'Bargaining theory and international conflict', *Annual Review of Political Science,* 5: 1–30.

Shukla, S.P. (2002) 'Correcting the WTO trajectory', *South Bulletin,* 44 (October). Available at: <www.southcentre.org/info/southbulletin>.

Singh, J.P. (2006) 'The evolution of national interests: new issues and north-south negotiations during the Uruguay Round', in J.S. Odell (ed.) *Negotiating Trade: Developing Countries in the WTO and NAFTA,* Cambridge: Cambridge University Press.

Steinberg, Richard H. (2002) 'In the shadow of law or power? Consensus-based bargaining and outcomes in the GATT/WTO', *International Organization,* 56 (2): 339–74.

Walton, Richard E., Cutcher-Gerchenfeld, Joel E. and McKersie, Robert B. (1994) *Strategic Negotiations: A Theory of Change in Labor–Management Relations,* Boston, MA: Harvard Business School Press.

Winters, L. Alan (2005) 'Developing country proposals for the liberalization of movements of natural service suppliers', in Ernst-Ulrich Petersmann (ed.) *Reforming the World Trading System: Legitimacy, Efficiency, and Democratic Governance,* Oxford: Oxford University Press.

World Bank (2003) *Global Economic Prospects 2004: Realizing the Development Promise of the Doha Agenda.*

WTO (2006) *WTO News – DDA June/July 2006 Modalities: Summary 1 July.* Available at: <www.wto.org/english/news_e/news06_e/mod06_summary_01july_e.htm>.

Zartman, I. William and Berman, Maureen R. (1982) *The Practical Negotiator,* New Haven, CT: Yale University Press.

2 Developing countries and the G20 in the Doha round

Javed Maswood

Introduction

Before the Doha Development Round (DDR) was launched in 2001 there were eight multilateral trade negotiating rounds. The general outcome in each was an example of collusion between the US and the EU, whether in terms of specific outcomes or on general principles to quarantine certain commodities from the liberalizing discipline of the General Agreement on Tariffs and Trade (GATT). The DDR, on the other hand, became a venue for North–South conflict. With a wide gap between the demands of each side and what the other was prepared to offer, deadlines to agree upon negotiating modalities on each of the key agenda items lapsed without any agreement. In September 2003, a ministerial meeting of the World Trade Organization (WTO) was convened in Cancun to review progress in the Round and, understandably enough, there was some pessimism that enough progress could be achieved at the meeting to move negotiations forward. But attempts by the EU to add the so-called Singapore issues to the agenda, against the wishes of the Group of Twenty (G20) developing countries, led to a collapse of the Cancun ministerial meeting.

This was not the first time a ministerial meeting had failed to produce an agreement. In Montreal in 1988, a mid-term ministerial meeting to review progress in the Uruguay round ended in similar disarray when a handful of Latin American countries, led by Brazil, refused to accept the terms of agreement prepared by the US and EU. The collapse of the Montreal ministerial meeting was however cleverly disguised as an adjournment and, consequently, attracted little media scrutiny. Talks resumed in Geneva and the Latin American countries buckled under intense pressure. The major source of contention was agriculture and the final agreement, the so-called Blair House Agreement, was a US and EU compact that was forced upon other contracting parties. The Uruguay round, as before, was a triumph of duopolistic control of multilateral negotiations, even considering the abolition of the Multi-Fibers Agreement (MFA).

In contrast to Montreal, Cancun could not be easily finessed. The high-profile role of the G20 meant that it was no longer possible to disguise the collapse. Cancun consequently became the first public display of developing country refusal to submit to deal-making by the big two actors of the WTO. Following the collapse of Cancun, a lengthy campaign followed to discredit the role and position of developing countries and the G20, and to force them to be more "accommodating." The collapse was blamed squarely on developing countries while developed countries presented themselves as models of conciliation, even to the point of unilateral concessions on some of the Singapore issues. Developing countries, likewise, blamed the West for not making genuine concessions on issues of interest to them, in particular agriculture. The acrimony only added to speculation that the rift spelt disaster not only for the Doha Development Round but for the newly established World Trade Organization.

One frequently made point was that developing countries, aided by some non-governmental organizations (NGOs), had been persuaded to adopt a radical posture even to the extent of being prepared to undermine global economic order. This is a misrepresentation. NGOs are easy targets for vilification, especially after Seattle, but on this charge of NGO involvement, the G20 actually had limited interactions with NGOs. During the Doha negotiations, NGOs were active in providing advice mainly to the smaller developing countries. These countries do not carry much weight in multilateral negotiations and, as an example, little is known of the G90 in the DDR, composed of the small and the least developed countries. By contrast, the G20 is familiar to all and played a crucial role in the DDR. More importantly, developing country participation in the DDR has been framed, from the start, as an attempt to reform and rebalance the unfair outcomes of the Uruguay round, not to destroy trade multilateralism. Developing countries are well aware that any descent into preferential trade agreements, not unlikely in the event of a collapse of multilateralism, would be far worse than the contemporary situation. Developing countries did not celebrate Cancun as a triumph of multilateralism; they were sobered by the obvious difficulties in reforming a system to make it fairer and more equitable.

Another criticism, following Cancun, of developing country participation in the DDR was that they opposed but did not propose in a constructive manner. The criticism had some merit but developing countries are held back by resource constraints that limit their capacity to intervene in the policy process with well-considered proposals. Most developing countries have very small missions attached to the WTO and they are easily overwhelmed by the extensiveness of the negotiating agenda. The South African mission, for example, with a staff of four is considered one of the larger developing country missions to WTO. The paucity of concrete proposals is a partial reflection of resource constraints.[1]

Developing countries, however, were unambiguous in demands that agricultural liberalization should be the core of any Doha round agreement. They were keen also to recover the lost ground of special and differential treatment, a principle that had been eroded by the Uruguay round agreements. As such, they talked of rebalancing existing inequities, not proportionate and reciprocal concessions. At Cancun, however, they were frustrated by the European Union and Japan. When trade ministers convened in Cancun the main outstanding issues were agriculture, market access (tariffs) and whether to include the Singapore issues (SI) on the agenda. Following a green-room meeting, the Singapore issues (investment, competition policy, transparency in government procurement and trade facilitation) were placed at the top of the agenda (Woolcock unpublished paper). Previously, in early May at a meeting of the Trade Negotiations Committee (TNC) of the WTO, the US had indicated that it was in agreement with the EU on the inclusion of Singapore issues on the agenda. Developing countries present at the TNC meeting did not object to this position and may have given the impression that they were prepared to negotiate. However, it later became clear that their failure to comment was consistent with the position that the Singapore issues were not "within the remit of the TNC, and that their views and comments on these and the progress at the working groups would be made at the General Council" (Raghavan 2003). At Cancun, developing countries spoke out against the Singapore issues, emphasizing that the Doha Ministerial Declaration had specifically noted that negotiations on SI would commence at Cancun only " on the basis of a decision to be taken, by explicit consensus ...."

The elevation of the Singapore issues was a spoiling strategy intended to shift focus away from agricultural liberalization. And developing countries collectively decided that it was better to walk away than to accept an unpropitious deal. While developed countries publicly declared the South uncooperative and intransigent, there also emerged a more subtle strategy to lower developing country expectations in the DDR. This reflected a realization that it had been a foolish mistake to declare Doha the Development Round, a mistake that had painted the EU and the West into a corner. The DDR promised benefits that were proving difficult to deliver and so, even in the context of multilateral trade negotiations, focus shifted to how much more important domestic policies were compared to whatever gains might be delivered by genuine liberalization through the DDR. For instance, while the World Bank estimates that agriculture and food reforms could contribute 63 percent of total welfare gains for developing countries, when this is further disaggregated, developed country policies account for 28 percent and developing country policies account for 35 percent (World Bank 2005: 133). The logical conclusion was that developing countries should concentrate on domestic policy reform rather than await a windfall from multilateral negotiations. It is certainly true that developing countries have to get policies right and many persist with measures that are a drag on their own economies (Birdsall *et al.* 2005)[2] but little is served by clouding the two issues together. Multilateral rules are unfair and discriminate against interests of developing countries, and those rules should be the focus of multilateral reform efforts. Even after that, developing countries may fail to take advantage of available opportunities with myopic or misguided policies but the prior objective must be to create a level playing field.

Inequities confronting developing countries

Until the last of the GATT negotiating rounds, developing countries were peripheral to the main agenda. They did not participate and were not expected to participate in negotiations. As a former US trade ambassador pointed out, developing countries remained on the sidelines and were not required to assume new obligations. They received all the most favored nations (MFN) concessions, which meant very little, and were not required to reciprocate (Schott 2004). That changed with the Uruguay round when they were forced to assume many new obligations in exchange for marginal benefits.

One casualty of the Uruguay round, for developing countries, was the principle of special and differential treatment (SDT), a concession they had struggled hard to achieve in the 1960s. The Generalized System of Preferences (GSP), the showpiece of special and differential treatment was approved in 1971 but apart from that, all multilateral negotiations gave developing countries special provisions. Of course, in all other aspects developing country interests were ignored and negotiations dealt mainly with industrial goods. But in the Uruguay round, all that developing countries managed to retain of SDT was an extended transition period to implement the same universally applicable outcomes. For instance, the TRIPS agreement provided uniform protection to patent holders with flexibility only in the phase-in period. Developed countries had to implement the new requirements by 1996, developing countries by 2000, and least developed countries by 2006 (extended later to 2016).

The Uruguay round Agreement was unbalanced in a range of issue areas. In textiles, for instance, liberalization of trade was required in four stages on the first day of 1995, 1998, 2002 and 2005 encompassing 16 percent, 17 percent, 18 percent and 49 percent of imports by volume against the base year of 1990. Liberalization was backended and in the first two stages only 33 percent of textiles and clothing were to be liberalized but in reality the United States liberalized only 1 percent, the EU 7 percent, and Canada 14 percent (Ryan 2005: 1).[3] It serves little purpose, however, to complain after the fact. Michalopoulos (2001: 199) writes that developing countries, in the period since the conclusion of the Uruguay round, have complained that benefits from textile liberalization had failed to materialize because the liberalization agreements were backloaded but that these complaints were pointless since "it was quite obvious at the time the agreement was signed that the benefits were to be backloaded, and that the developed countries could stay within the letter of the agreement without liberalizing meaningfully in the first few years."

Quotas were replaced with tariffs in 2005 and average tariffs tend to be very high – in the United States about 16 percent on textile and apparel products. Chinese exports not only have to cross a high tariff barrier but also growing protectionist sentiment as a result of a surge in textile exports to the US. In 2003, China had a 17 percent share of global textile markets but the following year the WTO estimated that its market share was likely to exceed 50 percent in three years (*Financial Times* 2004: 1). But a specter of protectionism hangs over the recently liberalized trade in textiles, and protectionist pressures, particularly in the US, may ultimately negate some of the benefits flowing from the abolition of export quotas.

Agriculture is a key issue for developing countries, and there are three problems: high tariffs, escalating tariffs, and domestic support and trade distorting subsidies. Average developed country tariffs are low by international standards but on agricultural commodities the tariff peaks can be very high. Moreover, tariff structures also contain an inherent bias against the export of processed grain where developing countries might be expected to significantly boost their manufacturing and developmental opportunities. Table 2.1 provides a summary of the escalating tariff rates in the main developed country markets.

The sliding-scale structure of agricultural protectionism in developed countries has been a disaster for developing countries by forcing them to specialize in exports with little processing and added value, and making it harder to move up the technology ladder. Protection levels in developed countries also tend to be low for commodities produced only in developing countries, such as coffee. This has encouraged expansion of coffee production in many more countries than in the past, resulting in oversupply and depressed prices in recent years. Export revenue and farm income have plummeted and farmers are discouraged from shifting to alternative crops because of protection structures in developed countries that will deprive them of export markets.

Quantitative restrictions have also been extensively employed by developed countries to exclude developing country exports. When agriculture first became part of multilateral negotiations in the Uruguay round, the main emphasis was on tariffication of quantitative restrictions. Negotiations, however, produced only modest reforms and if tariffication was meant to boost trade, the result was quite perverse. Tariffication resulted in a dual structure of in-quota tariffs and out-of-quota tariffs and high out-of-quota tariffs proved more restrictive than the quotas it replaced, such that there was no increase in trade in agricultural commodities. In many instances, the level of protection accorded to specific agricultural commodities in developed countries also increased as a result of the Uruguay round agreements. This happened because the bound tariff rates agreed to in the Uruguay round afforded higher protection than had existed in the base period of 1986–88. The obvious implication is that tariff rates will have to be cut substantially before there is any real improvement in market access for agriculture-exporting developed and developing countries.

Table 2.1 Tariff escalation rate in agriculture

	Raw	Intermediate	Final	Average	% of lines covered
Canada	6.3	9.6	15.2	11.2	85.5
Japan	1.6	4.0	7.5	4.7	71.8
US	4.6	10.2	16.0	10.9	84.8
EU	13.2	16.6	24.3	19.0	99.5

Source: John Nash, 'Issues and Prospects for Agricultural Trade Liberalization in Doha Development Agenda', paper presented at the World Bank, April 2003.

Subsidies are yet another nefarious feature of global agriculture trade. In absolute amounts, the bulk of OECD subsidies are provided by European and American governments and about one-third of total farm income is derived from various government programs in these countries. Globally, the rich countries spend nearly US$1 billion each day in subsidies for their farmers. In 2002, total OECD farm subsidies amounted to US$318 billion. This is about twice the total agricultural exports of developing countries. Between 2000 and 2002 average support to farmers as a percentage of gross farm receipts was less than 5 percent for Australia and New Zealand, less than 25 percent for the United States, Poland, Canada and Mexico, 35 percent for the EU, and 60 percent for Switzerland, Norway, South Korea and Japan (OECD 2003). For most OECD countries, subsidies, production and exports, are concentrated in a few product lines: meat, dairy products, cereals and sugar.

Subsidies have had a particularly damaging effect on developing countries. In 2002, the United States provided its 25,000 cotton producers US$3 billion in subsidies, an amount greater than the national income of Mali, one of the main African cotton-exporting countries. The effect of subsidies provided to farmers and of subsidized exports has been to depress commodities prices globally and it is estimated that the result has been a net income loss of US$60 billion annually for the developing countries (Orden *et al.* 2002). Cotton subsidies in the United States alone are reported to have resulted in lost revenues of US$200 million for West African countries (Watkins 2003: 13).

Theoretically, subsidies are provided to assist struggling farmers but many of the recipients are only part-time farmers. While, for instance, David Rockefeller does not need federal assistance, he received US$134,556 in subsidies in 2001 and Ted Turner received a more modest sum of US$12,925 (Dalton 2003: 17). Overall, the growth in subsidy payments to farmers has been pronounced since the 1980s, when the United States and the European Union became caught up in a subsidy war to protect traditional overseas markets and maintain exports. The subsidy war has of course damaged the commercial interests of the developing countries and Cairns Group, which do not have the financial resources to provide countervailing support to their farmers, but it has also damaged the government coffers in the US and EU. Budget constraint has forced the US and the EU to try to curb runaway expenditures on farm subsidies but in-principle agreement has not translated into agreement on specifics.

Tariff liberalization and withdrawal of subsidies can be expected to provide a major developmental boost through trade growth. A

World Bank report issued in September 2003 reported that elimination of agricultural subsidies and other protectionist measures could lift 144 million people out of poverty by 2015 and boost the income of developing countries by US$350 billion (Eccleston 2003: 13). While removal of all forms of protection is not realistically possible, the Doha Declaration included a commitment by WTO members to significantly reduce trade-distorting subsidies and barriers.[4]

Leaving aside implementation of the Uruguay round agreements, it is remarkable that developing countries agreed to the lopsided agreement of the Uruguay round in the first place. Finger and Nogues (2001) explain this in terms of lack of knowledge and information about actual realities and consequences and of clever strategies used by developed countries. In the Tokyo Round Codes, for example, developing countries could decline the obligations without losing protection of existing GATT rules but:

> The proposal to create a new organization to contain and administer the Uruguay Round agreements changed the rules of the game. The GATT/WTO heavyweights announced that as soon as the new organization existed they would withdraw from GATT. A country that voted "No" on joining the new organization would leave itself out in the cold – with neither GATT disciplines nor those of the new agreement to protect it.
>
> (Finger and Nogues 2001: 13)

The Doha round and the window of opportunity

With a history of being sidelined and ignored, developing countries had much at stake in the Doha round, not only to prevent a repeat of the unfair Uruguay round agreements but also to try to rebalance the uneven playing field. The importance of rebalancing is highlighted by the double standards embedded into the global trading regime. While not all developing countries were in favor of launching a new round so soon after completing the Uruguay round and before the Uruguay round agreements had been fully implemented, South Africa was one of the countries in favor of a new round, if only to level the playing field and remove some of the inequities. In the Uruguay round, developing countries were compelled even to agree to a new regime on intellectual property (TRIPS) without fully comprehending its long-term consequences.

The Doha round was the first time developing countries negotiated in earnest, to rebalance results of the Uruguay round and to participate in the rule-making process of the global economy. The former Director-General Mike Moore, in a speech to the Trade and Development Board of the United Nations Conference on Trade and Development (UNC-TAD) in October 1996, had observed that the post-war trading system had undergone a profound change and that institutions like the WTO were no longer simply writing the rules of interaction between separate national economies but were "writing the constitution of a single global economy..." (Raghavan n.d.). In the case of the WTO, this is easy enough to appreciate now that negotiations deal less with tariffs and border measures, and increasingly with "behind the border" issues, including regulatory structures, labor and environmental standards, intellectual property rights etc., that previously were the exclusive domain of governments of each of the "separate national economies."

It was fortunate, in that context, that a window of opportunity was opened to them. When the Doha round started, developed countries agreed to designate it the "development round" in order to overcome resistance from some developing countries to the launch of a new trade round. Developing countries did shed their resistance but put on a garb of, perhaps, inflated expectations that this round would deliver outcomes conducive to their developmental aspirations. But this was never going to be an easy task as it is always difficult to roll back subsidies and protection from sectors that have become accustomed to their privileged status. While not openly admitted, it has become obvious that developed countries regret the designation of Doha as the DDR because they never had the political will to overcome the resistance from vested groups in their society.

Regime change

Nonetheless, having secured commitment that the Doha round would address their demands, developing countries were buoyed by expectations and false hopes that the trade regime could be made more neutral in its outcomes. Regimes are incomplete institutions that gradually evolve and adapt to changing circumstances. They also embody a certain value structure that can be traced back to their hegemonic creation. As such, the process of adaptation rarely undermines embedded values and any attempt at regime change inevitably has to overcome the conservative bias. The inequities confronting developing countries in the trade regime is behind the drive to engineer reforms.

Theirs is a protest within the system rather than a protest about the system, because most developing countries also recognize the utility of operating within regime parameters. It is true that in 2003 when the Cancun ministerial meeting collapsed, some developing country trade representatives rejoiced at their new-found voice and influence but the Trade Minister of Bangladesh captured the downside for developing countries when he said, "I am really disappointed. This is the worst thing we poor countries could have done to ourselves" (*The Economist* 2003). The potential downside of Cancun was that developed countries might abandon multilateralism to pursue bilateral and regional free trade agreements that could leave developing countries out in the cold, without any protective disciplines of the WTO.

But developing countries individually lack the power and influence to push for substantive change. The only option is to form negotiating coalitions and pursue reforms through either a confrontational or a collaborationist negotiating strategy, in other words a coalition made up exclusively of members of the developing South or a broader coalition of like-minded countries across the North–South divide. The confrontational path has a long history, beginning with the UNCTAD and reaching a high point in the North–South debate of the 1970s and the demands for a new international economic order. UNCTAD was marginally successful in campaigning for the Generalized System of Preferences but the North–South debate, despite its initial promise, ended as an exercise in futility.

Failure of the South in this confrontational episode might be attributed to size and leadership issues but also to the encroachment of détente in the 1970s that made it less urgent, politically, to respond to southern demands (Bhagwati 1981: 4–5). Developing countries, with high protectionist policies, also had little to offer the Northern countries in return and as has been noted by some it is difficult to secure concessions in the absence of commensurate offers. Thus, critics of SDT, Hoekman *et al.*, argue that exempting developing countries from principles of reciprocity is the reason why they have not been able to negotiate a better deal in trade talks, that their inability to make offers has limited their capacity to demand concessions from developed countries, such that products of interest to developing countries continue to benefit from high protection in OECD countries (Hoekman *et al.* 2003).

Taking a position against confrontational politics, Sewell and Zartman identify, as more promising, the formation of negotiating alliances that cut across the North–South divide. They argue that, "Until the North–South divide can be bridged so that countries can form coalitions and associations of their real interests, progress in North–South negotiations is not likely to be great" (Sewell and Zartman 1984: 121). Whether by conscious design or coincidence, developing countries adopted a collaborationist strategy in the Uruguay round, when they decided to join together with some developed countries to form the Cairns Group and lobby for removal of developed country protectionist policies in agriculture. This was an ambitious intervention in multilateral negotiations but one that could potentially benefit a large number of developing countries as well as OECD countries that were relative fair traders, such as Australia. The Cairns Group, however, proved an abysmal failure because it decided to align itself to the initial US position of zero subsidies only to find itself left high and dry when the US and EU signed the compromise Blair House Accord.

In a formal sense, the Cairns Group has continued its free trade advocacy in the DDR but is a marginal force, at best. Its place has been taken over by the G20, whose formation marked a return to the policy of confrontation. It is composed entirely of developing countries and its strategy of open confrontation has thus far been employed with greater success, partly due to energetic leadership of the South by the G20 and by the leadership role of South Africa and Brazil within the G20. At the same time, the South is in a very different economic circumstance, compared to the 1970s, and the rapidly globalizing economies of India and China have much to offer in terms of market access to developed countries. The G20 possesses substantial economic weight and as long as it remains united in purpose and resolute in its determination, there is room for some optimism that this confrontational approach will have more success than either the collaborationist strategy of the 1980s or the confrontational approach of the 1970s.

Negotiating Doha and the formation of the G20

Despite the window of opportunity, negotiating a meaningful set of agreements proved a considerably difficult task. The Doha ministerial meeting had established target dates for agreement on modalities in each of the main issue areas, for example, end of 2002 for pharmaceuticals and March 2003 for agriculture, but all deadlines lapsed with no agreement. And as delegates headed to Cancun in September 2003, for a mid-term review of the DDR, the outlook was not very hopeful. The only bright spot was that just prior to the Cancun meeting, the United

States withdrew its objections to the pharmaceuticals package that other countries had already agreed upon.

For developing countries, the principal remaining agenda item was agriculture and they hoped to advance negotiations in each of the three components of agriculture trade: domestic subsidies, export competition, and market access. There was, however, little to suggest that the EU was prepared to offer meaningful concessions. In the lead-up to Cancun, in late July 2002, a mini-ministerial meeting, with 25 invited countries including the EU and US, was held in Montreal. It was announced that the US and EU were preparing a joint position on agriculture and this was declared as essential leadership by the big two without which there could be no forward movement. The need for leadership had been alluded to, earlier in May 2003, by the US at the Trade Negotiations Committee of the WTO. Suggestions of duopolistic leadership immediately raised suspicion among developing countries that they might again be confronted with a Blair House type agreement that had ended the Uruguay round but at considerable cost to them. Fischler, a Member of the European Commission, tried to ease suspicions by proclaiming that the EU, like developing countries, wanted a "Full House" not a "Blair House" agreement. Developing countries chose not to believe such rhetoric because it came interspersed with calls for US–EU leadership to break the stalemate.

The Blair House Agreement was grossly unjust. On paper it looked impressive: reduction of subsidies to a level that was 36 percent below the average for 1986–90, reduction of subsidized exports by 21 percent over six years, relative to the 1986–88 base period, and no extension of subsidies to new product lines. But there was no product-by-product requirement of cuts in subsidies, and compensation payments were exempt from cuts. The French government, however, still held out for a better deal and in December 1993, the EU and US agreed to substantially revise the Blair House Agreement, allowing each more subsidized exports in the transition period. Thus, the changes allowed

> the European Union to subsidize exports of an additional 8 million MT of wheat and flour, 362,000 MT of beef, and 250,000 MT of poultry above that which would have been possible under the original base-period requirement. Similarly, the United States will be able to subsidize exports of a total of 7.5 million MT of wheat and flour, 1.2 million MT of vegetable oil, and about

700,000 MT of rice more than would have been permitted under the terms of the Blair House accord.

(Schott 1994: 48).

Following the Montreal mini-ministerial meeting, the EU put forward suggestions that borrowed on the Uruguay Round formula: a 60 percent cut on trade-distorting domestic subsidies and a 36 percent tariff cut. The fear of another Blair House Agreement was instrumental in the establishment of the G20, a grouping of developing countries led by Brazil and a few of the larger developing countries. Its formation owed less to a perceived need to coordinate response than to the immediate need to block an unfavorable agreement on agriculture. The G20 represents more than half the world's population, and its economic weight, though weak in comparison to the US and EU, is not insubstantial. The US share of world trade in 2003 was about 29 percent whereas that of India, China and Brazil was a cumulative 12.6 percent and that of the entire G20 membership about 20 percent. It lobbied extensively in Cancun for greater access for agricultural commodities and received the support of Australia and the Cairns Group.

In Cancun, the G20 refused to accept a modalities agreement that was based on principles established in the Uruguay round and chose instead to walk away. Its actions shattered the comfort zone of developed countries and introduced into the WTO a real sense of multilateralism. According to Ambassador Rubens Barbosa, Brazil's Ambassador to the United States, "What the G20 really did – and this is probably the reason for such great discomfort in Brussels and Washington – was question for the first time the duopoly of the European Union and the United States in the WTO system" (Barbosa 2003).

For almost a year after Cancun, very little progress was achieved in bridging the North–South divide and countries appeared to focus their energies on negotiating bilateral agreements. The July Framework Agreement signed in August 2004, however, marked a breakthrough. The Framework Agreement established parameters for future negotiations and set out basic principles for liberalizing trade in agriculture, issues relating to special and differential treatment, services trade, non-agricultural market access, and trade facilitation. I will deal mainly with the first two.

On agriculture, the main issue of concern to developing countries, the Framework pointed to possible outcomes in each of the three areas of market access, domestic support and export competition.

On market access, it supported the principle of tiered tariff cuts such that high tariff goods will be subject to deeper tariff cuts. The goal was substantial improvement in market access but the definition of "substantial" remained unclear and, in any case, would be hard to achieve because of a decision to benchmark tariff cuts to bound tariffs (Walkenhorst and Dihel 2003: 234).[5] Bound tariffs can be much higher than applied tariffs with the result that applied tariffs might not change to any great extent, especially in developed countries.[6] This is because while average bound tariffs for developed countries are lower than those for developing countries, the former have a spread of tariffs which is seven times that of the latter. Thus, the average bound tariff for the EU is 17.4 percent but the peak bound tariff is 456.9 percent whereas the average bound tariff for Brazil is 35.5 percent and the peak bound tariff is only 55 percent. Moreover, Konandreas writes also that "the tariff profiles of the developed countries are highly skewed with many tariff lines at zero or very low single-digit levels and another set of tariff lines bound at very high level" (Konandreas 2004a: 6).

It was decided that future negotiations would define thresholds for the different tiers or bands and the type of tariff reduction in each band. The July Framework Agreement borrowed on the Harbinson formula and unless there are very large cuts in bound tariffs, there will be only marginal impact on applied tariffs and market access for developing countries. This was also pointed out by Walkenhorst and Dihel (2003: 242) who write that "reductions in bound rates do not necessarily translate into corresponding cuts in applied tariffs, but first merely squeeze out unused protection."

On domestic subsidies, the Framework Agreement called for reduction of all the main types of subsidies, classified in boxes. Blue box subsidies that deal with payments related to programs to limit production and Amber box subsidies that are to be reduced have to be cut substantially. Green box subsidies that are permitted now will require a more transparent process for categorizing payments in this category. The plan to make substantial cuts in domestic subsidies however might not amount to much as cuts were to be based on subsidies allowed under WTO rules and not the actual amounts. The US, for instance, spends only about half the permitted US$49 billion (*The Economist* 2004).

On trade-distorting subsidies, including export credits, it was agreed that there would be substantial cuts with a view to ultimate elimination of all such support mechanisms. Reductions were to be phased in over time, which meant that the EU and the US could always, as had happened with liberalization of textiles trade, use the phase-in period to continue existing practices and then undertake a "big bang" liberalization at the end of the designated period. This would effectively delay any potential benefit from the agreement to phase out subsidies.

At the same time, developed countries protected their interests by giving themselves the right to designate an "appropriate" number of commodities as "sensitive" and exempt from liberalizing discipline. In theory, developing countries were also given access to sensitive product provisions but were expected instead to favor provisions for special product designations. However, while sensitive products were to be self-designated, the designation of "special product" was to be based on a yet-to-be-determined approach that might include some objective criteria of food security etc., multilateral agreement or, indeed, self-designation. Depending on the final agreed criterion, this may make it difficult to obtain special product listing. The Framework Agreement established broad principles and modalities but the details remained to be negotiated, including the numbers of sensitive and special products for each country, the maximum permitted deviation for these products from the general tariff cut formula, and whether there was to be an equivalent level of compensation in another product area (Konandreas 2004b, 2004c). As far as the likely impact of sensitive product provisions, Kym Anderson and Will Martin estimated the potential gains and found that if only "2 percent of HS6 Agricultural tariff lines in developed countries are classified as sensitive, and are thereby subject to just a 15 percent tariff cut, the welfare gains from global agricultural reform would shrink by three-quarters" (Anderson and Martin 2005: 10–11).

It is likely that any tariff reduction formula will allow a lengthy phase-in period to facilitate structural adjustment of the affected industry. Trade related structural adjustment programs have a long history going back to the 1960s when the US introduced the Trade Related Adjustment Assistance at the start of the Kennedy round. Structural adjustment however has not been easy and instead the temptation has been to reintroduce protectionism, relying on safeguard measures, when liberalization leads to a surge in imports. A good recent example of this is the textiles agreement at the Uruguay round and the phase out of the Multi-Fibers Agreement. As mentioned above, in textiles, for instance, liberalization of trade was required in four stages on the first day of 1995, 1998, 2002 and 2005 covering 16 percent, 17 percent, 18 percent, and 49 percent of imports by volume against the base year of 1990. Liberalization was back-ended and in the absence of phased-in liberalization and structural adjustment, a surge in imports followed the removal of quantitative restrictions in 2005. Subsequent to that, governments in the US and European countries began the process of introducing safeguard protectionism, an outcome that effectively rewarded these countries for policy failures and non-compliance with the phase-in schedule at the expense of developing countries. The only country that used the phase-in period for the required structural adjustment was Australia and consequently it emerged in 2005 with an industry that was relatively resilient and able to withstand import competition. In the DDR, developing countries will have to try to ensure that they are not similarly dudded in agricultural liberalization.

On special and differential treatment (SDT) the Agreement affirmed that SDT was an integral part of WTO and supported the Doha Ministerial Directive to strengthen SDT in ways to promote development. Until then, developed countries had emphasized reciprocity rather than SDT and argued that if developing countries wanted benefits they had to offer reciprocal concessions, an approach that would diminish SDT. Whether developed countries will demonstrate a genuine willingness to strengthen SDT is uncertain but in early May 2005, the European Trade Commissioner boldly ventured that it was important to "map the way towards a world trade system that is at the same time more open and more inclusive – a system to which each country contributes according to its means and from which it receives according to its needs" (Mandelson 2005). It was odd for Peter Mandelson to resort to such Marxist phraseology and he will probably come to regret it just as others, by now, probably regret the designation of Doha as the Development Round.

Overall, the Framework Agreement had the potential to benefit developing countries. Developed country concessions included dropping three of the Singapore issues from the negotiating agenda. Assertive action by the G20 in Cancun also demonstrated that developed countries cannot easily ignore the interests of developing countries. In that sense, at least, the formation of the G20 must be regarded as a partial success.

Following the July Framework Agreement, the next main opportunity to kick-start negotiations and push the agenda towards completion was the WTO Ministerial Meeting in Hong Kong in December 2005. At this meeting, however, the European Union refused to commit itself to any specific timeline for dismantling export subsidies and instead went on the offensive, demanding more discipline on state trading entities (for example, the Australian Wheat Board) and on food aid programs (such as that of the United States). The EU also criticized the US for not offering meaningful cuts in export subsidies. The US offer to reduce the ceiling on trade-distorting subsidies to around US$23 billion was still greater than actual US subsidies of US$19.7 billion in 2005 (*The Australian* 2006: 27). The Ministerial did achieve some agreement on specifying the "bands" for tariff and subsidy cuts on agricultural trade but failed, as mentioned, to outline a timetable for these cuts to be phased in. At best, the highlight was that it had averted a repeat of Cancun without however providing a clear roadmap for future negotiations. According to Ken Heydon (2006: 12), achieving certainty in improved market access remains an "elusive goal and failure to seriously address this goal was undoubtedly Hong Kong's biggest shortcoming."

Conclusion: the "window of (lost/false) opportunity"

By mid 2006, negotiations in the Doha round had reached a point where "hard" deadlines might beat negotiators as they struggled to achieve a viable agreement. The principal hard deadline is the expiration of US Trade Promotion Authority[7] in July 2007, which essentially means that failure to achieve agreement by the end of 2006 will probably lead to a collapse of the Doha round. In mid-2006, the negotiating stalemate was not unlike the situation that confronted negotiators in the final stages of the Uruguay round. Then, as now, the main divide was between the EU and US, with each side accusing the other of hypocrisy and bad faith. The Uruguay round was salvaged at the last minute by a compromise deal between the two protagonists. The so-called Blair House Agreement also completely sidelined the Cairns Group which, like the G20, demanded aggressive liberalization of farm trade. Despite developing country expectations, Doha round negotiations were suspended indefinitely by Pascal Lamy in July 2006. The decision was a surprise but, perhaps, understandable given the gulf that separated the EU and US position on agriculture. It may even have been a calculated move to pressure the EU and the US to offer more meaningful concessions instead of accusing the other side of negotiating in bad faith.

Even if negotiations resume in 2007, the goal of reducing some of the inequities in the trading system, the basic objectives of the DDR, will have to be put off till a later occasion. The failure of the G20 to engineer substantial change will not, however, have been a result of inappropriate negotiating strategy. The G20 was not established to pursue a spoiling strategy to undermine further trade liberalization, and member countries have a genuine interest in a bargain that included significant liberalization of agricultural markets. The failure was partly a result of false expectations, unwittingly inspired by developed country negotiators, that opposition from domestic vested interest groups could be easily overcome. Managing an end to subsidies and protection is politically difficult. However, it is also true that many countries (both developing and transitional) have done precisely that and it is imperative that these hard decisions are also accepted by countries that have found it all too easy to prescribe.

It is remarkable also that the G20, despite being only a loose coalition, has held together with no major defection or fracture. The G20 is informally led by Brazil and India and while these two countries participate in the smaller FIPs (Five Interested Parties) that was crucial to the July Framework Agreement, they participate largely as representatives of the G20. Within the G20 there are disagreements between "offensive" and "defensive" liberalizers but these divisions have not undermined a basic commitment to realize outcomes that are broadly beneficial to developing countries.

The "success" to date of the G20 can be attributed to its determination to make the North–South dimension the primary focus of WTO negotiations instead of letting outcomes be subject to negotiations between the US and EU, with minimal input from a third party like the Cairns Group. Contrary to suggestions that developing countries have more to gain by forming alliances across the developmental divide, the G20 has achieved more than the Cairns Group, composed of both developed and developing countries, in the Uruguay round. Whether the G20 will survive beyond the Doha round is, however, uncertain. For the G20 to defy the weight of history, coercion and the inherent centrifugal forces within this diverse community of states will require considerable skill and determination. One advantage that the G20 possesses is that it is composed primarily of developing countries that might be called the offensive liberalizers. There are exceptions, such as India, but that makes it more likely that the G20 will be inclined to reject deal-making of the kind that happened in the Uruguay round to insist on genuine reforms. The G20 has effectively established a minimum floor that makes a Uruguay round settlement less likely. Despite being a loose coalition, the G20 has displayed an essential unity of purpose and held together as a grouping notwithstanding suggestions that internal contradictions make it unlikely that G20 will survive in its current form (*Australian Financial Review* 2003).

Notes

1 In recent years there has been considerable emphasis on providing financial and technical assistance to developing countries for capacity-building measures. For example the WTO and the World Bank, in locations in Geneva and across the world, hold short-term workshops and training sessions on various trade-related issues designed to enhance the negotiating capacity of developing country delegations. Yet, after Cancun, capacity building is not seen in an entirely positive light. Privately, some developed country delegates have linked Cancun to increased capacity. Apart from capacity, the failure of developing countries to put proposals on the negotiating table is a reflection also of lack of access points to policy-making. Despite all the high-sounding rhetoric about the democratic credentials of WTO, decision-making processes are opaque. Moreover, the practice of a few countries meeting behind closed doors, the so-called green room, to make decisions remains an entrenched feature of WTO decision-making.

2 The importance of domestic policy variables to national economic success is brought out also in a recent article by Nancy Birdsall, Dani Rodrik and Arvind Subramanian. Comparing Vietnam and Nicaragua and their differential economic performance since the 1990s, they arrive at the conclusion that the "answers are internal: history and economic and political institutions have trumped other factors in determining economic success."

3 Back-ending of trade liberalization was political expediency but has come back to haunt the US and EU. By not using the transition period to phase in cuts, they denied their own textile industries to undertake structural adjustment and prepare for the eventuality of trade liberalization. Consequently, when the back-ended reforms were finally implemented, domestic industry found itself incapable of meeting the new competition from Chinese textiles, forcing both US and EU governments to contemplate introduction of new quotas on a number of product categories as a way of providing relief to domestic industries. By contrast, Australia has not encountered the same problems because, unlike the US and EU, it lifted quotas during the 10-year phasing-in period rather than waiting until the last minute.

4 The flip side of agricultural liberalization is that the net food-importing developing countries will be worse off than before because they will have to pay higher prices for their imports.

5 A bound tariff is a tariff in respect of which there is a legal commitment not to raise it beyond that level. There can be a large gap between applied tariffs and bound tariffs but the principle of tariff binding is still considered important as a commitment not to increase applied tariffs beyond that

level. As part of the Uruguay round agreement, non-tariff barriers (NTBs) were converted into tariff equivalents (bound tariffs) and developed countries agreed to bind 99 percent of tariff lines while developing countries increased their binding of tariff lines from 22 percent to 72 percent. The practice of converting NTBs to bound tariffs was not properly administered and resulted in bound tariffs being set much higher than tariff equivalents of NTB. This led to "dirty tariffication."

6 Some developing countries are in breach of their tariff binding commitments. For instance, Thailand in 1995 had a tariff binding rate of 35 percent but its average applied tariff in 1997 was 37 percent. See http://www.ers.usda.gov/publications/aer796/aer796g.pdf.

7 The Trade Promotion Authority granted by Congress to the US Administration guarantees that any agreement reached before the expiration will be protected from any Congressional demands for amendments. This is important to American trading partners because it makes US ratification of agreement more secure, without which they may have little confidence to invest in time- and resource-intensive negotiations.

References

Anderson, K. and Martin, Will (2005) 'Agricultural trade reform and the Doha Development Agenda', paper prepared for a workshop prior to the Annual Conference of the Australian Agricultural and Resource Economics Society, Coffs Harbour, 8 February.

Australian Financial Review (2003) '"Poor nations" G22 Fall Apart', 10 October.

Barbosa, Rubens Antonio (2003) 'Why the Group of 20 was "Suddenly" Formed', Remarks made at the Cordell Hull Institute, Washington, DC, 25 November. Available at <http://www.sice.oas.org/Tunit/barbosa03_e.asp>.

Bhagwati, J.N. (1981) 'Introduction', in Jagdish N. Bhagwati, *The New International Economic Order: The North–South Debate,* Cambridge, MA: MIT Press.

Birdsall, Nancy, Rodrik, Dani and Subramanian, Arvind (2005) 'How to help the poor countries', *Foreign Affairs,* 84 (4), July/August.

Dalton, R. (2003) 'Snouts in trough for cash crop', *The Australian,* 8 September.

Eccleston, R. (2003) 'Lining up for trade talks ... and all with a barrow to push', *The Australian,* 8 September.

Financial Times (US edition) (2004) 'US textile manufacturers skeptical over China's proposed export curbs', 14 December.

Finger, J. Michael and Nogues, Julio J. (2001) 'The unbalanced Uruguay Round outcome: the new areas in future WTO negotiations', *Policy Research Working Paper 2732,* Development Research Group, The World Bank, December.

Heydon, K. (2006) 'After the WTO Hong Kong Ministerial Meeting: what is at stake?', *OECD Trade Policy Working Paper No. 27,* OECD, Paris.

Hoekman, B., Michalopoulos, Constantine and Winters, Alan L. (2003) 'More favorable and differential treatment of developing countries: toward a new approach in the WTO', World Bank Policy Research, Working Paper 3107, August.

Konandreas, P. (2004a) 'Incorporating constrained flexibility in tariff reductions: a dynamic formula', unpublished paper, 9 July.

—— (2004b) 'Implementing the special products (SPs) provision on the basis of an aggregate deviation from the general tariff cut formula', unpublished paper, 3 December.

—— (2004c) 'Implementing the sensitive products provision on the basis of an additional pro-rated TRQ commitment for non-compliance with the general tariff cut formula', unpublished paper, 3 December.

Mandelson, P. (2005) 'Towards a new map for world trade', *Financial Times*, 3 May.

Michalopoulos, C. (2001) *Developing Countries in the WTO*, Houndmills: Palgrave.

OECD (2003) 'Agricultural policies in OECD countries: monitoring and evaluation 2003', OECD.

Orden, David, Kaukab, Rashid S. and Diaz-Bonilla, Eugenio (2002) *Liberalizing Agricultural Trade and Developing Countries*, Carnegie Endowment for International Peace, Issue Brief, November.

Raghavan, C. (2003) 'US–EC to cut new "Blair House" Deal on DDA?', *TWN Africa*, 12 May. Available at <http://twnafrica.org/print.asp?twnID=315>.

—— (n,d) 'MAI not dead yet', *Third World Network*. Available at <http://www.twnside.org.sg/title/dead-cn.htm>.

Ryan, Colleen (2005) 'China threatens US in trade row', *Financial Times*, 16 May.

Schott, Jeffrey J. (1994) *The Uruguay Round: An Assessment*, Washington, DC: Institute for International Economics, November.

—— (2004) *Reviving the Doha round, Institute for International Economics*, May. Available at: <www.iie.com/publications/papers/schott0604.htm>.

Sewell, John W. and Zartman, William I. (1984) 'Global negotiations: path to the future or dead-end street?', in Jagdish N. Bhagwati and John Gerard Ruggie (eds) *Power, Passions, and Purpose: Prospects for North-South Negotiations*, Cambridge, MA: MIT Press.

The Australian (2006) 'Negotiating the obstacles to a Doha deal', 8–9 July.

The Economist (2003) 'The WTO under Fire' 20 September.

—— (2004) 'Now harvest it; World Trade', 7 August.

Walkenhorst, P. and Dihel, Nora (2003) 'Tariff bindings, unused protection and agricultural trade liberalization', *OECD Economic Studies*, No. 36, 2003/1:242.

Watkins, K. (2003) 'Reducing poverty starts with fairer farm trade', *Financial Times*, 2 June.

Woolcock, S. 'The Singapore Issues in Cancun: a failed negotiation ploy or a litmus test for global governance?', unpublished paper. Available at <www.lse.ac.us/collections/internationalTradePolicyUnit/pdf/theSingapore IssuesInCancunRev1.pdf>.

World Bank (2005) *Global Monitoring Report 2005*, Washington, DC: World Bank, Table 4.11.

3 Agricultural tariff and subsidy cuts in the Doha round[1]

Kym Anderson and Will Martin

Why all the fuss over agriculture?

Agriculture is yet again causing contention in international trade negotiations. It caused long delays to the Uruguay round in the late 1980s and 1990s, and it is again proving to be the major stumbling block in the World Trade Organization's Doha round of multilateral trade negotiations (formally known as the Doha Development Agenda, or DDA). For example, it contributed substantially to the failure of the September 2003 Trade Ministerial Meeting in Cancún to reach agreement on how to proceed with the DDA, after which it took another nine months before a consensus was reached on the Doha work program, otherwise referred to as the July Framework Agreement (WTO 2004).

It is ironic that agricultural policy is so contentious, given its small and declining importance in the global economy. The sector's share of global gross domestic product (GDP) has fallen from around one-tenth in the 1960s to little more than one-thirtieth today. In developed countries the sector accounts for only 1.8 percent of GDP and only a little more of full-time equivalent employment. Mirroring that decline, agriculture's share of global merchandise trade has more than halved over the past three decades, dropping from 22 percent to 9 percent. For developing countries its importance has fallen even more rapidly, from 42 to 11 percent (Figure 3.1).

Since policies affecting this declining sector are so politically sensitive, there are always self-interested groups suggesting it be sidelined in trade negotiations – as indeed it has been in numerous sub-global preferential trading agreements, and was in the GATT prior to the Uruguay round.[2] Today the groups with that inclination include not just farmers in the highly protecting countries and net food-importing developing countries but also those food exporters receiving preferential access to

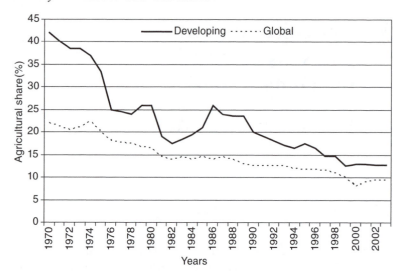

Figure 3.1 The declining share of agriculture and food in world and developing[a] countries' merchandise exports, 1970 to 2003

Source: COMTRADE data in the WITS database. Available at <www.wits.world bank.org>.

Note
Developing countries here do not include East Asia's newly industrialized economies of Hong Kong, Korea, Singapore and Taiwan.

those markets, including holders of tariff rate quotas, members of regional trading agreements, and parties to non-reciprocal preference agreements including all least-developed countries. However, sidelining agriculture in the Doha round would do a major disservice to many of the world's poorest people, namely those in farm households in developing countries. It is precisely *because* agricultural earnings are so important to a large number of developing countries that the highly protective farm policies of a few wealthy countries are being targeted by them in the WTO negotiations. Better access to rich countries' markets for their farm produce is a high priority for them.[3]

Some developing countries (DCs) have been granted greater access to developed-country markets for a selection of products under various preferential agreements. Examples are the EU's provisions for former colonies in the Africa, Caribbean and Pacific (ACP) program and more recently for least developed countries (LDCs) under the Everything But Arms (EBA) agreement. Likewise, the United States has its Africa Growth and Opportunity Act (AGOA) and Caribbean Basin Initiative (CBI). These schemes reduce demands for developed-country farm policy reform from preference-receiving countries, but they exacerbate the concerns of other countries excluded from such programs and thereby made worse off through declining terms of trade – and they may even be worsening rather than improving aggregate global and even developing country welfare.

Apart from that, many in developing countries feel they did not get a good deal out of the Uruguay round. From a mercantilistic view, the evidence seems to support that claim: Finger and Winters (2002) report that the average depth of tariff cut by developing countries was substantially greater than that agreed to by high-income countries. As well, developing countries had to take on costly commitments such as those embodied in the sanitary and phytosanitary measures (SPS) and TRIPS agreements (Finger and Schuler 2001). They therefore are determined in the Doha round that they get significantly more market access commitments from developed countries before they contemplate opening their own markets further.

Greater market access for developing countries' exporters, and especially for poor producers in those countries, is to be found in agriculture (and to a lesser extent in textiles and clothing). This can be seen from a glance at Table 3.1. It shows that developing country exporters face an average tariff (even after taking account of preferences) of 16 percent for agriculture and food, and 9 percent for textiles and clothing, compared with just 2.5 percent for other manufactures. The average tariff on agricultural goods is high not just in high-income countries but also in developing countries, suggesting even more reason why attention should focus on that sector (along with textiles) in the multilateral reform process embodied in the DDA.

If agriculture were to be ignored in the Doha negotiations, there is the risk that agricultural protection would start rising again. That is what happened throughout the course of industrial development in Europe and Northeast Asia (Anderson and Hayami 1986; Lindert 1991). It was only with the establishment of the World Trade Organization in 1995 that agricultural trade was brought under multilateral disciplines via the Uruguay Round Agreement on Agriculture (URAA).

That URAA was ambitious in scope, converting all agricultural protection to tariffs, and limiting increases in virtually all tariffs through tariff bindings. Unfortunately, the process of converting non-tariff barriers into tariffs (inelegantly termed "tariffication") provided numerous opportunities for backsliding that greatly reduced the effectiveness of the agreed disciplines (Hathaway and Ingco 1996). In

Table 3.1 Average applied import tariffs, by sector and region, 2001 (percent, ad valorem equivalent)

	Importing region		
Exporting region	High-income countries[b]	Developing countries[a]	World
Agriculture and food			
High-income countries[b]	18	18	17.8
Developing countries[a]	14	18	15.6
All countries	16	18	16.7
Textiles and wearing apparel			
High-income countries[b]	8	15	12.0
Developing countries[a]	7	20	9.3
All countries	8	17	10.2
Other manufactures			
High-income countries[b]	2	9	4.1
Developing countries[a]	1	7	2.5
All countries	1	8	3.5
All merchandise			
High-income countries[b]	3	10	5.4
Developing countries[a]	3	10	4.9
All countries	3	10	5.2

Source: Anderson, *et al.* (2006c, Table 12.2)

Notes

a These import-weighted averages incorporate tariff preferences provided to developing countries, unlike earlier versions of the GTAP database. They assume the EU is a single customs territory.

b High-income countries include the newly industrialized East Asian customs territories of Hong Kong, Korea, Singapore and Taiwan as well as Europe's transition economies that joined the EU in April 2004.

developing countries, the option for "ceiling bindings" allowed countries to set their bindings at high levels, frequently unrelated to the previously prevailing levels of protection. Hence agricultural import tariffs are still very high in both rich and poor countries, with bound rates half as high again as MFN applied rates (Table 3.2).

As well, agricultural producers in some countries are supported by export subsidies (still tolerated within the WTO only for agriculture) and by domestic support measures. Together with tariffs and other barriers to agricultural imports, these measures support farm incomes and encourage agricultural output to varying extents. The market price support component also typically raises domestic consumer prices of farm products. Figure 3.2 shows the value and the percentage of total

Table 3.2 Agricultural weighted average import tariffs, by region, 2001 (percent, ad valorem equivalent, weights based on imports)

	Bound tariff	MFN applied tariff[a]	Actual applied tariff
Developed countries	27	22	14
Developing countries	48	27	21
of which: LDCs	78	14	13
World	37	24	17

Source: Jean *et al.* (2006, Table 4.2)

Note

a Includes preferences and in-quota TRQ rates where relevant, as well as the ad valorem equivalent of specific tariffs. Developed countries include Europe's transition economies that joined the EU in April 2004. The "developing countries" definition used here is that adopted by the WTO and so includes East Asia's four newly industrialized tiger economies, which is why the 21 percent shown in column 3 is above the 18 and 14 percent shown in the first column of Table 3.1.

farm receipts from these support policy measures, called the Producer Support Estimate or PSE by the OECD secretariat.[4] For OECD members as a group, the PSE was almost the same in 2001–03 as in 1986–88, at about $240 billion per year. But because of growth in the sector, as a percentage of total farm receipts (inclusive of support) that represents a fall from 37 to 31 percent. Figure 3.2 also shows that there has been a significant increase in the proportion of that support coming from programs that are somewhat "decoupled" from current output such as payments based on area cropped, number of livestock, or some historical reference period.

Agricultural protection levels remain very high in these developed countries, especially when bearing in mind that 1986–88 was a period of historically very low international food prices and hence above-trend PSEs. And, as Figure 3.3 shows, the PSEs have fallen least in the most-protective OECD countries. By contrast, tariff protection to OECD manufacturing has fallen over the past 60 years from a level similar to that for OECD agriculture today (above 30 percent nominal rate of protection) to only one-tenth of that now. This means far more resources have been retained in agricultural production in developed countries – and hence fewer in developing countries – than would have been the case if protection had been phased down in both agriculture and manufacturing simultaneously.

Nonetheless, the achievements of the Uruguay Round Agreement on Agriculture provide some scope for optimism about what might be achieved via the WTO as part of the DDA and beyond. The current

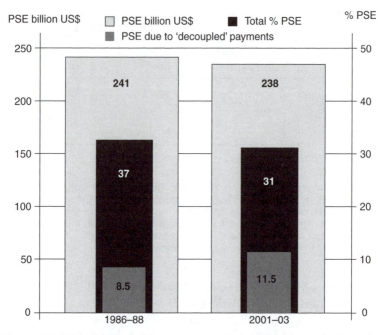

Figure 3.2 Agricultural producer support in high-income countries, by value, percent and type of support, 1986 to 2003 ($billion and percentage of total farm receipts from support policy meaures)

Source: PSE estimates from the OECD's database. Available at <www.oecd.org>.

Doha round has the advantage over the Uruguay round of beginning from the framework of rules and disciplines agreed in that previous round. In particular, it has the three clearly identified "pillars" of market access, export subsidies, and domestic support on which to focus. True, it took more than three years to agree on a framework for the current negotiations, reached at the end of July 2004 (WTO 2004), but now that July Framework Agreement is likely to guide the negotiations for some time. It therefore provides a strong basis for undertaking *ex ante* analysis of various options potentially available to WTO members during the Doha negotiations.

This chapter summarizes a recent study (Anderson and Martin 2006) that builds on numerous analyses of the Doha Development Agenda and agricultural trade, including five very helpful books that appeared in 2004. One edited by Aksoy and Beghin (2004) provides details of trends in global agricultural markets and policies, especially as they affect nine commodities of interest to developing countries.

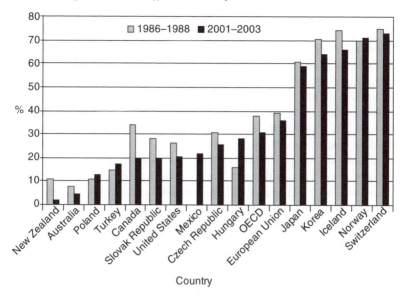

Figure 3.3 Agricultural producer support in high-income countries, by country, 1986 to 2003 (percentage of total farm receipts from support policy measures)

Source: PSE estimates from the OECD's database. Available at <www.oecd.org>.

Notes
Czech Republic, Hungary, Poland and the Slovac Republic data are for 1991–93 in the first period.
Austria, Finland and Sweden are included in the OECD average for both periods but also in the EU average for the latter period.

Another, edited by Ingco and Winters (2004), includes a wide range of analyses based on papers revised following a conference held just prior to the aborted WTO Trade Ministerial meeting in Seattle in 1999. The third, edited by Ingco and Nash (2004), provides a follow-up to the broad global perspective of the Ingco and Winters volume: it explores a wide range of key issues and options in agricultural trade reform from a developing country perspective. The fourth, edited by Anania *et al.* (2004), is a comprehensive tenth-anniversary retrospective on the Uruguay Round Agreement on Agriculture as well as a look ahead following numerous unilateral trade and subsidy reforms in developed, transition and developing economies. And the fifth focuses on implications for Latin America (Jank 2004).

All of those 2004 studies were completed well before the July Framework Agreement was reached in the early hours of 1 August 2004, and before the public release in December 2004 of the new

Version 6 database of the Global Trade Analysis Project (GTAP) at Purdue University. That Version 6 database is a major improvement over the previous version for several reasons. One is that it includes global trade and protection data as of 2001 (previously 1997). Another is that protection data are available, for the first time, on bound as well as applied tariffs, non-reciprocal as well as reciprocal tariff preferences, the ad valorem equivalents of specific tariffs (which are plentiful in the agricultural tariff schedules of many high-income, high-protection countries), and the effects of agricultural tariff rate quotas. In addition, key trade policy changes to the start of 2005 have been added for our analysis, namely, the commitments associated with accession to WTO by such economies as China and Taiwan (China), the implementation of the last of the Uruguay round commitments (most notably the abolition of quotas on trade in textiles and clothing at the end of 2004), and the eastward enlargement of the European Union from 15 to 25 members in April 2004.

Hence what distinguishes the present study from the above 2004 studies and other books with similar titles is that (a) its *ex ante* analysis focuses on the core aspects of the July Framework Agreement from the viewpoint of agriculture and developing countries, taking account also of what might happen to non-agricultural market access and the other negotiating areas, and (b) it does so in an integrated way by using the new GTAP Version 6 database (amended to account for key protection changes to early 2005) and the latest version of the World Bank's global, economy-wide Linkage model, details of which are documented in van der Mensbrugghe (2004).[5]

What questions are addressed in this study?

Among the core questions addressed in this study, following an intense program of integrated research during the latter half of 2004 by a complementary set of well-informed scholars from four continents, are the following:

- What is at stake in this Doha round, in terms of efficiency gains forgone by the various regions of the world because of current tariffs and agricultural subsidies?
- How much are each of the three "pillars" of agricultural distortions (market access, export subsidies and domestic support) contributing to those welfare losses, compared with non-agricultural trade barriers?

- How might the demands for Special and Differential Treatment for developing and least-developed countries be met without compromising the potential gains from trade expansion for those economies?
- What are the consequences, in terms of opening up to imports, of alternative formulas for cutting bound agricultural tariffs?
- In the case of products whose imports are subject to tariff rate quotas, what are the trade-offs between reducing in-quota or out-of-quota tariffs versus expanding the size of those quotas or the in-quota tariffs?
- To what extent would the erosion of tariff preferences, that necessarily accompanies MFN trade liberalization by developed countries, reduce the developing countries' interest in agricultural and other trade reform?
- What should be done about agricultural export subsidies, including those implicit in export credits, food aid, and arrangements for state trading enterprises?
- Based on recent policy changes in key countries, how might domestic farm support measures be better disciplined in the WTO?
- What are the consequences of reducing the domestic support commitments made in the Uruguay round, in terms of cuts to the actual domestic support levels currently provided to farmers?
- In particular, how might reductions in cotton subsidies help developing country farmers in West Africa and elsewhere?
- What difference does it make to expand market access for non-agricultural products at the same time as for farm goods under a Doha agreement?
- Which developing countries would have to reduce their farm output and employment as a result of such a Doha agreement?
- Taking a broad brush, and in the light of past experience and our understanding of the political economy of agricultural policies in rich and poor countries, how might reform of those policies best be progressed during the DDA negotiations?
- What would be the overall market and welfare consequences by 2015, for various countries and regions as well as globally, of the alternative Doha reform commitments considered in addressing each of the above questions?

What have we learned?

In addressing the above questions, the following are among the key messages that emerge from our study.

The potential gains from further
global trade reform are huge

Global gains from trade reform post-2004 are estimated to be large
even if dynamic gains and gains from economies of scale and
increased competition are ignored. Freeing all merchandise trade and
agricultural subsidies is estimated to boost global welfare by nearly
$300 billion per year by 2015 (Table 3.3), plus whatever productivity
effects that reform would generate.[6]

Developing countries could gain disproportionately
from further global trade reform

Welfare in the developing countries (as defined the WTO) would
increase by 1.2 percent from freeing all merchandise trade globally,
compared with an increase of just 0.6 percent for developed countries.
Developing countries (excluding the four Asian "tiger" economies)
would enjoy 30 percent of the global gain from complete liberalization of all merchandise trade, well above their one-fifth share of
global GDP. The developing countries' higher share is partly because
they have relatively high tariffs themselves (so they would reap substantial efficiency gains from reforming their own protection), and
partly because their exports are more concentrated in farm and textile
products whose tariffs in developed country markets are exceptionally
high (Table 3.1) – notwithstanding non-reciprocal tariff preferences
for many developing countries, which contribute to the losses associated with terms of trade deterioration shown in Table 3.3.

Benefits could be as much from South–South
as from South–North trade reform

Trade reform by developing countries is just as important economically to those countries as is reform by developed countries, including
from agricultural liberalization (Table 3.4). Hence choosing to delay
their own reforms or reforming less than developed countries, and
thereby holding back South–South trade growth, could reduce substantially the potential gains to developing countries.

Agriculture is where cuts are needed most

To realize that potential gain from opening up goods markets, it is in
agriculture that by far the greatest cuts in bound tariffs and subsidies

are required. This is because of the very high rates of assistance in that sector relative to other sectors. Food and agricultural policies are responsible for more than three-fifths of the global gain forgone because of merchandise trade distortions (column 1 of Table 3.4) – despite the fact that agriculture and food processing account for less than 8 percent of world trade and less than 6 percent of global GDP. From the point of view of welfare of developing countries, agriculture is at least as important as it is for the world as a whole: their gains from global agricultural liberalization represent almost two-thirds of their total potential gains, which compares with just one-quarter from textiles and clothing and one-ninth from other merchandise liberalization (columns 2 and 3 of Table 3.4).

The source of gains for developing countries varies by region, with agriculture being most important in Cairns Group countries

Most of the welfare gains for Cairns Group countries such as Australia, New Zealand, and Brazil would come from agricultural reforms, but that is also true for Sub-Saharan Africa. For more densely populated developing countries such as China and Indonesia the greatest gains would come from textiles and clothing tariff cuts, while for India it would be from reform in other manufacturing sectors (right-hand columns of Table 3.4).

Subsidy disciplines are important, but increased market access in agriculture is crucial

Extremely high applied tariffs on agricultural relative to non-farm products are the major reason for food and agricultural policies contributing 63 percent of the welfare cost of current merchandise trade distortions. Subsidies to farm production and exports are only minor additional contributors: 3 and 1 percentage points respectively, compared with 59 points due to agricultural tariffs.[7] This is even truer for developing countries than for developed ones (compare columns 1 and 2 of Table 3.5). Disciplining those domestic subsidies and phasing out export subsidies is nonetheless very important, so as to prevent re-instrumentation of assistance from tariffs to domestic subsidies and to bring agriculture into line with non-farm trade in terms of not using export subsidies.

Table 3.3 Impacts on real income from full liberalization of global merchandise trade, by country/region, 2015 (relative to the baseline, in 2001 dollars and percent)

	Total real income gain per annum ($billion)	Change in income due just to change in terms of trade ($billion)	Gain of trade effect due to improved efficiency of resource use net of terms of trade effect ($billion)	Total real gain as percentage of baseline income in 2015[a]
Australia and New Zealand	6.1	3.5	2.6	1.0 (0.4)
EU 25 plus EFTA	65.2	0.5	64.7	0.6 (0.6)
United States	16.2	10.7	6.5	0.1 (0.0)
Canada	3.8	-0.3	4.1	0.4 (0.4)
Japan	54.6	7.5	47.1	1.1 (1.0)
Korea and Taiwan	44.6	0.4	44.2	3.5 (3.5)
Hong Kong and Singapore	11.2	7.9	3.3	2.6 (0.8)
Argentina	4.9	1.2	3.7	1.2 (0.9)
Bangladesh	0.1	-1.1	1.2	0.2 (2.4)
Brazil	9.9	4.6	5.3	1.5 (0.8)
China	5.6	-8.3	13.9	0.2 (0.5)
India	3.4	-9.4	12.8	0.4 (1.5)
Indonesia	1.9	0.2	1.7	0.7 (0.7)
Thailand	7.7	0.7	7.0	3.8 (3.4)
Vietnam	3.0	-0.2	3.2	5.2 (5.5)
Russia	2.7	-2.7	5.4	0.6 (1.2)
Mexico	3.6	-3.6	7.2	0.4 (0.8)
South Africa	1.3	0.0	1.3	0.9 (0.9)
Turkey	3.3	0.2	3.1	1.3 (1.2)
Rest of South Asia	1.0	-0.8	1.8	0.5 (0.9)
Rest of East Asia	5.3	-0.9	6.2	1.9 (2.2)
Rest of LAC	10.3	0.0	10.3	1.2 (1.2)

	Total real income gain per annum ($billion)	Change in income due just to change in terms of trade ($billion)	Gain of trade effect due to improved efficiency of resource use net of terms of trade effect ($billion)	Total real gain as percentage of baseline income in 2015[a]	
Rest of ECA	1.0	-1.6	2.6	0.3	(0.8)
Middle East and North Africa	14.0	-6.4	20.4	1.2	(1.7)
Selected SSA countries	1.0	0.5	0.5	1.5	(0.8)
Rest of Sub-Saharan Africa	2.5	-2.3	4.8	1.1	(2.2)
Rest of the World	3.4	0.1	3.3	1.5	(1.5)
High-income countries	201.6	30.3	171.3	0.6	(0.5)
Developing countries	85.7	-29.7	115.4	0.8	(1.1)
Middle-income countries	69.5	-16.7	86.2	0.8	(1.0)
Low-income countries	16.2	-12.9	29.1	0.8	(1.4)
East Asia and Pacific	23.5	-8.5	32.0	0.7	(1.0)
South Asia	4.5	-11.2	15.7	0.4	(1.4)
Europe and Central Asia	7.0	-4.0	11.0	0.7	(1.1)
Sub-Saharan Africa	4.8	-1.8	6.6	1.1	(1.5)
Latin America and Caribbean	28.7	2.2	26.5	1.0	(0.9)
World total	287.3	0.6	286.7	0.7	(0.7)

Source: Authors' World Bank LINKAGE model simulations

Note

a Numbers in parentheses refer to that due to efficiency gains net of terms of trade effects. These are less than the total welfare gains where countries' benefit from favorable terms of trade effects, and more than the total gains where terms of trade effects are unfavorable.

Table 3.4 Effects on national, regional and global economic welfare of full trade liberalization in different groups of countries and sectors, 2015 (percent)

	World	All high-income countries	All developing *a* countries	Australia and New Zealand	Brazil	China	India	Indonesia	Sub-Saharan Africa
Developing a countries liberalize:									
Agriculture and food	17	9	33	24	6	137	−26	14	35
Textile and clothing	8	7	10	1	0	13	−7	5	11
Other merchandise	20	26	7	15	−2	−152	83	9	14
All sectors	45	42	50	40	4	3	50	28	60
High-income countries liberalize:									
Agriculture and food	47	54	30	73	93	−102	15	26	43
Textile and clothing	5	1	15	7	0	152	35	64	−0
Other merchandise	3	2	5	−20	3	80	0	−18	−3
All sectors	55	57	50	60	96	126	50	72	40
All countries liberalize:									
Agriculture and food	63	64	63	97	99	27	−11	40	78
Textile and clothing	14	8	25	8	0	150	28	69	11
Other merchandise	23	28	12	−5	−1	−77	83	−9	11
All sectors	100	100	100	100	100	100	100	100	100

Source: Authors' World Bank LINKAGE model simulations

Note

a High-income countries include the newly industrialized East Asian customs territories of Hong Kong, Korea, Singapore and Taiwan as well as Europe's transition economies that joined the EU in April 2004.

Table 3.5 Distribution of global welfare impacts of fully removing agricultural tariffs and subsidies, 2001 (percent)

Agricultural liberalization component	Beneficiary region:		
	High-income [a] countries	Developing countries	World
Import market access	66	27	93
Export subsidies	5	–3	2
Domestic support	4	1	5
All measures	75	25	100

Source: summarized from Hertel and Keeney (2006, Table 2.7)

Note

a High-income countries include the newly industrialized East Asian customs territories of Hong Kong, Korea, Singapore and Taiwan as well as Europe's transition economies that joined the EU in April 2004.

In developing countries the poor would gain most from multilateral trade reform

Full global merchandise trade liberalization would raise real factor returns for the poorest households most. This is implied in Table 3.6, where for developing countries the biggest factor price rise is for farm land, followed by unskilled labor. Since farmers and other low-skilled workers constitute the vast majority of the poor in developing countries, such reform would reduce both inequity and poverty.

Large cuts in domestic support commitments are needed to erase binding overhang

In turning from the potential gains from full liberalization to what might be achievable under a Doha partial reform package, the devil is going to be in the details. For example, commitments on domestic support for farmers are so much higher than actual support levels at present that the 20 percent cut in the total bound aggregate measurement of support (AMS) promised in the July Framework Agreement as an early installment will require no actual support reductions for any WTO member. Indeed a cut as huge as 75 percent for those with most domestic support is needed to get some action, and even then it would only require cuts in 2001 levels of domestic support for four WTO actors: the US (by 28 percent), the EU (by 18 percent), Norway (by 16 percent) and Australia by (10 percent) – and the EU and Australia have already introduced reforms of that

Table 3.6 Impacts of full global merchandise trade liberalization on real factor prices, 2015a (percentage change relative to the baseline in 2015)

	Unskilled wages	Skilled wages	Capital	Land owner rent	(CPI) Consumer price index
Australia and New Zealand	3.1	1.1	−0.3	17.2	1.2
EU 25 plus EFTA	0.0	1.3	0.7	−51.0	−1.3
United States	0.1	0.3	0.0	−9.2	−0.4
Canada	0.7	0.7	0.4	26.9	−0.9
Japan	1.3	2.2	1.1	−67.2	−0.1
Korea and Taiwan	6.5	7.1	3.8	−45.0	−0.7
Hong Kong and Singapore	3.2	1.6	0.3	4.4	1.1
Argentina	2.9	0.5	−0.7	21.3	0.3
Bangladesh	1.8	1.7	−0.2	1.8	−7.2
Brazil	2.7	1.4	1.6	32.4	2.2
China	2.2	2.2	2.8	−0.9	−0.4
India	2.8	4.6	1.8	−2.6	−6.0
Indonesia	3.3	1.5	0.9	1.0	0.5
Thailand	13.2	6.7	4.2	11.4	−0.6
Vietnam	25.3	17.6	11.0	6.8	−2.3
Russia	2.0	2.8	3.5	−2.2	−3.3
Mexico	2.0	1.6	0.5	0.6	−1.4
South Africa	2.8	2.5	1.8	5.7	−1.6
Turkey	1.3	3.4	1.1	−8.1	−0.3
Rest of South Asia	3.7	3.2	0.1	0.1	−2.7
Rest of East Asia	5.8	4.2	5.2	−0.9	−1.6
Rest of Latin America and Caribbean	5.7	1.4	−0.4	17.8	−1.2
Rest of E. Europe and Central Asia	2.3	4.2	2.1	−0.3	−2.6
Middle East and North Africa	4.1	4.1	2.6	2.4	−3.1
Other Southern Africa	6.0	1.6	0.0	4.6	0.4
Rest of Sub-Saharan Africa	8.2	6.5	2.2	5.2	−5.0
Rest of the World	4.4	2.7	1.1	6.3	−1.4

Source: Anderson *et al.* (2006c, Table 12.10)

order since 2001, so may need to do no further cutting under even that formula.

Large cuts in bound rates are needed also to erase binding overhang in agricultural tariffs

Table 3.2 shows there is substantial binding overhang in agricultural tariffs: the average bound rate in developed countries is almost twice as high as the average applied rate, and in developing countries the ratio is even greater. Thus large reductions in bound rates are needed before it is possible to bring about *any* improvements in market access. To bring the global average actual agricultural tariff down by one-third, bound rates would have to be reduced for developed countries by at least 45 percent, and up to 75 percent for the highest tariffs, under a tiered formula.

A complex tiered formula may be little better than a proportional tariff cut

It turns out that, because of the large binding overhang, a tiered formula for cutting agricultural tariffs would generate not much more global welfare – and no more welfare for developing countries as a group – than a proportional cut of the same average size (columns 1 and 2 of Tables 3.7, 3.8 and 3.9). This suggests there may be little value in arguing over the finer details of a complex tiered formula just for the sake of reducing tariff escalation. Instead, a simple tariff cap of, say, 100 or even 200 percent could achieve essentially the same outcome.

Even large cuts in bound tariffs do little if "Sensitive Products" are allowed, except if a cap applies

If members succumb to the political temptation to put limits on tariff cuts for the most sensitive farm products, much of the prospective gain from Doha could evaporate. Even if only 2 percent of HS6 agricultural tariff lines in developed countries are classified as sensitive (and 4 percent in developing countries, to incorporate also their "Special Products" request), and are thereby subject to just a 15 percent tariff cut (as a substitute for the tariff rate quota (TRQ) expansion mentioned in the Framework Agreement), the welfare gains from global agricultural reform would shrink by three-quarters. However, if at the same time any product with a bound tariff in excess of 200 percent had to reduce it to that cap rate, the welfare gain would shrink by "only" one-third (columns 3 and 4 of Tables 3.7, 3.8 and 3.9).

Table 3.7 Welfare effects of possible Doha reform scenarios, 2015 (percentage difference from baseline, and Equivalent Variation in income in 2001 $billion

| | Tiered agricultural tariff cuts[b] | Proportional agricultural tariff cuts[b] | Agricultural subsidy cuts[a] plus: | | | | |
| | | | Scenario 2 plus 2% SSP | Scenario 3 plus 200% cap | Scenario 1 plus 50% NAMA cut for HICs[c] | Scenario 1 plus 50% NAMA cut for HICs+DCs[d] |
	Scenario 1	Scenario 2	Scenario 3	Scenario 4	Scenario 5	Scenario 6
High-income[e] countries	0.20	0.18	0.05	0.13	0.25	0.30
Middle-income countries	0.10	0.10	0.00	0.01	0.15	0.21
of which: China	−0.02	−0.01	−0.05	−0.04	0.07	0.06
Low-income countries	0.05	0.04	0.01	0.00	0.18	0.30
Total world	0.18	0.16	0.04	0.10	0.23	0.28
(and in $billion)	74.5	66.3	17.9	44.3	96.1	119.3

Source: Anderson *et al.* (2006c, Table 12.14)

Notes
a Elimination of agricultural export subsidies and cuts in actual domestic support as of 2001 of 28 percent in the US, 18 percent in the EU, and 16 percent in Norway.
b In Scenarios 1 and 2 the applied global average tariff on agricultural products is cut by roughly one-third, with larger cuts in developed countries, smaller in developing countries, and zero in least developed countries. In Scenario 1 there are three tiers for developed countries and four for developing countries, following Harbinson (WTO 2003) but 10 percentage points higher.
c Non-agricultural market access (NAMA) is expanded by a 50 percent tariff cut for developed countries, 33 percent for developing countries, and zero in least developed countries.
d Developing and least developed countries cut all agricultural and non-agricultural tariffs as much as developed countries.
e High-income countries (HICs) include the newly industrialized East Asian customs territories of Hong Kong, Korea, Singapore and Taiwan as well as Europe's transition economies that joined the EU in April 2004.

Table 3.8 Dollar change in real income in alternative Doha scenarios, 2015 (change in real income in 2015 in 2001 $billion compared to baseline scenario)

	Scenario					
	1	2	3	4	5	6
Australia and New Zealand	2.0	2.2	1.2	1.2	2.4	2.8
EU 25 plus EFTA	29.5	28.2	10.7	10.9	31.4	35.7
United States	3.0	3.4	2.5	2.1	4.9	6.6
Canada	1.4	1.2	0.4	0.4	0.9	1.0
Japan	18.9	15.1	1.4	12.9	23.7	25.4
Korea and Taiwan	10.9	7.3	1.7	15.9	15.0	22.6
Hong Kong and Singapore	−0.1	−0.1	−0.2	−0.2	1.5	2.2
Argentina	1.3	1.4	1.1	1.0	1.3	1.6
Bangladesh	0.0	0.0	0.0	0.0	−0.1	−0.1
Brazil	3.3	3.2	1.1	1.1	3.6	3.9
China	−0.5	−0.4	−1.4	−1.1	1.7	1.6
India	0.2	0.1	0.2	0.2	2.2	3.5
Indonesia	0.1	0.2	0.2	0.0	1.0	1.2
Thailand	0.9	1.0	0.8	0.8	2.0	2.7
Vietnam	−0.1	−0.1	−0.1	−0.1	−0.5	−0.6
Russia	−0.3	−0.1	−0.7	−0.7	0.8	1.5
Mexico	−0.2	−0.2	−0.3	−0.3	−0.9	−0.2
South Africa	0.1	0.1	0.2	0.3	0.4	0.7
Turkey	0.6	0.5	0.1	0.0	0.7	1.4
Rest of South Asia	0.2	0.2	0.1	0.2	0.3	0.7
Rest of East Asia	0.1	0.1	0.1	1.0	0.3	0.6
Rest of Latin America and the Caribbean	3.7	3.7	0.5	0.4	3.9	4.0
Rest of Eastern Europe and Central Asia	−0.2	−0.2	−0.2	−0.2	−0.6	−0.7
Middle East and North Africa	−0.8	−0.9	−1.2	−1.2	−0.6	0.1
Other Southern Africa	0.1	0.1	0.0	0.0	0.1	0.2
Rest of Sub-Saharan Africa	0.0	0.0	−0.3	−0.3	−0.1	0.3
Rest of the World	0.4	0.3	0.0	0.0	0.6	0.6
High-income countries	65.6	57.2	17.8	43.2	79.9	96.4
Developing countries	9.0	9.1	0.1	1.1	16.1	22.9
Middle-income countries	8.0	8.3	0.0	1.0	12.5	17.1
Low-income countries	1.0	0.8	0.2	0.0	3.6	5.9
East Asia and Pacific	0.5	0.9	−0.4	0.6	4.5	5.5
South Asia	0.4	0.3	0.3	0.4	2.5	4.2
Eastern Europe and Central Asia	0.1	0.2	−0.9	−0.9	0.8	2.1
Middle East and North Africa	−0.8	−0.9	−1.2	−1.2	−0.6	0.1
Sub-Saharan Africa	0.3	0.3	−0.2	−0.1	0.4	1.2
Latin America and the Caribbean	8.1	8.0	2.5	2.1	7.9	9.2
World total	74.5	66.3	17.9	44.3	96.1	119.3

Source: Anderson *et al.* (2006c, Table 12.14)

Table 3.9 Percentage change in real income in alternative Doha scenarios, 2015 (change in real income in 2015 in percent compared to baseline scenario)

	Scenario					
	1	2	3	4	5	6
Australia and New Zealand	0.35	0.38	0.22	0.20	0.42	0.48
EU 25 plus EFTA	0.29	0.28	0.11	0.11	0.31	0.36
United States	0.02	0.02	0.02	0.01	0.03	0.05
Canada	0.15	0.13	0.05	0.05	0.10	0.11
Japan	0.38	0.30	0.03	0.26	0.48	0.51
Korea and Taiwan	0.86	0.58	0.14	1.26	1.19	1.79
Hong Kong and Singapore	−0.02	−0.02	−0.04	−0.04	0.35	0.52
Argentina	0.32	0.34	0.27	0.26	0.34	0.39
Bangladesh	−0.06	−0.06	−0.03	−0.04	−0.10	−0.09
Brazil	0.50	0.49	0.17	0.17	0.55	0.59
China	−0.02	−0.01	−0.05	−0.04	0.07	0.06
India	0.02	0.02	0.03	0.02	0.25	0.40
Indonesia	0.05	0.08	0.09	0.01	0.37	0.44
Thailand	0.43	0.49	0.38	0.38	0.99	1.33
Vietnam	−0.20	−0.22	−0.11	−0.16	−0.83	−0.97
Russia	−0.06	−0.03	−0.15	−0.15	0.16	0.31
Mexico	−0.02	−0.02	−0.04	−0.04	−0.11	−0.02
South Africa	0.06	0.09	0.11	0.17	0.25	0.49
Turkey	0.25	0.22	0.02	0.02	0.26	0.55
Rest of South Asia	0.13	0.11	0.06	0.14	0.17	0.39
Rest of East Asia	0.02	0.05	0.04	0.36	0.09	0.22
Rest of Latin America and the Caribbean	0.44	0.43	0.06	0.04	0.46	0.47
Rest of Eastern Europe and Central Asia	−0.06	−0.06	−0.09	−0.08	−0.22	−0.26
Middle East and North Africa	−0.07	−0.07	−0.10	−0.10	−0.05	0.01
Other Southern Africa	0.21	0.19	−0.03	−0.05	0.19	0.26
Rest of Sub-Saharan Africa	0.02	0.01	−0.14	−0.14	−0.02	0.13
Rest of the World	0.19	0.14	0.00	0.02	0.26	0.28
High-income countries	*0.20*	*0.18*	*0.05*	*0.13*	*0.25*	*0.30*
Developing countries	*0.09*	*0.09*	*0.00*	*0.01*	*0.16*	*0.22*
Middle-income countries	0.10	0.10	0.00	0.01	0.15	0.21
Low-income countries	0.05	0.04	0.01	0.00	0.18	0.30
East Asia and Pacific	0.01	0.03	−0.01	0.02	0.13	0.16
South Asia	0.03	0.02	0.03	0.03	0.21	0.36
Eastern Europe and Central Asia	0.01	0.02	−0.09	−0.09	0.08	0.21
Middle East and North Africa	−0.07	−0.07	−0.10	−0.10	−0.05	0.01
Sub-Saharan Africa	0.06	0.06	−0.04	−0.02	0.10	0.27
Latin America and the Caribbean	0.29	0.29	0.09	0.08	0.29	0.33
World total	*0.18*	*0.16*	*0.04*	*0.10*	*0.23*	*0.28*

Source: Anderson *et al.* (2006c, Table 12.14)

TRQ expansion could provide additional market access

Only a small number of farm products are subject to tariff rate quotas, but they protect over half of all developed countries' production and 44 percent of their agricultural imports (de Gorter and Kliauga 2006). Bringing down those products' (out-of-quota) MFN bound tariff could be supplemented by lowering their in-quota tariff or expanding the size of the quota. While this may increase the aggregate rent attached to those quotas and hence resistance to eventually removing them, the extent of binding overhang is such that quota expansion may be the only way to get increased market access for TRQ products in the Doha round – especially if they are among the ones designated as "sensitive" and hence subject to lesser cuts in their bound tariffs.

High binding overhang means most developing countries would have to make few cuts

Given the high binding overhang of developing countries, even with their high tariffs – and even if tiered formulae are used to cut highest bindings most – relatively few of them would have to cut their actual tariffs and subsidies at all (Jean *et al.* 2006). That is even truer if "Special Products" are subjected to smaller cuts and developing countries exercise their right – as laid out in the July Framework Agreement – to undertake lesser cuts (zero in the case of LDCs) than developed countries. Politically this makes it easier for developing and least developed countries to offer big cuts on bound rates – but it also means the benefits to them are smaller than if they had a smaller binding overhang.

Cotton subsidy cuts would help cotton-exporting developing countries

The removal of cotton subsidies (which have raised producer prices by well over 50 percent in the US and EU – see Sumner 2006) would raise the export price of cotton (although not equally across all exporters because of product differentiation). If those subsidies were removed as part of freeing all merchandise trade, that price rise is estimated to be 8 percent for Brazil but less for Sub-Saharan Africa on average. However, cotton exports from Sub-Saharan Africa would be a huge 75 percent larger, and the share of all developing countries in global exports would be 85 percent instead of 56 percent in 2015, vindicating those countries' efforts to ensure that cotton subsidies receive specific attention in the Doha negotiations.

Expanding non-agricultural market access would add substantially to the gains from agricultural reform

Adding a 50 percent cut to non-agricultural tariffs by developed countries (and 33 percent by developing countries and zero by LDCs) to the tiered formula cut to agricultural tariffs would double the gain from Doha for developing countries (compare Scenarios 1 and 5 in Tables 3.7, 3.8 and 3.9). That would bring the global gain to $96 billion from Doha merchandise liberalization, which is a sizable one-third of the potential welfare gain from full liberalization of $287 billion. Adding services reform would of course boost that welfare gain even more.

Adding non-agricultural tariff reform to agricultural reform helps to balance the exchange of "concessions"

The agricultural reforms would boost the annual value of world trade in 2015 by less than one-quarter of what would happen if non-agricultural tariffs were also reduced. The latter's inclusion also would help balance the exchange of "concessions" in terms of increases in bilateral trade values: in that case developing countries' exports to high-income countries would then be $62 billion, which is close to the $55 billion increase in high-income countries' exports to developing countries. With only agricultural reform, the latter's bilateral trade growth would be little more than half that of the former's (Table 3.10).

Most developing countries gain, and the rest could if they reform more

Even though much of the DC gains from that comprehensive Doha scenario go to numerous large developing countries (notably Brazil, Argentina and Other Latin America plus India, Thailand and South Africa), the rest of Sub-Saharan Africa gains too. This is particularly so when developing countries participate as full partners in the negotiations. An important part of this result comes from the increases in market access – on a non-discriminatory basis – by other developing countries.

Table 3.10 Effects on bilateral merchandise trade flows of adding non-agricultural tariff cuts to agricultural reform under Doha, 2015 (2001 $billion increase over the baseline in 2015)

Exports to:	Proportional agricultural reform only[a]		Agricultural plus non-agricultural reform[b]	
	High-income[c] countries	Developing countries	High-income[c] countries	Developing countries
Exports from:				
High-income[c] countries	20	11	80	55
Developing countries	18	5	62	16
Total world	38	16	142	71

Source: Anderson *et al.* (2006c, Table 12.16)

Notes
a Scenario 2 in Table 3.7;
b Scenario 5 in Table 3.7;
c High-income countries include the newly industrialized East Asian customs territories of Hong Kong, Korea, Singapore and Taiwan as well as Europe's transition economies that joined the EU in April 2004.

Preference erosion may be less of an issue than commonly assumed

Some least developed countries in Sub-Saharan Africa and elsewhere appear to be slight losers in our Doha simulations when developed countries cut their tariffs and those LDCs choose not to reform at all themselves.[8] These simulations overstate the benefits of tariff preferences for LDCs, however, since they ignore the trade-dampening effect of complex rules of origin and the grabbing of much of the rents by developed-country importers. Even if they would lose after correcting for those realities, it remains true that preference-receiving countries could always be compensated for preference erosion via increased aid at relatively very small cost to current preference providers – and in the process other developing countries currently hurt by LDC preferences would enjoy greater access to the markets of reforming developed countries.

Farm output and employment would grow in developing countries under Doha

Despite a few low-income countries losing slightly under our Doha scenarios when they choose to reform little themselves, in all the developing countries and regions shown the levels of output and employment on farms expand. It is only in the most protected developed countries of Western Europe, Northeast Asia and the US that these levels would fall – and even there it is only by small amounts, contrary to the predictions of scaremongers who claim agriculture would be decimated in reforming countries (Table 3.11). Even if there was a move to completely free merchandise trade, the developed countries' share of the world's primary agricultural GDP by 2015

Table 3.11 Effects of a comprehensive Doha reform on agricultural output and employment growth, by region, 2005 to 2015 (annual average growth rate)

	Output		*Employment*	
	Baseline	*Scenario 5*	*Baseline*	*Scenario 5*
Australia and New Zealand	3.5	4.3	0.4	1.0
Canada	3.5	4.0	0.2	0.6
United States	2.2	1.9	−0.8	−1.4
EU 25 plus EFTA	1.0	−0.3	−1.8	−2.8
Japan	0.5	−1.4	−2.7	−4.1
Korea and Taiwan	2.2	1.5	−1.3	−2.1
Argentina	2.9	3.5	0.9	1.5
Bangladesh	4.2	4.2	1.1	1.2
Brazil	3.3	4.4	1.1	2.2
China	4.3	4.3	0.8	0.8
India	4.3	4.4	1.0	1.0
Indonesia	3.0	3.0	−0.7	−0.6
Thailand	−0.1	0.4	−4.6	−4.3
Vietnam	5.8	5.9	3.9	4.0
Russia	1.5	1.4	−2.3	−2.4
Mexico	3.9	4.0	2.0	2.3
South Africa	2.5	2.6	0.0	0.1
Turkey	3.0	3.0	−0.5	−0.5
Rest of South Asia	4.8	4.9	2.0	2.1
Rest of East Asia	3.7	3.8	0.2	0.3
Rest of Latin America and Caribbean	4.4	5.3	1.9	2.6
Rest of Eastern Europe and Central Asia	3.3	3.3	0.0	0.0
Middle East and North Africa	4.0	4.0	1.5	1.5
Other Southern Africa	5.3	5.4	3.0	3.0
Rest of Sub-Saharan Africa	4.6	4.8	2.2	2.3
Rest of the World	5.0	5.5	2.4	2.7

Source: Anderson *et al.* (2006c, Table 12.17)

would be only slightly lower at 25 instead of 30 percent (but their share of global agricultural exports would be diminished considerably more: from 53 to 38 percent).

Poverty could be reduced under Doha

Under the full merchandise trade liberalization scenario, extreme poverty in developing countries (those where individuals earn no more than $1/day) would drop by 32 million in 2015 relative to the baseline level of 622 million, a reduction of 5 percent. The majority of the poor by 2015 are projected to be in Sub-Saharan Africa (SSA), and there the reduction would be 6 percent.[9] Under the Doha scenarios reported in Table 3.12, the poverty impacts are far more modest. The number of poor living on less than $1/day would fall by 2.5 million in the case of the core Doha Scenario 5 (of which 0.5 million are in SSA) and by 6.3 million in the case of Doha Scenario 6 (of which 2.2 million are in SSA). This corresponds to the relatively modest ambitions of the merchandise trade reforms as captured in these Doha scenarios.

Table 3.12 Changes in poverty (those earning <$1/day) in alternative Doha scenarios compared with full liberalization, 2015

	Base-line share	Full liberalization share	Shares under Doha scenarios		
			Doha 1	Doha 5	Doha 6
2015 headcount (%)					
East Asia and Pacific	0.9	0.8	0.9	0.9	0.9
Latin America and Caribbean	6.9	6.6	6.9	6.9	6.8
South Asia	12.8	12.5	12.8	12.7	12.6
Sub-Saharan Africa	38.4	36.0	38.4	38.3	38.1
All developing countries	10.2	9.7	10.2	10.2	10.1
	2015	*Decrease from baseline*	*Decrease from baseline (in millions)*		
2015 headcount (million)	*level*	*(in millions)*			
East Asia and Pacific	19	2.2	0.1	0.3	0.5
Latin America and Caribbean	43	2.1	0.3	0.4	0.5
South Asia	216	5.6	0.2	1.4	3.0
Sub-Saharan Africa	340	21.1	−0.1	0.5	2.2
All developing countries	622	31.9	0.5	2.5	6.3

Source: Authors' World Bank Linkage model simulations as reported in Anderson *et al.* (2006b, Table 17.7).

If only agriculture was reformed (Doha Scenario 1) there would be much less poverty alleviation globally and none at all in SSA. This shows the importance for poverty of including manufactured products in the Doha negotiations.

Developing countries could trade off Special and Differential Treatment for more market access

If developing countries were to tone down their call for Special and Differential Treatment (see Josling 2006), in terms of wanting smaller cuts and longer phase-in periods, reciprocity means they could expect bigger tariff and subsidy cuts from developed countries. Similarly, if they were to forgo their call for lesser cuts for "Special Products," they could demand that developed countries forgo their call for some "Sensitive Products" to be subject to smaller tariff cuts. A comparison of Scenarios 5 and 6 in Tables 3.7, 3.8 and 3.9 shows that the economic payoffs for low-income countries even if high-income countries do not reciprocate with larger offers is considerable. Moreover, by embracing those options to reform more in the context of the Doha round would make it harder for high-income countries to resist the call to respond with larger reforms themselves.

Key policy implications

Among the numerous policy implications that can be drawn from the above findings, the following are worth highlighting.

Prospective gains are too large to not find the needed political will to make Doha a success

With gains of the order of $300 billion per year at stake from implementing the July Framework Agreement (even if no reforms are forthcoming in services and if the counterfactual would be the status quo rather than protectionist backsliding), the political will needs to be found to bring the round to a successful conclusion, and the sooner the better. Multilateral cuts in MFN bindings are helpful also because they can lock in previous unilateral trade liberalizations that otherwise would remain unbound and hence be vulnerable to backsliding; and they can be used as an opportunity to multilateralize previously agreed preferential trade agreements and thereby reduce the risk of trade diversion from those bilateral or regional arrangements (as stressed in Sutherland *et al.* 2004).

Since developed countries would gain most, and have the most capacity and influence, they need to show leadership at the WTO

The large developed countries cannot generate a successful agreement on their own, but nor can the Doha round succeed without a major push by those key traders. Their capacity to assist poorer economies could hardly manifest itself more clearly than in encouraging global economic integration via trade reform, and in particular in opening developed country markets to the items of greatest importance to poorer countries, namely farm (and textile) products. The more that is done, the more developing countries will be encouraged to reciprocate by opening their own markets more – accelerating South–South trade in addition to South–North trade.

Outlawing agricultural export subsidies is the obvious first step

That will bring agriculture into line with the basic GATT rule against such measures, and in the process help to limit the extent to which governments encourage agricultural production by other means (since it would raise the cost of surplus disposal). China has already committed not to use them, and other developing countries too can find more efficient ways of stabilizing their domestic food markets than by dumping surpluses abroad.

Even more importantly, agricultural tariff and domestic support bindings must be cut hugely to remove binding overhang and provide some genuine market opening

Getting rid of the binding overhang that resulted from the Uruguay round, particularly with "dirty tariffication," must be a priority.[10] The highest-subsidizing countries, namely the EU, US and Norway, need to reduce their domestic support not just for the sake of their own economies but also to encourage developing countries to reciprocate by opening their markets as a quid pro quo. But more than that is needed if market access is to expand. If a choice had to be made, reducing MFN bound tariffs in general would be preferable to raising tariff rate quotas, because the latter help only those lucky enough to obtain quotas and crowd out non-quota holders. (Being against the non-discrimination spirit of the GATT, they deserve the same fate as textile quotas which were abolished at the end of 2004.) Exempting even just a few Sensitive and Special Products is undesirable as it would reduce hugely the gains from reform and would tend to divert resources into, instead of away from, enterprises in which countries have their least comparative advantage. If it turns out to be politically impossible not to designate some Sensitive and Special Products, it would be crucial to impose a cap such that any product with a bound tariff in excess of, say, 100 percent had to reduce it to that cap rate.

Expanding non-agricultural market access at the same time as reforming agriculture is essential

A balanced exchange of concession is impossible without adding other sectors, and it needs to be more than just textiles and clothing (which also benefit developing countries disproportionately) even though they are the other highly distorted sector. With other merchandise included, the trade expansion would be four times greater for both rich and poor countries – and poverty in low-income countries would be reduced considerably more.

South–South "concessions" also are needed, especially for developing countries, which means reconsidering the opportunity for developing countries to liberalize less

Since developing countries are trading so much more with each other now, they are the major beneficiaries of reforms within their own regions. Upper middle-income countries might consider giving least developed countries duty-free access to their markets (mirroring the recent initiatives of developed countries), but better than such discriminatory action would be MFN tariff reductions by them. Even least developed countries should consider reducing their tariff binding overhang at least, since doing that in the context of Doha gives them more scope to demand "concessions" (or compensation for preference erosion or other contributors to terms of trade deterioration) from richer countries – and yet would not require them to cut their own *applied* tariffs very much.

Conclusions

The good news in this chapter is that there is a great deal to be gained from liberalizing merchandise – and especially agricultural – trade under Doha, with a disproportionately high share of that potential gain available for developing countries (relative to their share of the global economy). Moreover, it is the poorest people in developing countries that appear to be most likely to gain from global trade liberalization, namely farmers and unskilled laborers in developing countries. To realize that potential gain, it is in agriculture that by far the greatest cuts in bound tariffs and subsidies are required. However, the political sensitivity of farm support programs, coupled with the complexities of the measures introduced in the Uruguay Round Agreement on Agriculture and of the modalities set out in the Doha Framework Agreement of July 2004, ensure the devil will be in the details of the final Doha agreement. It is for that reason that ex ante empirical analysis of the sort provided in the study summarized above is a prerequisite for countries engaged in the Doha round of negotiations.

What emerges from our analysis is that developing countries would not *have* to reform very much under Doha, because of the large gaps between their tariff bindings and applied rates. That is even truer if they exercise their right (as laid out in the July Framework Agreement) to undertake lesser tariff cuts than developed countries. In that case, they gain little in terms of improved efficiency of national resource use. Yet, as Panagariya (2004) and others have warned, for a non-trivial number of low-income countries their terms of trade could deteriorate, as shown in Table 3.3. For some that is because they would lose tariff preferences on their exports. For others it is because they are net food importers and so would face higher prices for their imports of temperate foods. To realize more of their potential gains from trade, developing and least developed countries would need to forgo some of the Special and Differential Treatment they have previously demanded, and perhaps also commit to additional unilateral trade (and complementary domestic) reforms, and to invest more in trade facilitation. High-income countries could encourage them to do so by being willing to open up their own markets more to developing country exports,[11] and by providing more targeted aid. To that end, a new proposal has been put forward to reward developing country commitments to greater trade reform with an expansion of trade-facilitating aid, to be provided by a major expansion of the current Integrated Framework which is operated by a consortium of international agencies for least developed countries (Hoekman 2005a, 2005b). This may well provide an attractive path for developing countries seeking to trade their way out of poverty, not least because linking aid to greater trade reform would help offset the tendency for an expanded aid flow to cause a real exchange rate appreciation (see Commission for Africa 2005: 296–97). As well, it is potentially a far more efficient way for developed countries to assist people in low-income countries than the current systems of tariff preferences.

In conclusion, the July Framework Agreement does not guarantee major gains from the Doha Development Agenda. On the one hand, even if an agreement is ultimately reached, it may be very modest. How modest depends on, among other things, the nature of the agricultural tariff-cutting formula, the size of the cuts, the extent to which exceptions for Sensitive and Special Products are allowed, whether a tariff cap is introduced, and the extent to which Special and Differential Treatment is invoked by developing countries in terms of their market access commitments. But what is equally clear, on the other hand, is that major gains are possible if only the political will to reform protectionist policies – especially in agriculture – can be mustered.

Acknowledgment

The authors are grateful for the collaboration of all their co-contributors to that project, especially Dominique van der Mensbrugghe and Tom Hertel, and for funding from the UK's Department for International Development. The views expressed are the authors' alone.

Notes

1 This chapter is based on a program of World Bank research on the implications of the Doha Agenda for developing countries. To access the chapters of the forthcoming book this chapter summarizes, and for a companion book on Doha and poverty alleviation, please visit www.worldbank.org/trade/wto.
2 The rules of the GATT are intended, in principle, to cover all trade in goods. However, in practice, trade in agricultural products was largely excluded from their remit as a consequence of a number of exceptions. Details are to be found in Josling *et al.* (1996) and in Anderson and Josling (2005).
3 According to the UN's Food and Agriculture Organization, 54 percent of the economically active population is engaged in agriculture in developing countries, which is nearly five times larger than the sector's measured GDP share (FAO 2004, Table A4). While some of that difference in shares is due to under-reporting of subsistence consumption, it nonetheless implies that these people on average are considerably less productive and hence poorer than those employed outside agriculture.
4 Until recently the PSE referred to the Producer Subsidy Equivalent. For more about the concept and its history, see Legg (2003).
5 This analysis is vastly more sophisticated than the *ex ante* analyses undertaken for the Uruguay round. At that time there were very few

economy-wide global models, so primary reliance was on partial equilibrium models of world food markets (see e.g. World Bank 1986; Goldin and Knudsen 1990; Tyers and Anderson 1992); estimates of protection rates were somewhat cruder and less complete; and analysts grossly overestimated the gains because they did not anticipate that tariffication would be so "dirty" in the sense of creating large wedges between bound and MFN applied tariff rates, nor did they have reliable estimates of the tariff preferences enjoyed by developing countries or the ad valorem equivalent of specific tariffs. Some of these limitations also applied to *ex post* analyses of the Uruguay round (see e.g. Martin and Winters 1996).

6 There is strong evidence that trade reform in general is also good for economic growth and, partly because of that, for poverty alleviation (Winters 2004; Dollar and Kraay 2004; Winters *et al.* 2004).

7 This result is very similar to that reported from a partial equilibrium study by Hoekman *et al.* (2004). In our initial empirical analysis we also included crude estimates of implicit forms of farm export subsidization such as via food aid, export credits or state trading enterprises, but even that was not enough to raise that export subsidy share above 1 percent.

8 As warned by Panagariya (2004) among others, some low-income countries' terms of trade could deteriorate either because they would lose tariff preferences on their exports or because they are net food importers and so would face higher prices for their imports of temperate foods.

9 The approach here has been to take the change in the average per capita consumption of the poor, apply an estimated income-to-poverty elasticity, and assess the impacts on the poverty headcount index. We have done this by calculating the change in the real wage of unskilled workers, deflating it by a food/clothing consumer price index which is more relevant for the poor than the total price index. That real wage grows, over all developing countries, by 3.6 percent, or more than four times greater than the overall average income increase. We are assuming that the change in unskilled wages is fully passed through to households. Also, while the model closure has the loss in tariff revenues replaced by a change in direct household taxation, the poverty calculation assumes – realistically for many developing countries – that these tax increases affect only skilled workers and high-income households. While these simple calculations are not a substitute for more detailed individual country case study analysis using detailed household surveys as in, for example, Hertel and Winters (2006), they are able to give a broad region-wide indication of the poverty impact.

10 As Francois and Martin (2004) have shown, any binding cut is useful for the long run even if it brings no immediate cut in applied rates.

11 Limao and Olarreaga (2005) suggest preference erosion could be addressed by replacing the current margin of preference with an equivalent import subsidy for products from preference-receiving countries, thereby retaining the preference status quo while taking away this reason not to undertake most-favored-nation tariff cuts.

References

Aksoy, M.A. and Beghin, J.C. (eds) (2004) *Global Agricultural Trade and Developing Countries*, Washington, DC: World Bank.

Anania, G., Bohman, M., Carter, C. and McCalla, A. (eds) (2004) *Agricultural Policy Reform and the WTO: Where Are We Heading?*, London: Edward Elgar.

Anderson, K. and Hayami, Y. (1986) *The Political Economy of Agricultural Protection: East Asia in International Perspective*, Boston, London and Sydney: Allen and Unwin.

Anderson, K. and Josling, T.E. (eds) (2005) *The WTO and Agriculture*, London: Edward Elgar Publishers.

Anderson, K. and Martin, W. (eds) (2006a) *Agricultural Trade Reform and the Doha Development Agenda*, New York: Palgrave Macmillan (co-published with the World Bank).

—— (2006b) 'Global impact of the Doha scenarios on poverty', Ch. 17 in *Putting Development Back Into the Doha Agenda: Poverty Impacts of a WTO Agreement*, T.W. Hertel and L.A. Winters (eds), New York: Palgrave Macmillan.

—— (2006c) 'Market and welfare implications of Doha reform scenarios', Ch. 12 in *Agricultural Trade Reform and the Doha Development Agenda*, K. Anderson and W. Martin (eds), New York: Palgrave Macmillan.

Commission for Africa (2005) *Our Common Interest*, London: UK Department for International Development, March.

de Gorter, H. and Kliauga, E. (2006) 'Consequences of TRQ expansions and in-quota tariff reductions', Ch. 5 in *Agricultural Trade Reform and the Doha Development Agenda*, K. Anderson and W. Martin (eds), New York: Palgrave Macmillan.

Dollar, D. and Kraay, A. (2004) 'Trade, growth and poverty', *Economic Journal*, 114: F22–F49, February.

FAO (2004) *The State of Food and Agriculture 2003–04*, Rome: UN Food and Agriculture Organization.

Finger, J.M. and Schuler, P. (2001) 'Implementation of Uruguay round commitments: the development challenge', Ch. 7 in *Developing Countries and the WTO: A Pro-Active Agenda*, B. Hoekman and W. Martin (eds), Oxford: Blackwell.

Finger, J.M. and Winters, L.A. (2002) 'Reciprocity in the WTO', Ch. 7 in *Development, Trade and the WTO: A Handbook*, B. Hoekman, A. Matoo and P. English (eds), Washington, DC: The World Bank.

Francois, J.F. and Martin, W. (2004) 'Commercial policy, bindings and market access', *European Economic Review*, 48 (3): 665–79, June.

Goldin, I. and Knudsen, O. (eds) (1990) *Agricultural Trade Liberalization: Implications for Developing Countries*, Paris: OECD.

Hathaway, D. and Ingco, M. (1996) 'Agricultural liberalization and the Uruguay Round', Ch. 2 in *The Uruguay Round and the Developing*

Countries, W. Martin and L.A. Winters (eds), Cambridge and New York: Cambridge University Press.

Hertel, T.W. and Keeney, R. (2006) 'What's at stake: the relative importance of import barriers, export subsidies and domestic support', Ch. 2 in *Agricultural Trade Reform and the Doha Development Agenda,* K. Anderson and W. Martin (eds), New York: Palgrave Macmillan.

Hertel, T.W. and Winters, L.A. (eds) (2006) *Putting Development Back Into the Doha Agenda: Poverty Impacts of a WTO Agreement,* New York: Palgrave Macmillan (co-published with the World Bank).

Hoekman, B. (2005a) 'Operationalizing the concept of policy space in the WTO: beyond special and differential treatment', *Journal of International Economic Law,* 8 (2): 405–24.

—— (2005b) 'Making the WTO more supportive of development', *Finance and Development,* pp. 14–18, March.

—— Ng, F. and Olarreaga, M. (2004) 'Agricultural tariffs versus subsidies: what's more important for developing countries?', *World Bank Economic Review,* 18 (2): 175–204.

Ingco, M.D. and Nash, J.D. (eds) (2004) *Agriculture and the WTO: Creating a Trading System for Development,* Washington, DC: World Bank and New York: Oxford University Press.

Ingco, M.D. and Winters, L.A. (eds) (2004) *Agriculture and the New Trade Agenda: Creating a Global Trading Environment for Development,* Cambridge and New York: Cambridge University Press.

Jank, M.S. (ed.) (2004) *Agricultural Trade Liberalization: Policies and Implications for Latin America,* Washington, DC: Inter-American Development Bank.

Jean, S., Laborde, D. and Martin, W. (2006) 'Consequences of alternative formulas for agricultural tariff cuts', Ch. 4 in *Agricultural Trade Reform and the Doha Development Agenda,* K. Anderson and W. Martin (eds), New York: Palgrave Macmillan.

Josling, T. (2006) 'Consequences of special and differential treatment for developing countries', Ch. 3 in *Agricultural Trade Reform and the Doha Development Agenda,* K. Anderson and W. Martin (eds), New York: Palgrave Macmillan.

—— , Tangermann, S. and Warley, T.K. (1996) *Agriculture in the GATT,* London: Macmillan and New York: St. Martin's Press.

Legg, W. (2003) 'Agricultural subsidies: measurement and use in policy evaluation', *Journal of Agricultural Economics,* 54 (2): 175–200.

Limao, N. and Olarreaga, M. (2005) 'Trade preferences to small developing countries and the welfare costs of lost multilateral liberalization', Policy Research Working Paper No. 3565, Washington, DC: World Bank.

Lindert, P. (1991) 'Historical patterns of agricultural protection', in *Agriculture and the State,* P. Timmer (eds), Ithaca: Cornell University Press.

Martin, W. and Winters, L.A. (eds) (1996) *The Uruguay Round and the Developing Countries,* Cambridge and New York: Cambridge University Press.

Panagariya, A. (2004) 'Subsidies and trade barriers: alternative perspective 10.2', pp. 592–601 in *Global Crises, Global Solutions*, B. Lomborg (ed.), Cambridge and New York: Cambridge University Press.

Sumner, D.A. (2006) 'Reducing cotton subsidies: the DDA cotton initiative', Ch. 10 in *Agricultural Trade Reform and the Doha Development Agenda*, K. Anderson and W. Martin (eds), New York: Palgrave Macmillan.

Sutherland, P. et al. (2004) *The Future of the WTO*, Report by the Consultative Board, Geneva: World Trade Organization.

Tyers, R. and Anderson, K. (1992) *Disarray in World Food Markets: A Quantitative Assessment*, Cambridge and New York: Cambridge University Press.

van der Mensbrugghe, D. (2004) *Linkage technical reference document: version 6.0*, mimeo, Washington, DC: World Bank. Available at: <http://siteresources.worldbank.org/INTPROSPECTS/Resources/334934 –1100792545130/LinkageTechNote.pdf>.

Winters, L.A. (2004) 'Trade liberalization and economic performance: an overview', *Economic Journal*, 114: F4–F21, February.

—— , McCulloch, N. and McKay, A. (2004) 'Trade liberalization and poverty: the empirical evidence', *Journal of Economic Literature*, 62 (1): 72–115, March.

World Bank (1986) *World Development Report 1986*, New York: Oxford University Press.

WTO (2003) 'Negotiations on agriculture: first draft of modalities for the further commitments', TN/AG/W/1/Rev.1, Geneva: World Trade Organization, 19 March (The Harbinson Draft).

—— (2004) 'Doha work programme: decision adopted by the General Council on 1 August 2004', WT/L/579, Geneva: World Trade Organization (The July Framework Agreement).

4 Making and keeping negotiating gains

Lessons for the weak from the negotiations over intellectual property rights and access to medicines

Peter Drahos

Introduction

Much of the literature on international negotiation tends to concentrate on the antecedents of negotiation, the process itself and the variables that explain why there was or was not a successful outcome. Little attention has been paid to the fact that a hard-won negotiating gain can be eroded or lost in a subsequent negotiation. Longitudinal studies of distinct but linked negotiations are in short supply. Perhaps this is for the same reason that there are many more books written about how to make a fortune than on the seemingly mundane task of keeping what one has won. But clearly, avoiding the loss of what one has gained is just as important as making gains.

This chapter examines a set of distinct but linked negotiations in the World Trade Organization (WTO) over issues that are broadly referred to as access-to-medicines issues. Drawing on the experience of these access-to-medicines negotiations in the WTO, the chapter derives the following four lessons:

1. In a situation where a coalition of weak bargainers obtains a negotiating gain there has to be a strategy that is aimed at the realization of that gain.
2. Weak actors have to be alert to the dangers of negotiating fatigue.
3. Where a coalition of weak bargainers obtains a negotiating gain that requires high levels of rule complexity to implement, it reduces its chances of successfully realizing that gain.
4. Where a coalition of weak bargainers obtains a negotiating gain it must have a strategy for countering forum shifting by a powerful losing state that is aimed at recapturing that gain.

The problems that patents cause for access to medicines have been a structural issue for developing country consumers for many decades (Gereffi 1983). For the purposes of this chapter, one can trace the political genealogy of the current crop of negotiations over access to medicines back to the emergence of the Agreement on the Trade-Related Aspects of Intellectual Property Rights (TRIPS), an agreement that came into operation on 1 January 1995. TRIPS was the outcome of a sophisticated networked power wielded by a coalition of dominant developed states and corporate actors seeking greater economic rents for their intellectual property assets. Section 2 briefly sets out the negotiating reality of TRIPS. Over time as the patent provisions of TRIPS came to be better understood, the opposition to TRIPS began to grow. In November 2001 at the Ministerial Conference of the WTO in Doha, Qatar a coalition of developing states and civil society actors secured a major negotiating victory in the form of the Declaration on the TRIPS Agreement and Public Health (Doha Declaration).[1] Amongst other things, the Doha Declaration affirmed the right of states to use, under certain conditions, patents without the permission of the patent owner. In practice, however, this right could not be exercised by a country if there was no capacity in a country to manufacture the needed pharmaceutical product and there were legal problems in being able to import the needed medicine from another country. TRIPS had added to these complications by imposing a requirement that where a patented good had been manufactured under a compulsory license, the use of that good had to be "predominantly for the supply of the domestic market."[2] Once a state began to export more than 50 percent of what had been manufactured it left itself open to the argument that it had breached its obligation under Article 31 of TRIPS. WTO Members in Paragraph 6 of the Doha Declaration instructed "the Council for TRIPS to find an expeditious solution to this problem." The solution that was adopted by the WTO General Council on 30 August 2003 took the form of waivers of the obligations in Article 31.[3] The waivers would only operate if a number of conditions were met. The Paragraph 6 solution, as it is often referred to, received a more muted reception from public health advocates.[4] The basic problem was that the Paragraph 6 solution took the form of a system of rules that many saw as promoting uncertainty, the very thing that potential exporters of generic medicines along with importers of those medicines would want. Some saw the Paragraph 6 solution as a defeat for developing countries (Baker 2004).

At the same time as these WTO negotiations had been taking place the US (and to a lesser extent the EU) had been negotiating bilateral agreements relating to intellectual property (Drahos 2001). The US had been on this parallel negotiating track since the 1980s, but beginning with Jordan in 2000 it began to insert into regional trade agreements (more commonly referred to as free trade agreements (FTAs)) comprehensive chapters on intellectual property standards. Many of these standards go beyond what is required under TRIPS or create new obligations altogether. A recent report by the Committee on Government Reform in the United States House of Representatives examined a number of these FTAs and came to the conclusion that "US trade negotiators have repeatedly used the trade agreements to restrict the ability of developing nations to acquire medicines at affordable prices."[5]

If we simplify these complex negotiations in win–loss terms (using the US and developing countries as representatives of opposing coalitions) we end up with the summary below:

TRIPS 1995	(WIN – US)
Doha Declaration 2001	(WIN – developing countries)
Paragraph 6 Solution 2003	(LOSS – developing countries)
IP Chapters of US FTAs	(WIN – US (beginning with US–Jordan FTA 2000))

There are two important points to make about this win–loss sequence. The most-favored nation clause (Article 4) in TRIPS picks up any higher standard of protection that WTO members may agree to in a FTA. In the context of access to medicines this means that when a developing country agrees with the US to an increase in patent standards, the benefit of that increase in protection is available to the nationals of all WTO members. A second point worth noting about this win–loss sequence is that the one win for developing countries, the Doha Declaration, takes the form of a declaration. The status of declarations in international law is not a topic to be pursued here, but we can observe that the degree of legal entrenchment of the principles won in the Doha negotiation does not match the entrenchment by hard law that the US has achieved for its negotiating wins. By way of example, TRIPS began the process of placing conditions and restrictions on the capacity of states to issue compulsory licenses, a process that has been continued by subsequent FTAs. The Doha Declaration articulates the principle that nothing in TRIPS prevents WTO members "from taking measures to protect public health," but it does not stop WTO members from agreeing to restrictions on the measures available to them for the purposes of protecting public health. US

FTAs that impose new restrictions on the capacity of states to regulate intellectual property for public health purposes take advantage of the fact that the Doha Declaration does not establish peremptory norms for this purpose.

TRIPS

The claim that the Doha Declaration was a negotiating success for a coalition of weak actors can only be understood by reference to the negotiations that had produced TRIPS. Susan Sell (2003) points out that some 12 US corporations were primarily responsible for the lobbying that brought TRIPS into being. Others have come to a similar conclusion. TRIPS was a stunning negotiating victory that was made possible because a small group of individuals saw in the 1980s the possibilities of networked governance, especially when those networks could capture and deploy a "big stick" in the form of US trade threats. TRIPS was the product of politically powerful and linked networks deploying a regulatory pyramid with the threat of trade sanctions at its apex.[6] Within these intersecting networks there were pools of technical expertise upon which to draw for the purposes of producing a draft agreement, while other networks steered the draft through a multilateral trade negotiation involving more than 100 states that lasted from 1986 to 1993. Important to this achievement were a small number of business actors who created ever-widening circles of influence that enrolled more actors in networks that had TRIPS as their mission. In the actual negotiations developing countries were not part of the informal groupings where much of the real negotiating was done and where the consensus and agreement that mattered was obtained. A list of these groups in roughly their order of importance would be:

1. US and Europe.
2. US, Europe, Japan.
3. US, Europe, Japan, Canada (Quad).
4. Quad "plus" (membership depended on issue, but Switzerland and Australia were regulars in this group).
5. Friends of Intellectual Property (a larger group that included the Quad, Australia, and Switzerland).
6. 10+10 (and the variants thereof such as 5+5, 3+3). The US and the European Community were always part of any such group if the issue was important. Other active members were Japan, Nordics, Canada, Argentina, Australia, Brazil, Hong Kong, India, Malaysia, Switzerland and Thailand.)

7. Developing country groups (for example, the Andean Group – Bolivia, Colombia, Peru and Venezuela; Argentina, Brazil, Chile, China, Colombia, Cuba, Egypt, Nigeria, Peru, Tanzania and Uruguay combined to submit a developing countries draft text in 1990).
8. Group 11 (the entire TRIPS negotiating group – about 40 countries were active in this group).

(Drahos 2002a:161)

It was the first three circles of consensus that really mattered in the TRIPS negotiations. Through the use of these circles the process became one of hierarchical rather than democratic management. Those in the inner circle of groups knew what TRIPS had to contain. They worked on those in the outer circle until the agreement of all groups to a text had been obtained. TRIPS was much more the product of the first three groups than it was of the last five.

TRIPS covers a range of intellectual property rights and has a number of legal and economic consequences for developing countries. It achieves one thing in its provisions on patents that is essential to understanding the debates around access to medicines. Article 27.1 of TRIPS obliges all Members of the WTO to recognize patents on products in all fields of technology. Before TRIPS some countries (India, for example) did not recognize patents on pharmaceutical products. Product patents are the foundation stone of complex patent portfolios that are built by large pharmaceutical companies around the basic compound they wish to protect. Once the product patent is in place they use other types of patents such as formulation patents, process patents and method-of-treatment patents to build a wall of protection around the original compound. Generic companies have to wait for the product patent to expire before they can enter the market. They may well encounter dozens of other patents around the basic molecule, but many of these are of doubtful validity (and therefore may be litigated) or can be circumvented (e.g. another process of manufacture can be found). It is product patents that are the fundamental building blocks of protection. By globalizing product patent protection for pharmaceuticals, TRIPS released a wave of change in pharmaceutical markets that will be felt for many years to come.

During the 1990s public health experts began to develop an understanding of TRIPS. They began to ask what would happen to the supply of medicines, especially for HIV/AIDS, if pharmaceutical multinationals began to register large numbers of patents in the relatively small number of developing countries that had generic industries with export capacity.[7] Product patents in pharmaceuticals potentially confer enormous market power because of the fact that often there are no ready substitutes for the product. In order to deal with this market power developed countries have over a long period of time used a range of regulatory tools, including compulsory licensing and parallel importation of pharmaceuticals. These are available under TRIPS.[8] Public health advocates aimed to make clear to developing countries that these flexibilities were available to them and that they should not hesitate to use them. Building the institutional capacity to regulate the use of intellectual property does not happen overnight. One important purpose of the Doha Declaration was to clear the air of the uncertainty that had arisen in many developing countries surrounding the use of TRIP flexibilities because of a lack of experience and administrative know-how in these countries in the regulation of patents.

Winning Doha

During the TRIPS negotiations international NGOs and African states were not significant players. The two most striking features in terms of actors involved in the post-TRIPS scene has been the engagement of international NGOs in TRIPS issues and the leadership of the Africa group on health and biodiversity issues. The Organisation of African Unity (OAU), Ethiopia, Kenya, the Third World Network and the Institute for Sustainable Development have been prime movers in developing model legislation for African states which sets out regulatory principles for the ownership and use of biological resources and related local community knowledge. The special sessions of the TRIPS Council on the issue of intellectual property rights and access to medicines, the first of which was held in June of 2001, were inspired by a proposal from the African Group that was discussed and agreed to at a TRIPS Council meeting in April of 2001. This initiative ultimately culminated in the Doha Declaration.

There is little doubt that the rise in influence of the Africa Group has been enabled by a partnership with NGOs. In a study conducted for the UK Commission on Intellectual Property Rights, every single developing country negotiator that was interviewed commented on the positive role that NGOs have played in the debate over TRIPS and access to medicines (Drahos 2002b). (The role of the Quaker Geneva Secretariat came in for express mention. Another interviewee said "what negotiators like me failed to accomplish Oxfam and MSF [Médecins Sans Frontières] have accomplished.")

Northern NGOs have broadly followed the reactive sequence of regulatory change that Braithwaite and Drahos (2000: 33) identify empirically as one of the sequences that results in global regulatory change. This sequence begins with a crisis that sees a regulatory entrepreneur seize the initiative by putting a regulatory model on the table, a model that eventually globalizes. The death toll in Africa from AIDS has created one of the greatest international public health crises in history. Using this crisis NGOs have reframed the contest of principles surrounding intellectual property rights. During the TRIPS negotiations, US multinationals framed the contest as one between the protection of private property rights versus piracy by developing countries. During the late 1990s NGOs presented the contest as one between the rights of states to protect public health versus the extension of patent monopoly power. The Doha Declaration, the outcome of this contest, elevates the former principle over the latter.

The Doha Declaration is a case of a weak coalition making a gain that an observer would not have predicted given the power resources of the US-led coalition. The explanation for this success lies in the fact that we live in a networked world and in such a world, as John Braithwaite (2006) has observed, "the prescription for potency is not to sit around waiting for your own power to grow ... [r]ather the prescription is to actively network with those with power that you do not yourself control." Through networking the weak actor becomes connected to other pools of capacity/power, pools that can then flow through the network to achieve the goals of members of the network. The Africa Group could never have achieved the Doha Declaration because they were and remain a weak group. But an Africa Group that joined with a large coalition of developing countries that included Brazil and India, that drew on the power of Northern NGOs to work the Northern mass media, that gained the quiet support of some European states, that drew on independent technical expertise to evaluate draft text, and that gained resources from Geneva-based NGOs, was a group strengthened by many ties.[9] If TRIPS was about a form of networked governance in which the powerful built ever-larger circles of consensus in the shadow of credible threats of trade coercion, the Doha Declaration was about the weak networking networks that surrounded and eventually isolated the US and in the final instance its pharmaceutical industry. At Doha the then USTR Robert Zoellick faced a choice between appearing to be against access to medicines or abandoning the US pharmaceutical industry. Neither were especially palatable alternatives; he chose the latter. There was also another factor at play. The networking of networks by the weak had created a form of sanction that cast its shadow over Doha: that of the court of global public opinion. Northern NGOs had succeeded in reducing the complexities of patent law and HIV/AIDS down to a simple choice readily understood by mass publics. Moreover, WTO negotiations were globally visible and transparent in ways that FTA negotiations were simply not. With the world's press watching, the US-led coalition was faced with coming out in support of a declaration that unambiguously helped to prevent millions of needless deaths or declaring itself in favor of putting patents and profit first. The former was a basic moral canon understood by all. No individual, country or organization could be seen to be deciding the latter.

Frail victory – the Paragraph 6 solution

We saw in the introduction to this chapter that the Doha Declaration had left the TRIPS Council with a task that was defined in Paragraph 6. The Council had to find a solution to the problem of how developing countries that lacked manufacturing capacity in the pharmaceutical sector could make use of the flexibilities of TRIPS, which the Doha Declaration stated were available, when TRIPS itself imposed a limit on export under compulsory license. This solution had to be found against a background in which trade law, patent law and treaty law all converged to produce a high level of legal complexity. From the point of view of US pharmaceutical multinationals, a Paragraph 6 solution had the potential to make it easier for developing country exporters such as India to export medicines that were needed by other countries. One of the key long-term objectives of US pharmaceutical multinationals was to create an international patent regime that would make it difficult for generic exporters to contest the US market or third markets in cases where a product had gone off patent or a compulsory license had been issued. In particular, US corporations were worried about the use that India, which was the principal developing country exporter, might make of a Paragraph 6 solution. India had always been the main target of the TRIPS negotiations, because it had not bowed to US bilateral pressure during the 1980s. Moreover, US pharmaceutical companies were not content with TRIPS standards for India, as the following extract from a letter from Pfizer written in 1994 to the United States Trade Representative makes clear:

> Finally, GATT does not do it. Many Indians mistakenly (often very honestly) believe that if they endorse GATT they will have solved their IP and pharmaceutical patent issue. Not so, particularly if

they truly want to create an environment that attracts investment and provides better medicine – legalistically agreeing to something (GATT) that brings this into play in ten years or more achieves neither of these two objectives.[10]

When the solution to the Paragraph 6 problem was adopted by the WTO General Council on 30 August 2003 it took the form of six pages of rules that specified conditions under which an importing country would be able to bring in a consignment of drugs from an exporting country. For present purposes, it is important to note that the solution is characterized by a high degree of rule complexity. Rule complexity has some basic indicators: density, technicality, differentiation and uncertainty (Schuck 1992). The Paragraph 6 solution covers the import/export transaction (density of coverage), it requires specialist expertise to apply (technicality), it involves the application of domestic and treaty law (differentiation) and it requires a number of conditions to be satisfied before it can be applied (uncertainty). Civil society advocates in particular were keen on a solution that kept rule complexity to a minimum. For this reason key players such as CPTech and Médecins Sans Frontières pushed what became known as an Article 30 solution.[11]

Article 30 is an important provision in TRIPS that recognizes that states may limit the right of the patent holder for certain purposes. The Article 30 principle of a limitation of rights could potentially be used to create new exceptions and limitations on patent rights. In its simplest form an Article 30 solution could have seen WTO members simply agreeing that in cases where a country lacked manufacturing capacity and needed medicines, Article 30 would permit the creation of an exception to the restriction imposed by Article 31(f) of TRIPS. Over time a state practice around this exception would have emerged as states implemented this approach into their national laws. Disagreements over the scope of the Article 30 solution could have been dealt with through negotiation, consultation and ultimately the WTO's dispute resolution process. An Article 30 solution could have laid the basis for the evolution of a responsive state practice and custom on public health and intellectual property issues. The important point for present purposes is that a principle-based solution was available. What WTO members actually negotiated was a rule-intensive solution. We shall see in the next section that this type of solution has real costs for weaker actors when it comes to realizing the gains of a negotiation.

Rule complex solutions – costs and lessons from Doha

We can now turn to the four propositions that we put forward at the beginning of this chapter and show how they are supported by the negotiations around the Doha Declaration and the Paragraph 6 solution.

In a situation where a coalition of weak bargainers obtains a negotiating gain there has to be a strategy that is aimed at the realization of that gain

Negotiating wins or gains may or may not turn into real gains. Within the context of trade negotiation an example of a negotiating gain that is turned into a real gain is where a state wins a tariff concession and the state granting the concession does nothing to frustrate its grant with the result that the first state gains a share of an export market that it did not have before.[12] Much of trade law can be read as providing mechanisms for ensuring that states stick to the concessions that they have negotiated and that they do not use other devices and stratagems for defeating the thrust of those concessions. In the case of international negotiations, a negotiating win is most likely to be realized where the parties to the agreement both have strong interests in meeting their promises or where the breach of a promise by one party is likely to be detected and there is a robust enforcement mechanism that will deliver a sanction for that breach. Where mutual gains providing for self-enforcement do not exist or where there is no strong enforcement mechanism there is a real danger that a negotiating win, especially one by a weaker actor, will not be realized. Under these conditions if a negotiating win is not accompanied by some strategy of post-negotiation implementation there is a real risk that the gain will never be realized.

The Doha Declaration is an example of a rare negotiating win for developing countries in the context of intellectual property rights. However, developing countries had no common or even individual strategy for exploiting its potential. The negotiations over the Doha Declaration were not about trade gains in any conventional sense. Instead, as the opening paragraph makes clear, the negotiation was about recognizing that developing countries were facing severe public health problems and TRIPS (and therefore the WTO) had to be part of the solution rather than part of the problem. The Declaration does not create new rights that override TRIPS. Rather it provides a constitutional-like ordering of principle in which the principle of intellectual property protection is expressly subordinated to the right of states to protect public health. Following on from this constitutional ordering in Paragraph 4 of the Doha Declaration, Paragraph 5 lists some of the flexibilities that TRIPS contains and that can be used to serve the principle of protecting public health.

Winning a contest of principles, however, is only the beginning of securing a desired regulatory outcome. Principles are by their nature open-ended and so have to be secured through practices and rules that institutionalize those principles. Victory in a contest of principles that is not secured through institutionalization can be lost, if the losing party shifts the contest to another forum or if the losing party counters by generating a rule complexity that does not support the spirit of the principle.

Following the Doha Declaration, developing states had the opportunity to create forms of state practice around the Doha Declaration and TRIPS that would have clearly established that intellectual property rights were the regulatory servants of public health. The kinds of practices that states might have engaged in would have been to begin routinely issuing compulsory licenses for needed medicines, establishing an exhaustion regime for patents that best suited their circumstances and if necessary making use of Article 30. This sounds very much like a bootstraps enterprise, but this is a form of enterprise that international law expressly recognizes.[13] States can through practice and custom create law and give meaning to treaties. More important than the rules of international law are the politics. If developing countries had collectively, vigorously and with media savvy pursued the kind of options outlined above would the US in particular have opposed them by, for example, threatening litigation in the WTO? Bearing in mind the public relations disaster of the litigation by pharmaceutical multinationals against South Africa (Odell and Sell 2006: 85, 98) and the fact that the US would have been globally seen to be undermining the Doha Declaration as a moral canon, one suspects that the costs to the US of a WTO litigation strategy would have been simply too high. The more widespread the practices of developing countries became, the more weight as a matter of international law those practices would have gained.

As it turned out, developing countries did not have any such post-negotiation implementation strategy in place for the realization of the gains of Doha. Table 4.1 illustrates just how little activity actually took place on the ground in developing countries in the first three years after Doha. Instead, developing countries became drawn into another negotiation in the WTO on the Paragraph 6 issue. It is from this negotiation that our next two propositions are derived.

Table 4.1 Compulsory licenses after the Doha Declaration, 2001–04

Country	Year	License activity
Brazil	2001	From 2001 Brazil has on a number of occasions threatened the use of compulsory licenses but no license has been issued to date.
Indonesia	2004	On 5 October 2004, Indonesia issued a compulsory license for lamivudine and nevirapine.
Korea	2002	Application for compulsory non-exclusive license for importation of Glivec from India. Rejected 2003.
Malaysia	2003	On 29 October 2003, the Malaysian Minister of Domestic Trade and Consumer Affairs issued a two-year compulsory license for importation of didanosine (ddI), zidovudine (AZT) and lamivudine+zidovidine (Combivir) from Cipla, India.
Mozambique	2004	On 5 April 2004, Mozambique's Deputy Minister of Industry and Commerce issued a compulsory license for patent rights to lamivudine, stavudine and nevirapine.
South Africa	2003	On 10 December 2003, South Africa's Competition Commission reached a settlement with GlaxoSmithKline and Boehringer Ingelheim. The complaint charged these corporations with excessive pricing in respect of ritonavir, lamivudine, ritonavir + lamivudine and nevirapine.
Zambia	2004	On 21 September 2004, the Zambian Minister of Domestic Trade and Consumer Affairs issued a compulsory license for lamivudine, stavudine and nevirapine. The license was granted to Pharco Ltd, a local producer, which will produce a triple fixed-dose combination.
Zimbabwe	2004	On 27 May 2004, Zimbabwe's Minister of Justice, Legal and Parliamentary Affairs declared a Period of Emergency in order to override anti-retroviral drug patents. With assistance from India, Zimbabwe has begun local production of anti-retrovirals.

Source: Available at: <http://www.cptech.org/ip/health/cl/recent-examples.html>.

Note: This table is compiled from the page that is kept by the Consumer Project on Technology on compulsory licenses and health matters. It is the best public source of information on this issue that is known to the author.

Weaker actors have to be alert to the dangers of "negotiating fatigue"

During their fieldwork at the WTO in the early 1990s Braithwaite and Drahos (2000: 196) found that senior personnel saw the organization as suffering from "negotiating fatigue:"

A situation of negotiating fatigue "suits the US and Europe" with their large infrastructure for trade negotiation in Geneva. They want the WTO to take on "more and more good things" that will liberalize trade, knowing that only they can resource the committees properly. "Big players can afford to play cat and mouse ... when they are suffering less negotiating fatigue than others."

(WTO official)

One only needs to look at the meeting schedule of the WTO on any given day in Geneva, along with other relevant meetings in organizations such as UNCTAD or the World Intellectual Property Organization (WIPO) to see that developing and many middling developed country economies have little capacity to service negotiations on so many fronts on which there are constant demands. Drahos (2002b), in a separate fieldwork exercise conducted in 2001, found that the cycle of negotiating fatigue had intensified since the early 1990s. He interviewed developing country representatives that had responsibility for up to a dozen different areas across a number of international organizations. Expert tracking of so many areas is not, as the interviewees readily conceded, a realistic possibility. Instead many negotiators stumble from one meeting to another with little evidence-based understanding of what they are dealing with, largely repeating what they have picked up in conversation or read in a summary briefing paper that has found its way onto their desk.

The Paragraph 6 negotiations provide a useful illustration of the dangers of negotiating fatigue. They also illustrate that in a world of perpetual negotiation all negotiating wins should be treated as temporary. Any other attitude to victory leaves one open to the dangers of hubris and nemesis.

An alliance of developing countries and civil society actors using a combination of evidence-based analysis and skillful public campaigning along with the issue of credible threats (No Doha Declaration, No Doha round) won the Doha Declaration. After the Doha Declaration two fundamental things happened. The US pharmaceutical industry, realizing the dangers to it of Doha's guarantees and freedoms for public health, came to the Paragraph 6 negotiations with the clear objective of finding a "solution" that would limit the freedoms of Doha. The Paragraph 6 negotiations became an opportunity for the US industry to recoup its losses. At the same time, the US intensified its strategy of obtaining stronger standards of intellectual property protection through FTAs. Developing countries by contrast were not especially well prepared for another negotiation on intellectual property rights and public health. The launch of the Doha Trade Round meant that their already strained trade bureaucracies would confront extra demands. Facing this situation, developing countries would have done better to postpone the Paragraph 6 negotiation and concentrate on developing supportive state practices that would have released the full potential of the Doha Declaration. Instead they entered into another WTO negotiating cycle at a time when the US had also opened up a bilateral front on intellectual property.

Negotiating fatigue is a real phenomenon. The US and EU know that pressure-ridden negotiating cycles over complex issues will strain and eventually overwhelm the capacities of most weaker actors. For weaker actors part of the art of negotiation is knowing when to walk away, when not to be drawn into a cycle of negotiation and when to put on the negotiating agenda items that they can service in terms of analysis and personnel. Agreeing to tight negotiating schedules and deadlines creates pressures that the stronger actor is better able to absorb. Where these pressures produce a negotiating impasse between the stronger and weaker actor, the subsequent political intervention to resolve that impasse may also favor the stronger actor. The political representatives of the stronger party will generally be in a better bargaining position than the representatives of the weaker party.

Where a coalition of weak bargainers obtains a negotiating gain that requires high levels of rule complexity to implement, it reduces its chances of successfully realizing that gain

We saw earlier that the Paragraph 6 solution is an example of rule complexity. The decision covers all aspects of the export/import transaction in tiny detail (for example, the licensee before shipment has to post on a website information as to quantities and product labeling). It requires technical advice to implement within a national system of patent law and technical advice about how to use it. The implementation and use of the system requires the application of multiple sources of law, including patent law, treaty law and trade law. There is a multi-dimensionality of multiple factors that has to be taken into account before a country can implement or use the decision. If, for example, a country has a free trade agreement with the US its obligations under that free trade agreement may impede the effective use of the system. It is worth noting that a 64-page guide to the Paragraph 6 decision published by the World Bank cautions the following:

[T]his Guide can only provide a starting point. The actual implementation of the Paragraph 6 Decision will take place within the
contours of each country's existing legislative and regulatory
framework, practice and jurisprudence. The authorities of each
country will have to work with their own legal experts to arrive at
a solution that is right for their situation.

(Abbott and Van Puymbroeck 2005: 3)

The real gain to developing countries of the Paragraph 6 decision, as
opposed to the negotiating gain, is if large numbers of generic companies use the Paragraph 6 system to export medicines to developing
countries. The more generic companies that enter the system the
greater will be the real gains. Developing countries will have access to
a wider range of medicines (generic companies specialize e.g. in medicines taken by means of injection vs medicines taken orally). Increased
numbers of generic companies also mean greater competition on
price, the first necessary condition of access.

At base if the Paragraph 6 solution is to work it must provide
generic exporters with enough certainty about access to export markets so as to induce them to enter those markets. Many of the costs of
medicines in developing countries related to the treatment of diseases
such as HIV Aids, tuberculosis and malaria are being met by a combination of private–public initiatives from developed countries.
Organizations like MSF, the Clinton Foundation, The Bill and Melinda
Gates Foundation and developed country governments acting indepen-
dently or together through mechanisms like the Global Fund have
created global export markets for medicines in developing countries
where none existed before. The crucial issue then becomes whether, as
a matter of commercial reality, the Paragraph 6 solution as presently
cast helps generic exporters to enter these new markets. This is an
empirical question about the future conduct of companies. Roberto
Danino, Senior Vice President and General Counsel of the World Bank,
in his foreword to the World Bank's Guide observes that despite the
wide coverage the Paragraph 6 decision has been given, "the decision
has still not been used to bring affordable, life-saving medicines to
countries" that need them (Abbott and Van Puymbroeck 2005: v).

One factor that may help to explain the slow uptake of the decision
is its very rule complexity. Clear rules that bring transparency and certainty to decisions about investment are essential to encouraging
investment activity of any kind. Rules do not always deliver certainty.[14] Patent rules are standardly justified as a means for offering
investors the certainty that for a limited period they will have the right

to exploit the product of their investment. However, from the point of view of social welfare, which the patent system is meant to serve, it is just as important that the rules about the end of the patent period are equally certain. Investors in generic companies need to know that there really is a pharmaceutical market in which they may freely compete with other companies to produce the product. Clear and simple rules about when a product goes off patent are fundamental to the operation of competitive markets in pharmaceuticals.

One problem with the Paragraph 6 solution may be that it is generating additional uncertainty that will lead generic companies not to use it. All companies have to live with the brute fact of risk and uncertainty. Rule-based regulatory complexity is a fact of life for pharmaceutical companies. But at some point a company will conclude that additional risks and uncertainty are not worth any potential reward i.e. the company will adopt a risk-averse strategy. This may well turn out to be the case for many generic companies when they look at the Paragraph 6 decision. The present author as part of a project that is looking at the impact of free trade agreements on public health interviewed five generic companies based in Australia.[15] All those interviewed saw the WTO solution as somewhat remote from their interests and plans. Dealing with risk and uncertainty was a recurring theme in the interviews with the companies reporting that they were seeing higher levels of patenting by brand companies and that navigating through these patents was increasing their costs. The companies were not well informed about the details of the Paragraph 6 solution. In the one or two cases where they had more information about it they saw no real value in it. The companies interviewed in Australia spoke about the need for simple clear export rules that would allow them to access markets in a timely fashion. One company pointed out that in any implementation of the Paragraph 6 solution, where a large pharmaceutical company was given the opportunity to hinder or stop export by a generic company, that large company would always take that opportunity. This would be a rational business practice. This kind of observation is consistent with the gaming of patent rules that can be seen more broadly within the pharmaceutical industry.[16]

Of course, other generic companies in other parts of the world may study the Paragraph 6 decision and come to a different conclusion to these Australian companies. Many, one suspects, will reach a similar conclusion. There is a real possibility that developing country negotiators have agreed to a solution that is simply not rooted in the realities of commercial life. The obvious cost of encasing a negotiating outcome in complex rules is the risk of losing the gains that were meant to flow from the negotiated solution. There may also be other costs that flow from complex rule solutions. The solution may be sold to concerned mass publics as having solved the problem. Mass publics, which in any case have short attention spans, are hardly likely to follow the technical details of implementation in the improbable event that the press chooses to report them. The passage of the Paragraph 6 rules was an important symbolic ritual that allowed the WTO and its supporters to claim that the trade regime had done what it could do about the HIV/AIDS pandemic and now it was time to move on to the real business of trade liberalization.[17] The rule complexity of Paragraph 6 had handed the reframing initiative back to US and the pharmaceutical industry. What Paragraph 6 and its supporting rhetoric concealed was that the opportunity to create more competitive pharmaceutical markets for poor people around the world had been sacrificed in favor of perpetuating the pharmaceutical monopoly interests of the US and Europe.

This raises the question of how weaker actors can avoid or minimize the risk of rule complexity. A basic but important point is that negotiators must be aware of the risk before they can decide what, if anything, they will or are able to do about the risk. This leads directly into the issue of information, or rather the lack of it. Generally, the problem of imperfect information (or bounded rationality) in the context of negotiation relates to lack of information that negotiators have about each other's bottom lines, preferences, goals, etc. In the case of the Paragraph 6 solution we are dealing with information about the workability of a solution that was available, or least enough information was available to make a better probability calculation about the chances of the solution working. This information could have been obtained from generic companies, many of which had had years of experience with the export of pharmaceuticals and the gaming of rules by brand pharmaceutical companies. Even the small number of interviews conducted by the author in Australia turned up enough information to show that the risks of gaming complex rules for the export of pharmaceuticals was very real. This example suggests that where weaker actors can correct for imperfect information they should do so. As John Odell (2006: 1, 10) correctly observes, there are times in negotiations when negotiators have to operate using rules of thumb. But there are other occasions when they should not economize on obtaining information, especially where that information is reasonably available. The investment of resources into finding out about the workability of any proposed Paragraph 6 solution would have repaid itself many times over, given what was at stake in the negotiation – the structure of pharmaceutical export markets for poor people. A corollary of correcting for imperfect information is that weaker actors should not be drawn into deadlines and negotiating timetables (which in any case promote negotiating fatigue) until that information is obtained.

Where a coalition of weak bargainers obtains a negotiating gain, it must have a strategy for countering forum shifting by a powerful losing coalition that is aimed at negotiating that gain away

Forum shifting is a practice that has been utilized primarily by the US since the Second World War (Braithwaite and Drahos 2000: 29). Essentially it allows the US to increase its opportunities to play for a win by not confining the pursuit of its negotiating agenda to one international forum. Three basic strategies are involved. A negotiating agenda may be moved from one international organization to another, a negotiating agenda may be pursued in parallel in more than one international organization, or an international organization may be abandoned by the strong player. Forum shifting has been fundamental to the globalization of intellectual property rights. The US shifted its agenda on strong enforceable intellectual property rights from the World Intellectual Property Organization to the GATT during the 1980s. That move led to TRIPS. During the 1990s the US made little progress in the TRIPS Council on the issues that mattered to it. The US was sending impressive delegations of intellectual property experts to TRIPS Council meetings only to be confronted by developing country coalitions pushing issues related to health and biodiversity, issues that the US did not see as related to trade in intellectual property rights.[18] The US switched its negotiating agenda on intellectual property to FTAs. Since the FTA with Jordan in 2000 it has maintained an impressive track record of securing TRIPS plus standards through FTAs (Thomas 2005).

One clear effect of these FTAs is to restrict the rights that a country would otherwise have had under TRIPS to protect public health by inserting in them provisions that delay the approval of generic drugs, require patent extensions, link drug approval to patent status, restrict compulsory licensing, prohibit parallel importation and expand patent protection.[19] Here we have a very clear case of successful forum shifting. The US would never have been able to obtain in the WTO the standards on intellectual property that it has in FTAs.

From the point of view of the US the shift to a FTA has the effect of taking the target state out of an effective WTO coalition and reinstating an inequality of bargaining power that existed before the coalition came into existence. Even if, as is usually the case, the economics of the FTA do not favor the weaker state (Freund 2003), the leaders from that weaker state may see political benefit in having a bilateral relationship with the world's strongest state. Political leaders from a weak state may well be ready to give up hard-won negotiating gains in other fora as part of the price of securing a "special" relationship with the US. In this context it is worth recalling Robert Keohane's (1969) insight of the "Al Capone alliance" between small and great powers. In this type of alliance,

> remaining a faithful ally protects one not against the mythical outside threat but rather against the great power ally itself, just as, by paying "protection money" to Capone's gang in Chicago, businessmen protected themselves not against other gangs but against Capone's own thugs.

From the point of view of the strong state, forum shifting is all about cycling through fora to find one at a moment in time where its power is optimized and the advantages of negotiation for the weak are minimized. From the point of view of weak states, forum shifting poses a great danger because when the weak states make clear negotiating gains, as did developing countries with the Doha Declaration, a stronger actor may simply recontest that outcome in another forum. Forum shifting means that some negotiations are never really over. It also suggests that some negotiations are best studied longitudinally and as linked sequences rather than statically and as individual case studies. This is certainly the case for trade negotiations where in the last decade there has been an explosion in free trade negotiations (Crawford and Fiorentino 2005).

Turning now to the question of what lesson to derive from the negotiations around access to medicines, it is important to bear in mind that this latest example of forum shifting by the US is part of a 25-year pattern on intellectual property issues. Developing country responses to this pattern represent a record of failure. Developing country negotiators can point to individual successes like the Doha Declaration, but those successes are being undermined by the greater power and capability of the US, much as structural realist theory would predict. If an answer to this problem is to be found it lies in developing countries evolving superior kinds of organizational forms for the conduct of negotiations that have a clear longitudinal and spatial dimension. If it is efficient to hold the line on the globalization of patent monopolies in Geneva in the WTO it is also efficient to do so back in the capitols in the context of a FTA.

The possibility of developing states evolving a joint negotiating strategy to defeat the rent-seeking politics of intellectual property rights that is robust over time and place is, of course, no small challenge. Nevertheless it is a challenge that developing countries must begin to address. The starting point is to focus on the differences in performance between coalitions and networks. For present purposes we can distinguish coalitions and networks by stipulating that the former consist of governments that coordinate (Odell 2006: 1, 13) while the latter consist of nodal actors (whether state or non-state) that coordinate. Stating the distinction in this way we can say that the coalitionist in a negotiation places the emphasis on enrolling governments while the networker looks more widely to enrolling nodal actors that can help the cause.

Developing country coalitions in the WTO have tended to be temporary, informal, single issue groups with little emphasis on institutionalization beyond a single negotiation (Drahos 2003). Perhaps the best example of an institutionalized coalition that does not fit this generalization has been the Cairns Group on agriculture that was formed during the Uruguay Round of the GATT.[20] Site specific and temporary coalitions are not a strong organizational form for dealing with negotiations in which a strong actor has the capacity to cycle that negotiating agenda through a number of fora. A coalition of weak actors that arises in one organization may, for a variety of reasons, simply not arise in another. Developing countries with limited resources may simply concentrate their attention on the WTO and limit, for example, their participation in WIPO, or they may send different representatives to WIPO who may not coalesce in the same way on an issue in WIPO as their counterparts do in the WTO. Moreover, if the strong actor shifts to a bilateral negotiation the possibility of a coalition to oppose the strong actor is simply removed.

All developing countries have, as the Doha Declaration demonstrated, strong interests in access to medicines. Coalitions have proven not to be a successful means of longitudinal coordination on this issue and have failed to counter the strategy of forum shifting. Developing states have to find ways of protecting negotiating gains on access to medicines across fora and across time. One way of achieving this kind of coordination is through an institutionalized network that has enrolled in it as many nodal actors as possible. The core of the network would be those states that were prepared to unite around the basic premise of the Doha Declaration. The network could start as a

Cairns-style, Health and Intellectual Property (HIP) group. As with the Cairns Group it would have a secretariat. The HIP group, however, would place the emphasis on enrolling actors whether state or non-state to increase its capacity and power. For example, the strategy of framing, which was central to the success of developing countries in the Doha Declaration, requires the assistance of media savvy NGOs. More importantly and unlike the Cairns Group, the HIP group would operate as a network to coordinate the positions of its members across fora whenever the issue of public health and intellectual property was being negotiated (for example, in WIPO, WTO, WHO and FTAs). The goal would be to avoid defections by single states in any negotiating context that end up compromising the goal of the overall group (for example, the FTA between Australia (a Cairns Group leader) and the US has probably undermined the goal of the Cairns Group in the WTO). Coalitions of weak actors that are site specific cannot prevent this kind of defection. By joining the HIP group, states would be signaling that they would only agree to intellectual property standards that did not compromise their right to protect public health. States that stayed out of the HIP group would have to account to various NGOs and ultimately their publics as to why they were staying out of a network designed to protect public health.

The HIP network could remain a single issue network, just as the Cairns Group is a single issue group. This would help avoid the fragmentation of the network. The goal of the network would be to enroll as many nodal actors as possible on the single issue of public health and intellectual property rights, with a view to isolating the proponents of stronger intellectual property protection at the expense of public health. Developing countries would simply agree that the issue of access to medicines was of such fundamental importance that they would develop a common bargaining strategy around it. A joint strategy of this kind would not prevent them from going their different ways on other issues such as services or government procurement. This limited joint form of bargaining would be a means of ensuring that any gains from negotiations over public health and intellectual property were realized rather than being recaptured over time by the US through a strategy of forum shifting. Irrespective of how developing countries respond to forum shifting, the clear lesson from the access to medicines negotiations is that they must respond. In a trade world of perpetual negotiation and many fora the negotiating gains of the weak are fragile and may end up being taken away.

Conclusion

Weak actors do make negotiating gains. The Doha Declaration is a case in point. However, before one can conclude much about the role of negotiation and the limits of structural power in the world one has to recognize that a strong state like the US will shift fora in order to recapture negotiating gains. The FTAs that the US has negotiated since the Doha Declaration are rapidly eroding the gains of the Declaration for developing countries. The experience of developing countries with the Doha Declaration is part of a deeper game of forum shifting around intellectual property that has been in play for at least 25 years. It is only by studying negotiation in this area longitudinally, as a series of connected episodes, that we can gain a real understanding of the possibilities and limits of negotiation as a tool through which weak actors can make gains. Intellectual property is an area where structural power meets and usually trumps the negotiating coalitions and tactics of the weak. Depending on how one draws the boundaries of property around knowledge and information, US, European and Japanese multinationals will get richer or poorer. They would like to get richer. Developing countries also want to get richer. Intellectual property rights are all about transfers of wealth. Negotiations over them will not end any time soon.

For weaker actors the lessons of the Doha Declaration are clear. They must have strategies for realizing the gains of negotiation, acting where they can on the basis of self-help and unilateral action. They have to avoid concessions that are encased in rule complexity. Most importantly, they have to find ways to develop a joint bargaining strategy on at least some intellectual property issues that will counter forum shifting by the US. The key to finding this strategy lies in exploring the possibilities offered by a world of networked governance.[21] Traditional coalition formation will be of little use to developing states in this regard. Instead they must escalate their networking across time and place in order to protect precious negotiating gains made in one time and place.

Notes

1 See WT/MIN(01)/DEC/W/2, 14 November 2001.
2 See Article 31(f). This condition does not apply where the compulsory license is issued as part of an anti-competitive remedy. See Article 31(k).
3 Implementation of Paragraph 6 of the Doha Declaration on the TRIPS Agreement and Public Health, Decision of the General Council of 30 August 2003, WT/L/540, 1 September 2003.

4 See, for example, *MSF Comments on the Draft Chairman's Statement of 21 August '03*, available at < http://www.accessmed-msf.org/prod/publications.asp?scntid= 26820031712133&contenttype =PARA&> and *Joint NGO Statement on TRIPS & Public Health*, available at <http://www.oxfam.org.uk/what_we_do/issues/health/wtodeal_300803.htm>.

5 *Trade Agreements and Access to Medications Under the Bush Administration*, United States House of Representatives, Committee on Government Reform-Minority Staff, Special Investigations Division, June 2005, I. Available at: <www.reform.house.gov/min>.

6 For an explanation of how the theory of the regulatory pyramid applies to US trade regulation as well as the theory of the nodally coordinated pyramid see Peter Drahos (2004).

7 Only a small number of developing countries possess reverse engineering capabilities on an industrial scale. A study in 1992 by UNIDO pointed out that only five developing countries had innovative capabilities in the pharmaceutical sector (defined as the capability of producing new drugs by a process of reverse engineering). These countries were Argentina, China, India, Korea and Mexico (See Balance *et al.* 1992). Since the UNIDO study a number of developing countries have, as a result of the HIV/AIDS crisis, placed resources into the pharmaceutical sector and as a result have a much stronger sector. Brazil and Thailand are leaders in the manufacture of cheap anti-retroviral drugs.

8 See generally, Musungu *et al.* (2004).

9 For a detailed account of how these factors played out in the negotiation see Odell and Sell (2006: 85).

10 Letter from C.L. Clemente, Senior Vice President – Corporate Affairs, Pfizer Inc to Joseph Papovich, Deputy Assistant US Trade Representative for Intellectual Property, 7 June 1994.

11 For an explanation as to why CPTech, MSF, Oxfam and Health Action International preferred an Article 30 solution see 'Letter from CPTech, Oxfam, MSF and HAI to WTO Delegates regarding 16 December 2002 Chairman's Text for "solution" to Paragraph 6 of the Doha Declaration on TRIPS and Public Health'. Available at: <http://www.accessmed-msf.org/prod/publications.asp?scntid=6120031111255&contenttype=PARA&>.

12 In economic terms the state granting the concession also wins, but this is not how it is seen in the world of trade negotiators. See Finger (2005).

13 For example, Article 31(3) (b) of the Vienna Convention on the Law of Treaties 1969 states that "any subsequent practice in the application of the treaty which establishes the agreement of the parties regarding its interpretation" shall be taken into account.

14 For an argument for simpler rules see Epstein (1995).

15 (With Tom Faunce and David Henry) Discovery Grant from the Australian Research Council, 'The Impact of International Trade Agreements on the Regulation and Provision of Medicines in Australia'.

16 See Federal Trade Commission (2002). For an account of the gaming of aspects of Canadian patent regulations from the perspective of the Canadian generic industry see Hore (2004).

17 See the press release by the WTO, *Decision removes final obstacle to cheap drug imports*, Press/350/Rev.1. Available at <http://www.wto.org/english/

news_e/pres03_e/pr350_e.htm>. See also *Statement of the US Trade Representative Robert B. Zoellick on TRIPS and Access to Medicines,* 30 August 2003. Available at <http://www.ustr.gov/Document_Library/Press_Releases/2003/ August/Statement_of_US_Trade_Representative_Robert_B_Zoellick_on_TRIPS_access_to_medicines.html>. The Pharmaceutical Research and Manufacturers of America also viewed the Paragraph 6 solution as positive and welcomed its codification. See its press release of 6 December 2005. Available at <http://www.phrma.org/news_room/press_releases/phrma_ welcomes_trips_ and_public_health_agreement/>.

18 Interview in USTR's Office, Geneva, 2001.

19 See *Trade Agreements and Access to Medications Under the Bush Administration, United States House of Representatives, Committee on Government Reform-Minority Staff, Special Investigations Division, June 2005, I.* Available at: <www.reform.house.gov/min>.

20 The Cairns Group was formed in 1986 and continues as a group in the WTO. See <http://www. cairnsgroup.org/milestones.html>.

21 On the possibilities in general for developing countries see Drahos (2004) and Braithwaite (2004).

References

Abbott, Frederick M. and Van Puymbroeck, Rudolf V. (2005) Compulsory Licensing for Public Health: A Guide and Model Documents for Implementation of the Doha Declaration Paragraph 6 Decision, World Bank Working Paper No. 61, Washington, DC: World Bank.

Baker, Brook K. (2004) 'Arthritic flexibilities for accessing medicines: analysis of WTO action regarding Paragraph 6 of the Doha Declaration on the TRIPS Agreement and Public Health', *Indiana International & Comparative Law Review,* 14: 613.

Balance, Robert, Progany, Janos and Forstener, Helmet (1992) 'The world's pharmaceutical industries: an international perspective on innovation, competition and policy', UNIDO.

Braithwaite, John (2004) 'Methods of power for development: weapons of the weak, weapons of the strong', *Michigan Journal of International Law,* 26.

—— (2006) 'Responsive regulation and developing economies', *World Development,* 34: 884, 892.

—— and Drahos, P. (2000) *Global Business Regulation,* Cambridge: Cambridge University Press.

Crawford, Jo-Ann and Fiorentino, Roberto V. (2005) 'The changing landscape of regional trade agreements', Discussion Paper No. 8, World Trade Organization.

Drahos, Peter (2001) 'BITS and BIPS: bilateralism in intellectual property', *Journal of World Intellectual Property,* 4: 791.

—— (2002a) 'Negotiating intellectual property rights: between coercion and dialogue', in Drahos and Mayne (eds) *Global Intellectual Property Rights: Knowledge Access and Development,* Hampshire and New York: Palgrave Macmillan.

—— (2002b) *Intellectual Property Standard Setting and Developing Countries,* paper for the UK Commission on Intellectual Property Rights, Study Paper 8. Available at: <http://www.iprcommission.org>.

—— (2003) 'When the weak bargain with the strong: negotiations in the World Trade Organization', *International Negotiation,* 8: 79–109.

—— (2004) 'Intellectual property and pharmaceutical markets: a nodal governance approach', *Temple Law Review,* 77: 401.

Epstein, Richard A. (1995) *Simple Rules for a Complex World,* Cambridge: Harvard University Press.

Federal Trade Commission (2002) 'Generic Drug Entry Prior to Patent Expiration', July.

Finger, Michael J. (2005) 'A diplomat's economics: reciprocity in the Uruguay Round negotiations', *World Trade Review,* 4: 27.

Freund, Caroline (2003) *Reciprocity in Free Trade Agreements,* World Bank, April. Available at: <http://www.sice.oas.org/geograph/mktacc/freund.pdf>.

Gereffi, Gary (1983) *The Pharmaceutical Industry and Dependency in the Third World,* Princeton, NJ: Princeton University Press.

Hore, Edward (2004) 'Patently Absurd: evergreening of pharmaceutical patent protection under the Patented Medicines (Notice of Compliance) Regulations of Canada's Patent Act', available from the Canadian Generic Pharmaceutical's Association.

Keohane, Robert (1969) 'Lilliputians' dilemma: small states in international politics', *International Organization,* 23: 291, 302.

Musungu *et al.* (2004) 'Utilizing TRIPS flexibilities for public health protection through south-south regional frameworks', South Centre, Geneva.

Odell, John S. (2006) 'Introduction', in John S. Odell (ed.) *Negotiating Trade: Developing Countries in the WTO and NAFTA,* Cambridge: Cambridge University Press.

—— and Sell, Susan K. (2006), 'Reframing the issue: the WTO coalition on intellectual property and public health, 2001', in John S. Odell (ed.), *Negotiating Trade: Developing Countries in the WTO and NAFTA,* Cambridge: Cambridge University Press.

Schuck, Peter (1992) 'Legal complexity: some causes, consequences, and cures', *Duke Law Journal,* 42: 1.

Sell, Susan (2003) *Private Power, Public Law: The Globalization of Intellectual Property Rights,* Cambridge: Cambridge University Press.

Thomas, John R. (2005) 'Intellectual Property and the Free Trade Agreements: innovation policy issues', Congressional Research Service, Library of Congress, 21 December.

5 Services

The importance of further liberalization for business and economic development in the region[1]

Christopher Findlay and Alexandra Sidorenko

Introduction

Developing countries have considerable interests in export markets for services and they stand to gain significantly from reform of their own services sectors. Despite these interests, and the complementarities between developed and developing countries in these markets, negotiations in the WTO on services are proceeding only slowly. Partly this is due to the two-way linkages across broad negotiating areas, particularly the linkage with the agricultural negotiations. Our interest in this chapter, however, is restricted to aspects of the services negotiations themselves, developing country interests in commitments in those sectors, and the ways in which those commitments contribute to economic and business development. This includes especially the use of those commitments to support unilateral domestic reform which is not directly connected to offers of market access made by trading partners.

The next section provides a brief overview of the main characteristics of world trade in services. We then review the links between trade and development, with special attention to studies of the effects of services liberalization. These general points are illustrated by reference to a number of sectoral case studies, and by remarks about the effects of the liberalization of the movement of labor, a key interest of developing countries. We then review the current state of the WTO negotiations and conclude with some remarks on options for their acceleration and on regional interests in those options.

World trade in services

World services exports grew from about 17 percent of world total trade in 1987 to 20 percent of total trade in 2003.[2] The growth rate of goods and services exports for high, middle and low income countries has persistently outpaced income growth: according to the World Bank, average annual growth rate of GNP over 1965–98 was 3.2 percent for the world, 5.9 percent for the low-income countries, 3.7 percent for the middle-income countries and 3.0 percent for the high-income countries. Corresponding growth rates of exports are 5.7 percent, 7.0 percent, 6.1 percent and 5.7 percent.

Services are more important components of high-income economies: the share of services in GDP ranges from 46 percent in LDCs to 54 percent in middle-income countries, 59 percent in upper-middle-income countries, and 71 percent in high-income countries according to the World Bank definitions (see Figure 5.1). Developed countries are also the largest exporters and importers of services (Tables 5.1 and 5.2). The share of services trade attributed to the developing countries is small. A significant number of the international services transactions are linked to movement of people, or its substitute (in some cases) involving cross-border transactions: the share of developing countries in cross-border exports of services has been fluctuating between 22 percent and 23 percent over 1998–2003 (see Figure 5.2). At the same time, the share of services in total exports has dwindled from 17.5 percent in 1998 to 14.5 percent in 2003 on average among the developing countries, and from 21.3 percent to 15.9 percent in the LDCs (Figure 5.3). Some services export areas are of more interest to developing countries as export markets, including maritime transport, tourism, health services, and construction services (Nielson and Taglioni 2004).

Trade and development

A positive link between trade liberalization and economic growth has been established in trade literature. Statistical work finds a positive relationship between income per capita and the ratio of trade to the GDP,[3] yet the trade share itself may be endogenous and the direction of causality may not be in one direction (Helpman 1988; Rodrik 1995a). Adding measures of countries' trade openness also does not rectify the problem, for countries with more liberal trade policy may also have free-market domestic policies, as well as stable fiscal and monetary policies in place, which in turn would explain their higher level of income (Sala-I-Martin 1991: 368–78). A gravity model of

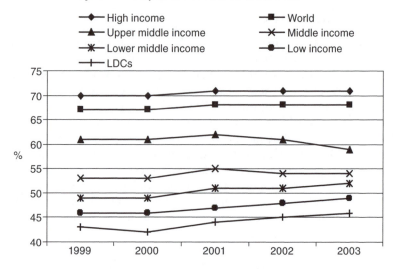

Figure 5.1 Share of services in GDP versus GDP per capita, 1999–2003

Source: World Development Indicators database: 2002 and 2003 values for High Income and World aggregates are not available, plotted at 2001 level

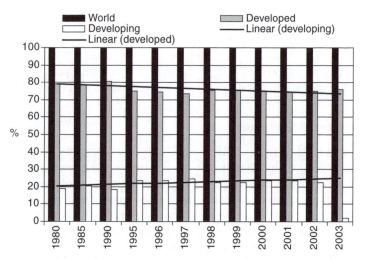

Figure 5.2 The developing countries' share in world total export of services, 1980–2003

Source: UNCTAD

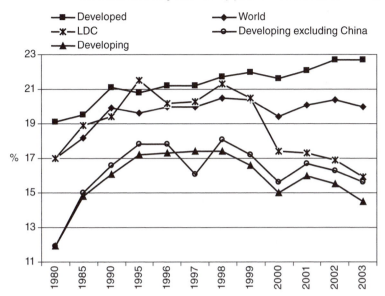

Figure 5.3 Export of services as percentage of country's total trade, 1980–2003

trade demonstrates that geographic location is one of the determinants of volumes of bilateral trade (Linnemann 1966; Frankel 1997). Nevertheless, the generally accepted wisdom is that a quantitatively large and robust positive effect exists between trade and income (Frankel and Romer 1999).

Growth in trade through trade liberalization has been found to induce a significant increase in productivity (Frankel and Romer 1999). Pressure on domestic industries by competing imports stimulates technological innovations and increased productivity. The significant contribution of trade openness to productivity gains and its impact on the risk premium attached to the country is another effect to be taken into account (Stoeckel *et al.* (1999). The major gains to the developing countries from trade liberalization accrue, according to Dornbusch (1992), through the following channels:

- improved allocative efficiency;
- access to superior technology and intermediate inputs;
- greater variety of goods;
- advantages of economies of scale and scope;
- increased domestic competition; and
- creation of growth externalities through knowledge transfers.

Table 5.1 Top 20 exporters of commercial services, 2000 ($US million)

Rank	Country	Total services	Transport	Travel	Other services
1	United States	296,347	50,490	97,944	147,913
2	United Kingdom	119,542	19,058	21,769	78,715
3	Germany	83,095	19,955	18,555	44,586
4	France	80,917	18,546	30,981	31,390
5	Japan	69,238	25,599	3,373	40,267
6	Italy	56,556	9,291	27,493	19,772
7	Spain	53,540	7,843	30,979	14,718
8	Belgium–Luxembourg	49,789	10,665	7,447	31,676
9	Netherlands	49,318	16,786	7,197	25,335
10	Canada	40,230	7,539	10,778	21,912
11	China, Hong Kong SAR	38,736	12,772	5,906	20,057
12	Austria	31,342	4,354	9,998	16,990
13	Korea, Republic of	30,534	13,687	6,834	10,012
14	China	30,431	3,671	16,231	10,529
15	Singapore	29,099	11,879	5,202	12,017
16	Switzerland	28,881	4,538	7,777	16,566
17	Denmark	24,107	14,232	4,058	5,817
18	Turkey	20,429	2,955	7,636	9,838
19	Luxembourg	20,301	1,331	1,686	17,283
20	Sweden	20,252	4,359	4,064	11,829

Source: UNCTAD

Studies of the benefits of reform generally show large, but varying, values. The OECD estimated that welfare benefits of full implementation of Uruguay Round commitments would exceed US$200 billion. According to the GTAP model (Hertel 1997), cutting the level of protection in agriculture, manufacturing and services in half would deliver an annual gain to the world economy of over US$400 billion. Full elimination of all barriers would produce an annual gain to the global economy of $US750 billion (DFAT 1999). Modeling work by the Australian Productivity Commission found that the net benefit to the world as a whole from elimination of all post-Uruguay Round barriers to trade in goods and services is in excess of US$260 billion, with half of this gain (US$130 billion) resulting from removal of impediments to trade in services (Dee and Hanslow 2000).

Trade-related reforms alone may not produce significant benefits without institutional capacity, including enforceable property rights, commercial codes and bankruptcy rules as well as sound corporate

Table 5.2 Top 20 importers of commercial services, 2000 ($US million)

Rank	Country	Total services	Transport	Travel	Other services
1	United States	224,908	65,699	67,043	92,166
2	Germany	137,253	25,541	52,824	58,889
3	Japan	116,864	35,096	31,884	49,883
4	United Kingdom	99,134	24,132	38,262	36,740
5	France	61,044	17,979	17,906	25,159
6	Italy	55,601	13,140	15,685	26,776
7	Netherlands	51,337	12,886	12,191	26,260
8	Canada	44,118	9,373	12,438	22,308
9	Belgium–Luxembourg	41,868	8,386	10,182	23,300
10	China	36,031	10,396	13,114	12,521
11	Korea, Republic of	33,381	11,048	7,132	15,201
12	Spain	31,283	8,172	5,476	17,636
13	Ireland	31,272	2,627	2,525	26,121
14	Austria	29,653	2,995	8,463	18,195
15	Singapore	26,938	12,478	4,547	9,913
16	China, Taiwan Province of	26,647	6,247	8,107	12,293
17	Saudi Arabia	25,262	2,247	–	23,015
18	China, Hong Kong SAR	24,584	6,241	12,502	5,841
19	Sweden	23,440	3,640	8,048	11,752
20	Denmark	21,488	11,021	5,101	5,366

Source: UNCTAD.

and public governance. Nevertheless, trade reforms and economic liberalization may help create a demand for the development of such institutions. These institutional questions are of special importance in services. Winters (2004) summarizes empirical evidence on the relationship between trade liberalization and growth and concludes that in general, liberalization induces at least transitory but possibly also a longer-term increase in growth. A large component of this effect is caused by increased productivity, but other factors such as regulatory institutions, property rights and investment regimes, transparency and anti-corruption measures, and human capital development play an important role. Santos-Paulino (2005) surveys the literature on trade liberalization and economic performance in developing countries.

Availability of cheaper intermediate service inputs through the inter-industry input-output relations and the total factor productivity (TFP) growth through import-embodied technology transfer produce welfare gains to developing countries in the modeling analysis by

Robinson *et al.* (2002) using a CGE with transport (international shipping) costs. Konan and Maskus (2004) find large gains from services trade liberalization using CGE model of Tunisia's economy, with benefits accruing more evenly across factors than in the goods liberalization scenario, and with smaller adjustment costs. Modeling results for Egypt demonstrate that liberalization of services trade through foreign investment (commercial presence) is responsible for the largest share in estimated welfare gains (Konan and Kim 2004). Romer (1994) points out that trade restrictions result in the reduced supply of intermediate goods to an economy with an infra-marginal effect on productivity. The argument can be extended to services such as those provided in the infrastructure, communications and financial sectors. Dollar and Kraay (2004) find that globalizing developing countries that have implemented trade liberalization reform by reducing tariff barriers in the 1980s are enjoying higher per capita growth rates decades later and are catching up with the developed economies. Developing countries that failed to open up to trade are lagging behind. Absolute poverty levels in the globalizing countries have also reduced, supporting the evidence for the pro-poor economic growth through trade liberalization.

The Australian Productivity Commission (using the multi-region FTAP model which includes foreign investment) found that completely liberalizing trade in telecommunications and financial services would increase world real gross national product (GNP) by 0.2 percent. The global gains from removing barriers to trade in these sectors come from three sources: improvements in the allocation of resources, increased returns to the world stock of capital, and increased product variety. In essence, imposing a barrier to trade of any kind distorts primary factor markets, generating a "rent" (a mark-up of price over opportunity cost) to the incumbent and a "tax" on local capital users. Liberalizing trade in financial services is estimated to increase world GNP by 0.1 percent, with an additional 0.1 percent GNP gain stemming from the liberalization of telecommunications (Verikios and Zhang 2003; Verikios and Zhang 2004).

Whalley (2004) provides a critical review of the current body of literature on quantifying welfare effects of the services trade liberalization, including the problems associated with constructing measures of trade restrictiveness and modeling methodology. He concludes that liberalization of foreign establishment and the movement of people are of the greatest importance to developing countries: "If service trade liberalization is a surrogate for improved functioning of global factor markers in which more capital flows to developing countries and more labor flows from them, developing countries could benefit in a major way" (p. 1250).

Nielson and Taglioni (2004) review the major studies of the effect of barriers to trade and investment in services. They point out the differences between types of barriers to trade, which can be rent creating and/or cost creating. Some impediments to trade and investment have the effect of limiting competition and raising prices, thereby adding to the profits of incumbent producers. Liberalizing these measures may create efficiency gains but would also lead to relatively large transfers between producers and consumers. Other impediments have the effect of adding to costs, and liberalizing those measures can provide gains to both incumbent producers and downstream consumers. Welfare gains from this reform will also be significant. These distinctions suggest the political economy of managing reform will differ between types of impediments.

A number of studies have attempted to assess the extent and impact of impediments between economies and across sectors. In their review of these studies Nielson and Taglioni conclude that:

- on average, developing countries have more restrictive barriers than developed economies;
- those economies are expected to gain more from liberalization; and
- the estimates are that gains from services liberalization are of the order of five times those of the gains from goods liberalization.

There is however considerable variation in the estimates of these gains, reflecting the methodology used to estimate the scale of the impediments and the nature of their effects (rent vs. cost creating). The gains from reform are even greater when capital mobility and options for foreign direct investment are made explicit, and when the likely imperfectly competitive nature of services markets is recognized. Further comment is offered below on studies which focus on Mode 4 delivery. The key point however from this review of studies is the following:

> for most countries, including many developing countries, export-related gains from services liberalisation are neither the only nor the largest basis of expected gains. A large portion of benefits from services liberalisation derive, not from seeking better market access abroad, but from the increased competitiveness and efficiency of the domestic market.
>
> (Nielson and Taglioni 2004: abstract)

Thus the greater gains are available not from removal of barriers to exports or establishment in foreign markets, but from domestic reform in ways which do not simply remove impediments to foreign entry but which remove impediments to entry by all firms (foreign or domestic) and which create more competitive markets.

Sectoral case studies

The following sections report case studies of the effects of restrictions in banking, telecommunications and health services, and also examine some of the key issues involved in the liberalization of restrictions on the movement of people.

Banking and financial services

Financial contracts are crucial in facilitating the settlement of trade and distributing resources efficiently across time and space. Risk management and liquidity are very important to the smooth functioning of financial markets. The ability to access, process and use financial information more efficiently benefits providers of financial services, allowing them to respond faster and expand the range of products and services they can offer. Market access allowed to foreign service providers creates extra competition in the market and leads to technology transfer.

Mattoo (1999) examines patterns of market access commitments in financial services (banking and direct insurance) made under the General Agreement on Trade in Services (GATS) negotiations (the FSA 1997 package of commitments). The developing economies of Asia and Latin America appeared to be lagging behind in liberalization of their financial sector compared to the Eastern European and African participants. The degree of financial sector protection in developing countries exceeds that in the developed countries as demonstrated in Figure 5.4. Murinde and Ryan (2003) provide further discussion of the African banking sector performance in view of the potential entry of foreign service providers due to the market liberalization commitments made under GATS. Analyzing the pattern of commitments in banking services, Harms *et al.* (2003) find that agricultural and textile exporters have scheduled fewer market access measures in banking services, raising the question of whether services negotiations are being used as a bargaining chip by developing countries with strong export interests in the protected markets of developed members.

Dee and Nguyen-Hong (2003) reports an index of restrictions to foreign entry into banking; the index provides a measure of discrimination against foreign entrants embedded in the non-prudential domestic regulations and rules. Economies with more liberal market access provisions for foreign service providers are statistically associated with higher GNP per capita (Figure 5.5).[4]

Trade liberalization measures including market access commitments have to be coordinated with the state of development of domestic regulatory framework, with sequencing of reform and liberalization measures becoming an important issue. An empirical study by Fink *et al.* (2003), encompassing 86 geographically dispersed developing countries, has found that the gains from the simultaneous privatization and introduction of competition regulation in the telecommunications market are higher than those resulting from privatization followed by competition policy reform. Effective competition policies implemented in domestic markets are essential to ensure that liberalization of market access does not result in foreign service providers capturing monopoly rents and impeding entry of other players.

Restrictive public policy measures are not the only impediments to international trade in services. Private business practices in the markets exempt from application of the national competition laws (such as maritime transport conferences) result in higher prices to the consumer. Fink *et al.* (2002b) demonstrate that restrictive business practices have a stronger effect on international shipping prices than public policies, and propose a set of measures to bring maritime shipping cartels under the umbrella of domestic competition law and of strengthening multilateral disciplines using GATS Article IX.

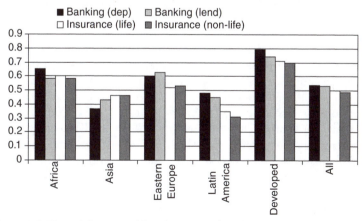

Figure 5.4 Financial services liberalization indices based on GATS FSA 1997 commitments

Source: Mattoo (1999)

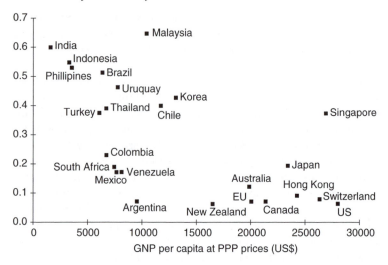

Figure 5.5 Banking foreign restrictiveness indices and GNP per capita at PPP prices, 1996 (US$)

Source: Dee and Nguyen-Hong (2003: 78–105), based on McGuire and Schuele (2000: 201–14)

Telecommunications and transport

Infrastructure services such as telecommunications and financial services are intermediate inputs into production of all other goods and services. Availability of cheap and efficient financial and telecommunications services has also been demonstrated to facilitate international trade.

Fink *et al.* (2002a) estimate a gravity model which includes telecommunications costs and find that international variations in communications costs influence bilateral trade flows, with the larger impact on differentiated products whose production uses telecommunications services more intensively than the production of homogeneous products. Fink *et al.* (2001) analyze the state of telecommunications reform in Asia and find evidence for a slow unilateral liberalization process since the adoption of the Reference Paper on basic telecommunications. Their econometric analysis confirms that telecommunications reform (including privatization, competition and regulation) yields higher market outcomes such as fixed lines penetration, service quality and labor productivity. The authors conjecture that to stimulate further liberalization of the sector in the region, there must be other members with significant interest in telecommunications willing to make concessions in other sectors of export interest to the developing countries, such as agriculture, textiles and movement of individual service providers.

Findlay *et al.* (2005: 111–44) have examined actual policy scores in the telecommunications sector for Asia-Pacific Economic Cooperation (APEC) economies and found that actual policies have improved over 1998–2002 in a number of East Asian countries, including Thailand, China, South Korea and Singapore. Even so, a significant number of ASEAN economies (those in the lower left quadrant of Figure 5.6) show a less than average degree of openness of their telecommunications market, and have made only limited unilateral progress over the period 1998–2002.

Benefits of trade openness in sectors such as transport and distribution have been analyzed by Robinson *et al.* (2002) using a CGE model with transport costs (international shipping), Fink *et al.* (2002b) and Findlay and Fink (2005). Figure 5.7 demonstrates that developing countries are lagging behind in making market access commitments in transport and distribution sectors, with the significant exception of maritime transport.

Health services

Developing countries have recognized their cost advantage in providing health care services to the ageing population of the developed

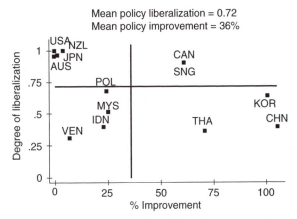

Figure 5.6 Telecommunications policy liberalization and the rate of liberalization, 1998–2002

Source: Findlay *et al.* (2005: 119)

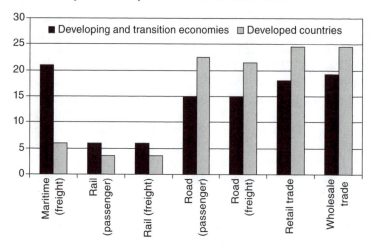

Figure 5.7 Number of WTO members scheduling transport and distribution services

Source: Findlay and Fink (2005)

countries. ASEAN member economies have included healthcare as one of the priority sectors for advanced integration. Competitive cost structures, the availability of a skilled medical workforce, technological advancement along with the natural endowments, geographical position and cultural links all create a comparative advantage for several ASEAN economies to export health services.

The costs and benefits of liberalization of trade in health services are outlined in Sidorenko and Findlay (2003) and Sidorenko (2003: 276–323). Notwithstanding the high level of protection of the healthcare sector in most of the developed countries and the high share of publicly provided services in the total mix, developing countries have scheduled even fewer liberalizing commitments in several healthcare-related sectors, especially in those granting market access to foreign medical professionals and nurses (see Figure 5.8). Where some commitments are made, however, their depth is limited.

Movement of natural persons (Mode 4)

International mobility of workers has increased dramatically over the recent decades, including both unskilled and skilled workers. A large share of this flow represents unregulated (illegal) migration between neighboring countries, but there is also a growing mobility

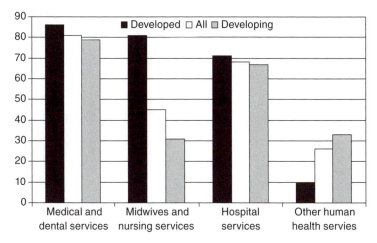

Figure 5.8 GATS commitments in health services: market access

Source: Sidorenko (2003: 286)

of professional skilled labor (see OECD 2001; OECD 2002a; OECD 2003). Demographic shifts and the ageing of populations in developed countries has created domestic labor market imbalances and an increased demand for foreign labor.

There are potentially large benefits to both sending and receiving countries resulting from the increased mobility of workers. Gains to sending countries include remittances. Receiving countries benefit from satisfaction of the otherwise unfilled demand for certain types of skills.

Within East Asia, there has been a significant increase in cross-border flows of labor over the past two decades. Demand for skilled labor has also increased in countries such as Japan, South Korea, Taiwan, Singapore and Malaysia as they have advanced in the development of knowledge-based economies. It has been estimated that temporary skilled migrants accounted for up to a quarter of all higher level workers in Singapore, and around 5–10 percent in Malaysia and Thailand in recent years (Manning and Bhatnagar 2004). Regional opportunities to further facilitate mobility of professional services providers in ASEAN are further examined in Manning and Sidorenko (2005). Economic importance of international mobility of labor for ASEAN countries is illustrated by the growing share of workers' remittances in GDP of the labor-exporting members such as the Philippines and Cambodia (see Table 5.3). At the same time, countries such as the Philippines and India are taking advantage of their skilled English-speaking workforce endowment, and export the "IT-enabled services" including computer

Table 5.3 Workers' remittances as percentage of GDP, selected ASEAN countries, 1995–2001

Country	Workers' remittances as % of GDP						
	1995	1996	1997	1998	1999	2000	2001
Cambodia	0.35	0.34	0.35	2.38	2.49	3.05	3.31
Indonesia	0.32	0.35	0.34	1.01	0.79	0.79	0.74
Lao People's Dem. Rep.	1.24	2.42	2.34	3.89	0.04	0.04	0.04
Malaysia	0.13	0.16	0.19	0.26	0.41	0.38	0.42
Myanmar	0.36	0.51	0.57	0.50	0.38	0.25	0.23
Philippines	7.23	5.88	8.26	7.87	9.08	8.18	8.56
Thailand	1.01	0.99	1.10	1.27	1.19	1.38	1.09

Source: UNCTAD, June 2005

related services and business process outsourcing such as call centers, medical prescription services, payment systems and financial processing (Mattoo and Wunsch-Vincent 2004).

Winters *et al.* (2003) estimate that an increase in inflow of temporary skilled and unskilled foreign workers from developing countries (equal to 3 percent of the developed countries' total workforce) would generate an additional US$156 billion per annum in world welfare (equivalent to an 0.6 percent of the world GNP). The gains will be shared between developed and developing countries, with most of the gains attributed to the liberalization of restrictions on unskilled rather than skilled labor.

The contribution of skilled professional migration and overseas graduate students to the US knowledge economy has been evaluated in Chellaraj *et al.* (2005). The authors found strong positive impact of the number of foreign graduate students and skilled migrants on the number of patent applications, patents awarded to the US universities and other non-university entities. Amin and Mattoo (2005) in a game-theoretical model find that Pareto improvement can be realized not through more liberal commitments by host countries to allow temporary entry, but rather to enable host countries to commit to repatriation. If the source country undertakes obligations such as pre-movement screening of temporary migrants, facilitation of their return and commitments to combat illegal migration, the joint outcome may correct the current problem of too little temporary and too much permanent migration.

Major impediments to movement of natural persons are: lack of transparency in entry requirements and procedures; complicated visa application process; lack of recognition of previous training, qualifications and degrees; and labor market (economic needs) tests (Chanda 2001).

Chaudhuri *et al.* (2004) assess the current state of GATS commitments on Mode 4 and propose a framework for negotiating further liberalization of movement of natural persons. Concerns such as cultural identity, the drain on public resources and problems of assimilation are not nearly as relevant to the increased mobility of professionals as they are for unskilled foreign labor. What really worries policy-makers, preventing them from making any binding commitments under Mode 4, are issues of national security and difficulties in enforcing temporariness. If temporary workforce shortages filled by recruiting foreign labor correct themselves and the temporary entrants change their status to permanent in the interim, a new labor market imbalance is created, with longer-term costs such as the need to re-train those temporarily unemployed. Chaudhuri *et al.* (2004) proposed a model schedule on Mode 4 commitments based on broad horizontal commitments and supplemented by deeper sectoral commitments where possible. The schedule is supplemented by a Reference Paper that formulates measures to improve transparency in temporary entry requirements and procedures, and minimum disciplines for domestic regulation under Article VI:4 (qualification requirements and procedures, technical standards and licensing requirements). The proposal seeks the extension of current GATS commitments on Mode 4 to go beyond the categories linked to commercial presence (such as intra-company transferees, managers and specialists) and include individual service providers and contractual service suppliers.

Services in regional agreements

Liberalization of trade in services may advance in a unilateral, plurilateral or multilateral way. The major argument against a preferential trade agreement (PTA) as opposed to multilateral liberalization is its trade creation versus trade diversion effects. The relative welfare effects of the PTA depend on the relative magnitude of these effects. Apart from the trade creation and trade diversion phenomena, there is also, as a rule, some redistribution of the revenue within the newly created preferential trade area, with its winners and losers. The aggregate effect of the PTA on the total welfare thus is ambiguous, depending on the particular conditions.[5] To yield unambiguous welfare gains, the PTA must involve those sectors in which the partner economy is the sole source of imports. In such a situation, there will be no trade diversion effect, and no associated welfare losses. Even if this is the case, multilateral liberalization will always provide even larger gains. The mercantilist rationale used to justify regional and multilateral bargaining over reduction of tariffs and non-tariff barriers in goods trade does not extend immediately to services trade, as pointed out in Dee and Sidorenko (2005: 200–26). Several levels of product differentiation (by economy, firm and even individual consumer) are inherent in services. This high differentiation of services along with the regulatory nature of barriers to their international tradability weakens the case for preferential liberalization and favors non-preferential and unilateral measures.

The potential liberalizing effect of the regional trade arrangement depends on the breadth of coverage and on the structure of the agreement. This is especially the case for services liberalization. One will often find a gap between the actual levels of policy openness/restrictions, and the level legally bound in the agreement. The legal structure of the agreement itself may be more or less liberalizing, depending on whether a negative or a positive list approach is used. The schedules of country-specific commitments in the ASEAN Free Trade Area (AFTA) follow the GATS and are built upon the positive list approach. The schedule of commitments in the North American Free Trade Agreement (NAFTA) and the Australia New Zealand Closer Economic Relations Trade Agreement (CER), to the contrary, is constructed by the negative list approach. Although the negative list approach is usually preferred on liberalization grounds, there are a number of difficulties associated with compiling negative lists and a permanent exclusion of sensitive sectors (Sauvé 2000: 72–85).

Most of the modeling studies confirm that the benefits of multilateral liberalization exceed those resulting from the regional liberalization. The benefits are very significant: for example, the FTAP model used by the Australian Productivity Commission demonstrated the net benefit to the world as awhole from elimination of all post-Uruguay Round trade barriers to be in excess of US$260 billion. Half of this gain (US$130 billion) comes from liberalization of services trade. Liberalization of agriculture contributes US$50 billion in benefits, with the remaining gain of US$80 billion attributed to manufactured goods (Dee and Hanslow 2000).

Dee and Gali (2003) provide an ex-post evaluation of 18 recent PTAs (traditional and new-age) on merchandise trade and investment, and find the evidence of trade diversion exceeding trade creation in all but six cases. The non-(goods)trade provisions of PTAs (in particular, those related to investment and services), are estimated to produce a more positive effect. The authors conclude that real progress may be achieved if regional negotiations are used to advance negotiations on investment, services, competition policy and government procurement, and the outcomes extended on a non-preferential basis. Stephenson (2002) examines recent regional agreements in services involving developing countries (including the ASEAN Framework Agreement on Services (AFAS), the Common Market of the South (MERCOSUR), NAFTA, and the Caribbean Community and Common Market (CARICOM)) and finds that such agreements may yield significantly higher degrees of market openness for member service providers. The challenge is to translate these achievements into the progress in the multilateral setting as well.

Some regional fora have undertaken their own steps in advancing Mode 4 liberalization. The ASEAN Framework Agreement on Services (AFAS) signed in December 1995 was conceived as a GATS-plus agreement. The ultimate objective is to achieve the free flow of services between the ASEAN member economies before 2020. By June 2005, four packages of commitments on the liberalization of services trade were concluded resulting from three rounds of negotiations under AFAS. Assessing achievements in liberalization of Mode 4, Manning and Sidorenko (2005) find that those are mostly at the level of the GATS, and the development of meaningful liberalizing measures has been slow. Among the priority sectors for advanced liberalization are "e-ASEAN" and healthcare services.[6] The Roadmap for Integration of e-ASEAN Sector scheduled (Article XIV) and the Roadmap for Integration of Healthcare Services (Article XIX) both envisage facilitation of professional mobility in these sectors.

Doha round negotiations

Recommendations to developing countries on the most beneficial way to advance GATS negotiations formulated in Mattoo (2000) remain relevant. They include eliminating restrictions to market access through improved Article XVI commitments, liberalization of Mode 4, developing pro-competitive principles for network sectors following the telecommunications Reference Paper, development of disciplines for domestic regulation, and other rule-making objectives (safeguards, government procurement and subsidies).

With the mandate to enter the negotiations no later than 1 January 2000, most of the WTO members failed to meet the initial agreed deadline of 30 March 2003 to submit their services offers. By

February 2005, only 47 offers were received, 37 by developing countries, representing 71 members (the EU offer counted as representing 25 member states). A new deadline of 31 May 2005 was proposed to submit improved services offers. Based on the report by the Chairman to the Trade Negotiations Committee WTO (2005), the total number of initial offers by 1 July 2005 was 68 representing 92 members. Some 24 developing countries' offers remained outstanding, and if the LDCs (31) are added, there were 55 initial services offers still outstanding in this round of negotiations. Two ASEAN LDC members (Cambodia and Myanmar) had failed to submit an initial offer.

The Chairman was disappointed with the quality of the submitted offers, with majority failing to provide any significant improvement. The average number of commitments as offered at that time would improve from 51 to 57. Less than half scheduled commitments in distribution, postal and courier services, or road transport, or offered improved horizontal commitments under Mode 4. Sectoral analysis of the initial offers is represented in Figure 5.9. Overall, there was a much smaller liberalization offered by developing countries in all sectors but health services (included in 17 percent of all developing countries' offers), and an equal reticence in making market-opening commitments in audiovisual services (10 percent of both developed and developing members offered any commitments in this area). Sectors in which commitments show the most liberalizing activity included financial services, computer and related services, telecommunications and other business services.

The common assessment of these offers is that they offered little more than "standstill commitments," and in the case of some developing countries, including in ASEAN, are not even committing those countries to policies which are already in place. This situation prompted discussion of how more meaningful offers can be prompted from WTO members, and more specifically how "meaningful" might be measured. The extent of sectoral coverage (either the absolute number of sectors or the percentage of heretofore-uncommitted sectors) of the offers made (even with reservations) was one indicator which was under discussion.[7] Some members proposed that scores be applied to commitments.[8] Others suggested that the benchmarking approach would facilitate linkages with other negotiations, particularly in agriculture.

As a consequence of this debate, it was agreed that the bilateral process of negotiation within the WTO was not working. At the Hong Kong WTO Ministerial meeting in December 2005, Ministers agreed to adopt a plurilateral approach. This approach would not be

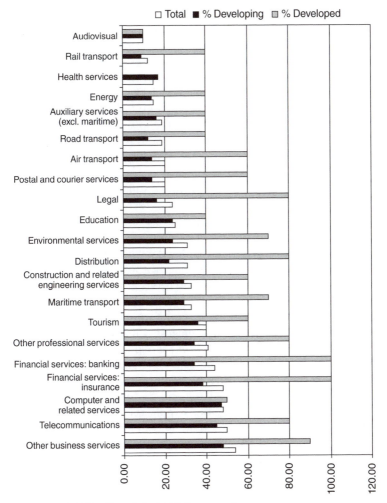

Figure 5.9 GATS offers, July 2005 (by sector)

Source: WTO (2005)

mandatory; however, the expectation was that addressees of plurilateral requests were asked to "consider" them. The GATS specifies that services liberalization "shall be advanced" in round through bilateral, plurilateral and multilateral negotiations but the plurilateral approach had not been used before. Collective requests on specific sectors were to be submitted by the end of February 2006, with revised offers of commitments to be submitted by 31 July.

Small groups then formed around a number of sectors and collective requests were drawn up. These requests were supposed to be confidential but some were leaked and made available on the website of the US Coalition of Services Industries.[9] The US CSI has also produced a table showing the sectoral coverage (more than 20 topics) of the plurilateral negotiations, the chairs of each group as well as the demandeurs and the "target group." Only the process of negotiation is plurilateral, and not the result. All commitments made as a result of these negotiations would be applied without discrimination. There is also the understanding in these plurilateral negotiations that if a WTO member asks for a commitment from another member then it is also willing to make that commitment itself (if it has not already done so). More recent reports (July 2006) were that these plurilateral negotiations we're at a "standstill" because of the lack of progress in agricultural and non-agricultural market access. Then on 24 July 2006, the whole negotiating round was suspended without any clear indication of when it would recommence, mainly as a result of divisions among members on the agricultural negotiations.

Progress in services negotiations had been made on the treatment of domestic regulation, and some suggested it was the "only area of the services talks which (had) been showing concrete progress" (*Bridges Weekly Trade News Digest* 2006). These negotiations refer to domestic regulatory measures such as licensing and technical standards. A draft text prepared at the end of June 2006 proposed to make disciplines on these regulations applicable to all services sectors in which a member had made a binding commitment. However, further negotiation would have been required since the paper presents options for the application of disciplines. Members were also reported to differ in their priorities in these negotiations. The US put more weight on transparency and preferred sector-specific rather than horizontal disciplines which may be "too general." The EU was more concerned with disciplines on licensing. Developing countries were divided, some stressing the "right to regulate" and others the value of horizontal disciplines. A third group put more weight on regulation affecting Mode 4.

Next steps

The research shows that the significant gains for developing countries are associated with domestic reform of the impediments to competition that affect both foreign and domestic suppliers. Reforms of this type create larger gains than those which remove impediments to foreign entry. Even in those cases, larger gains are available from commitments which are made multilaterally. With the Doha round suspended, attention may shift to bilateral negotiation. However, Dee's (2005) conclusion is that there may be a few areas where PTAs can supplement a domestic regulatory reform program, and because they tend to be preferential they also divert the efforts of reform away from the areas where the large gains are available.

In this context, what is the value of commitments in the WTO process? It has much to offer to support domestic reform. Findlay and Fink (2005), drawing on Mattoo (2002: 280–9), suggest the following:

> First ... an international agreement may provide an opportunity for domestic service providers to secure access to export markets (and the) market access opportunities that trading partners might provide as part of a package of commitments may be sufficient to shift the balance in the domestic policymaking process to support reform at home.
>
> Second, a trade commitment can add to the credibility of the policy change .... A trade agreement has the potential to add value, as commitments are binding under international law – including those to be applied at a future date. If the policy change is not made, trading partners have recourse to dispute settlement and may impose trade sanctions.
>
> Third, trade agreements may offer a forum for regulatory cooperation. Such cooperation can ... underpin market-opening commitments by assuring traders and investors that liberal market access will not be impaired by the imposition of regulatory barriers, (establish) regulatory principles that governments promise to fulfil, ... aid the harmonisation of regulatory standards and promote recognition of foreign regulations in order to open markets to international competition.

To this list could be added the contribution of commitments to the transparency of policy-making processes. Commitments also oblige members to apply the GATS principles of domestic regulation in the relevant sectors.

Developing countries have export market interests in services, which add to the contribution of these negotiations, but their main value is through their support for domestic reform. Success in that respect therefore requires the statement of a development plan, which includes an assessment of the priority areas for domestic reform (that is, an assessment of sectors in which restrictions on entry are relatively high and whose removal would create significant welfare gains), and the derivation of negotiating positions from that development plan.

Given these contributions of international commitments, Findlay and Fink (2005) identify some activities that might support the negotiations when they resume. This includes further work to identify gains from exchange of commitments either within sectors (perhaps across modes) or across sectors. They also stress the value of putting reform programs together with capacity building. On the latter they suggest that:

> Developing countries, for example, may be cautious to commit to greater market opening in transport and distribution, fearing their regulatory systems are ill prepared for the additional complexities of international competition. ... Commitments by developed countries to technical assistance and international enforcement of competition law could be explicitly linked to developing countries' market opening commitments.

To this list might be added the production of model schedules of commitments (freight logistics is an example of a sector where a group of WTO members have developed a model for others to follow). There is also the scope for all WTO members to at least bind current policy, which will add to the transparency of their policies and provide reassurance to trading partners, including those considering establishment as the best mode of supply.

Findlay and Fink (2005) observe that implementation of these steps requires careful preparation and coordination among different ministries (a feature of service sector impediments is the number of agencies involved in the administration of the various elements) and with the private sector (see OECD 2002b). It is valuable therefore, they suggest, to establish procedures and institutional arrangements for consultation within government and with a range of private sector interests: the latter should include not just import competing firms but also those with export interests and those who are significant consumers of services.

Notes

1 An earlier version of this chapter appeared in UN ESCAP 'Delivering on the WTO Round: A High Level Government-Business Dialogue', Studies in Trade and Investment, No. 56, UN, New York 2005 (ST/ESCAP/2393).
2 UNCTAD online database, accessed July 2005.
3 Rodrik (1995b: 2925–82) provides a review of literature on this subject.
4 The index was based on policy information up to 31 December 1997, hence most of the recent unilateral liberalization activities in the financial sector have not been reflected in the calculations.
5 See Panagariya (2000) for an excellent discussion of the theory of preferential trade liberalization and its welfare implications.
6 ASEAN Framework Agreement for the Integration of Priority Sectors, Vientiane, 29 November 2004.
7 In a speech before the Coalition of Service Industries, St Regis Hotel, Washington on 20 September 2005, USTR Portman said that the US would seek "high quality commitments from key developing countries" in financial services, telecommunications, computer-related services, express delivery, distribution and energy services. He mentioned that "unrestricted direct investment and unlimited supply of cross border services" were listed as elements of the "quality" of commitments.
8 More details of these proposals and the plurilateral agreements are reported in *Bridges Weekly Trade News Digest* (2005). Proponents of the benchmarking approach include the EU, Australia, Korea, New Zealand, Taiwan and Switzerland.
9 See <http://www.uscsi.org/wto/crequests.htm>. The table referred to in the next sentence is available at <http://www.uscsi.org/publications/papers/collective/Table.pdf>.

References

Amin, M. and Mattoo, A. (2005) 'Does temporary migration have to be permanent?', *World Bank Policy Research Working Paper 3582.*
Bridges Weekly Trade News Digest (2005) 9 (31), 21 September.
Bridges Weekly Trade News Digest (2006) 10 (16), 19 July.
Chanda, R. (2001) 'Movement of natural persons and the GATS', *World Economy,* 24 (5): 631–54.
Chaudhuri, S., Mattoo, A. and Self, R. (2004) 'Moving people to deliver services: how can the WTO help?', *Journal of World Trade,* 38 (3): 363–93.
Chellaraj, G., Maskus, K.E. and Mattoo, A. (2005) 'The contribution of skilled immigration and international graduate students to U.S. innovation', *World Bank Policy Research Working Paper 3588.*
Dee, P. (2005) 'East Asia trade strategies and their impact on future growth', paper presented to the international conference on Advancing East Asian Economic Integration, Bogor, August.

Dee, P. and Gali, J. (2003) 'The trade and investment effects of preferential trading arrangements', *NBER Working paper W10160.*

Dee, P. and Hanslow, K. (2000) 'Multilateral Liberalisation of Services Trade', Staff Research Paper, Canberra: Productivity Commission.

Dee, P. and Nguyen-Hong, D. (2003) 'Domestic regulatory reform and liberalisation of trade in infrastructure services', in A. Sidorenko and C. Findlay (eds) *Regulation and Market Access,* Canberra: Asia Pacific Press, ANU.

Dee, P. and Sidorenko, A. (2005) 'The rise of services trade: regional initiatives and challenges for the WTO', in H. Soesastro and C. Findlay (eds) *Reshaping the Asia Pacific Economic Order,* London: Routledge.

DFAT (1999) *Global Trade Reform: Maintaining Momentum,* Canberra: Department of Foreign Affairs and Trade, Commonwealth of Australia.

Dollar, D. and Kraay, A. (2004) 'Trade, growth, and poverty', *Economic Journal,* 114 (493): F22–49.

Dornbusch, R. (1992) 'The case for trade liberalization in developing countries', *Journal of Economic Perspectives,* 6 (1): 69–85.

Findlay, C. and Fink, C. (2005) 'Trade in transport and distribution services', mimeo.

Findlay, C., Lee, R.C., Sidorenko, A. and Pangestu, M. (2005) 'Telecommunications', in E.M. Medalla (ed.) *Competition Policy in East Asia,* London: Routledge.

Fink, C., Mattoo, A. and Rathindran, R. (2001) 'Liberalizing basic telecommunications: the Asian experience', *World Bank Policy Research Working Paper 2718.*

Fink, C., Mattoo, A. and Neagu, I.C. (2002a) 'Assessing the impact of communication costs on international trade', *World Bank Policy Research Working Paper 2929.*

Fink, C., Mattoo, A. and Neagu, I.C. (2002b) 'Trade in international maritime services: how much does policy matter?', *World Bank Economic Review,* 16 (1): 81–108.

Fink, C., Mattoo, A. and Rathindran, R. (2003) 'An assessment of telecommunications reform in developing countries', *Information Economics and Policy,* 15 (4): 443–66.

Frankel, J.-A. (1997) 'Regional Trading Blocs in the World Economic System', Washington, DC: Institute for International Economics.

Frankel, J.-A. and Romer, D. (1999) 'Does trade cause growth?', *American Economic Review,* 89 (3): 379–99.

Helpman, E. (1988) 'Growth, technological progress, and trade', *Empirica,* 15 (1): 5–25.

Hertel, T.W. (ed.) (1997) *Global Trade Analysis: Modeling and Applications,* Cambridge: Cambridge University Press.

Konan, D.E. and Kim, K.E. (2004) 'Beyond border barriers: the liberalisation of services trade in Tunisia and Egypt', *World Economy,* 27 (9): 1429–47.

Konan, D.E. and Maskus, K.E. (2004) 'Quantifying the impact of services liberalization in a developing country', *World Bank Policy Research Working Paper 3193*.

Linnemann, H. (1966) *An Econometric Study of International Trade Flows*, Amsterdam: North-Holland.

McGuire, G. and Schuele, M. (2000) 'Restrictiveness of international trade in banking services', in C. Findlay and T. Warren (eds) *Impediments to Trade in Services: Measurement and Policy Implications*, London and New York: Routledge.

Manning, C. and Bhatnagar, P. (2004) 'Liberalizing and facilitating the movement of individual service providers under AFAS: implications for labour and immigration policies and procedures in ASEAN', *Final Report REPSF Project 02/004*, ASEAN Secretariat.

Manning, C. and Sidorenko, A. (2005) 'Movement of workers in ASEAN: health care and IT sectors', *Draft Final Report REPSF Project 04/007*, ASEAN Secretariat.

Mattoo, A. (1999) 'Financial services and the World Trade Organization: liberalization commitments of the developing and transition economies', World Bank Policy Research Working Paper 2184.

Mattoo, A. (2000) 'Developing countries in the new round of GATS negotiations: towards a pro-active role', *World Economy*, 23 (4): 471–89.

Mattoo, A. (2002) 'Negotiating improved market access commitments', in B. Hoekman, A. Mattoo and P. English (eds) *Development, Trade and the WTO: A Handbook*, Washington, DC: The World Bank.

Mattoo, A. and Wunsch-Vincent, S. (2004) 'Pre-empting protectionism in services: the GATS and outsourcing', *Journal of International Economic Law*, 7 (4): 765–800.

Murinde, V. and Ryan, C. (2003) 'The implications of WTO and GATS for the banking sector in Africa', *World Economy*, 26 (2): 181–207.

Nielson, J. and Taglioni, D. (2004) 'Services trade liberalisation: identifying opportunities and gains', *OECD Trade Policy Working Paper No. 1*, February.

OECD (2001) 'Innovative people: mobility of skilled personnel in national innovation systems', OECD proceedings. Paris and Washington, DC: OECD.

OECD (2002a) 'Migration and the labour market in Asia: recent trends and policies'. Paris: OECD.

OECD (2002b), 'Managing "request-offer" negotiations under the GATS', Working Party Paper of the Trade Committee, TD/TC/WP(2002) 13, Paris: OECD.

OECD (2003) 'Service providers on the move: labour mobility and the WTO general agreement on trade in services', *OECD Policy Brief*, Paris: OECD.

Panagariya, A. (2000) 'Preferential trade liberalization: the traditional theory and new developments', *Journal of Economic Literature*, 38 (2): 287–331.

Robinson, S., Wang, Z. and Martin, W. (2002) 'Capturing the implications of services trade liberalization', *Economic Systems Research,* 14 (1): 3–33.

Rodrik, D. (1995a) 'Getting interventions right: how South Korea and Taiwan grew rich', *Economic Policy: A European Forum,* 0 (20): 53–97.

Rodrik, D. (1995b) 'Trade and industrial policy reform', in Behrman, Jere and Srinivasan (eds) *Handbook of Development Economics. Volume 3B. Handbooks in Economics, vol. 9,* Amsterdam, New York and Oxford: Elsevier Science North Holland.

Romer, P. (1994) 'New goods, old theory, and the welfare costs of trade restrictions', *Journal of Development Economics,* 43 (1): 5–38.

Sala-I-Martin, X. (1991) 'Growth, macroeconomics, and development: comments', in Blanchard, Olivier, Jean, Fischer and Stanley (eds) *NBER Macroeconomics Annual 1991,* Cambridge and London: MIT Press.

Santos-Paulino, A.U. (2005) 'Trade liberalisation and economic performance: theory and evidence for developing countries', *World Economy,* 28 (6): 783–821.

Sauvé, P. (2000) 'Making progress on trade and investment: multilateral versus regional perspective', in S. Stephenson (ed.) *Services Trade in the Western Hemisphere: Liberalization, Integration, and Reform,* Washington, DC: Organization of American States, Brookings Institution Press.

Sidorenko, A. (2003) 'Regulatory impediments to international trade in health services', in A. Sidorenko and C. Findlay (eds) *Regulation and Market Access,* Canberra: Asia Pacific Press, ANU.

Sidorenko, A. and Findlay, C. (2003) 'The costs and benefits of health services trade liberalisation: the case study of Australia, Singapore and Malaysia', report to APEC study CTI 17/2002T, APEC Secretariat.

Stephenson, S.M. (2002) 'Regional versus multilateral liberalization of services', *World Trade Review,* 1 (2): 187–209.

Stoeckel, A., Tang, K. and McKibbin, W. (1999) 'The gains from trade liberalisation with endogenous productivity and risk premium effects', technical paper prepared for the seminar *Reason versus emotion: requirements for a successful WTO Round,* Seattle, 2 December.

Verikios, G. and Zhang, X.-g. (2003) 'Liberalising trade in financial services: global and regional economic effects', *Journal of Economic Integration,* 18 (2): 307–35.

Verikios, G. and Zhang, X.-g. (2004) 'The economic effects of removing barriers to trade in telecommunications', *World Economy,* 27 (3): 435–58.

Whalley, J. (2004) 'Assessing the benefits to developing countries of liberalisation in services trade', *World Economy,* 27 (8): 1223–53.

Winters, L.A. (2004) 'Trade liberalisation and economic performance: an overview', *Economic Journal*, 114 (493): F4–21.

Winters, L.A., Walmsley, T.L., Wang, Z.K. and Grynberg, R. (2003) 'Liberalising temporary movement of natural persons: an agenda for the development round', *World Economy*, 26 (8): 1137–61.

WTO (2005) 'Special Session of the Council for Trade in Services: Report by the Chairman to the Trade Negotiations Committee', TN/S/20, W Trade O.

6 The future of Singapore issues

Pradeep S. Mehta and Nitya Nanda

Introduction

The controversial Singapore issues supposedly played an important role in the collapse of the Cancun Ministerial of the WTO. Many believe that the Ministerial failed because the EU insisted on commencing negotiations on these issues while most developing countries were equally opposed to this agenda item. There are others who of course feel that the real intention of the EU was to balance progress on agriculture subsidies and hence they linked it to these issues, in particular investments (Jonquières 2003).

Developing countries, in general, were against the inclusion of new issues at the WTO. The Singapore issues, namely trade and investment together with trade and competition policy, were launched at Singapore, hence the prefix. They came about as part of the built-in agenda under Article 9 of the Trade-Related Investment Measures (TRIMS) agreement (WTO 2002), but even during the run up to the Singapore Ministerial the developing world had voiced their opposition to any such broadening of trade negotiations. Ultimately, the Ministerial Declaration adopted the Singapore issues as study programs rather than as a negotiating project. At the same time, a study process was also launched on trade facilitation and transparency in government procurement. While trade facilitation was not a particularly difficult issue for developing countries, government procurement was largely a plurilateral issue and developing countries were puzzled by its inclusion but buckled under pressure and the assurance that only a study was being proposed and that, too, was limited to transparency of government purchase programs.

These issues got a boost at the Doha Ministerial Meeting when the Declaration noted that negotiations on modalities will be launched soon (WTO 2001). This was the pound of flesh for Europe, which agreed to eliminate all export subsidies on farm goods. However, the agreement did not cover production subsidies or tariffs.

At Cancun, most developing countries felt that any further obligations at the multilateral level meant additional expenditure on structural adjustment and enforcement mechanisms to meet such obligations. Developed countries, as usual, promised technical and financial assistance but developing countries remained suspicious as to whether the promised assistance would be forthcoming and suspected that the obligations would, in the end, become millstones around their necks.

Let us examine how the Singapore issues came up on the WTO plate. Despite strong resistance from most developing countries, the EU successfully pushed for their inclusion in the Singapore Ministerial Declaration, leading to the establishment of working groups to analyze issues related to investment, competition policy and transparency in government procurement, directing the Council for Trade in Goods to "undertake exploratory and analytical work [...] on the simplification of trade procedures in order to assess the scope for WTO rules in this area."

At the Doha Ministerial, as stated above, further progress was made on these issues as the case for a multilateral agreement on them was *recognized* in the Doha Declaration. At Cancun, the Chair of the Ministerial Conference, Mexican Foreign Minister Luis Ernesto Derbez, abruptly ended the meeting in view of the sharply differing positions among many WTO members. Following Cancun, after a series of informal "green room"-style consultations, a breakthrough was achieved in the General Council on October 21, 2003, where members indicated some willingness to continue Doha round talks in Geneva on a number of key areas – including the Singapore issues.

In the following months, informal meetings at the Heads of Delegation level discussed other approaches to the Singapore issues. One was a plurilateral approach to investment. This was proposed by the EU, but again rejected by several developing countries (DCs). A willingness to discuss trade facilitation emerged by the first week of December 2003 as Bangladesh, on behalf of the least-developed country (LDC) group and supported by 15 other developing countries, including China and India, submitted a communication on the Singapore issues requesting that investment, competition and transparency in government procurement be dropped.[1] This showed their willingness to discuss trade facilitation only.

The debate remained largely unchanged until April 2004, when a "core-group" of developing countries and LDCs said they were prepared to discuss trade facilitation, but only for the purpose of clarifying substantive modalities for negotiations. In addition to insisting that negotiations must be based on "explicit consensus," the conditionality imposed in the Doha Declaration, they called for the remaining Singapore issues to be dropped altogether from the WTO work program, and expressed a desire to see prior movement in issues such as agriculture before starting discussions on trade facilitation.

Finally, in the July Package (2004), WTO Members agreed on the basis of "explicit consensus" in the General Council to formally launch negotiations on trade facilitation, while dropping the more contentious issues of investment, competition policy, and transparency in government procurement from the Doha Work Program.

Given this background, it is indeed good news for developing countries that three of the Singapore issues have now been dropped, at least for the time being. However, these issues remain on the WTO agenda and as such may be revived in the future. How should developing countries respond to such an eventuality? Let us briefly look into each of the issues from the perspective of developing countries.

Trade and investment

Even during the Uruguay Round (UR) trade negotiations, developed countries advanced the idea of framing multilateral rules to further liberalize the foreign investment regime. Developing countries were opposed to any such idea, primarily because they were unwilling to embark on multilateral negotiations on investment under the GATT, which was essentially devoted to trade relations. Eventually, developing countries agreed to negotiate on four clusters of investment-related matters. The four agreements under the auspices of GATT that relate to investment issues are:

- Trade Related Investment Measures (TRIMs)
- General Agreement on Trade in Services (GATS)
- Trade Related Aspects of Intellectual Property Right (TRIPS)
- Agreement on Subsidies and Countervailing Measures (ASCM)

TRIMs deals explicitly and exclusively with "negative investment measures," issues such as local content requirement, export balancing, etc. The agreement on TRIPS also has a bearing on foreign direct investment (FDI) matters in that the definition of these rights and the adherence to the international standards and procedures constitutes part of the framework within which foreign investment takes place. The GATS relates to FDI matters as it recognizes the establishment of a local company, either as a subsidiary or a joint venture, by a foreign service provider as a mode of trade in services. With respect to ASCM, certain investment incentives lie within the definition of a subsidy and as such are prohibited.

The demand for a comprehensive investment agreement was revived at the Singapore Ministerial Conference of the WTO. Many developing countries were not convinced, as there was no evidence that an international investment agreement would increase investment flows to developing countries. Empirical studies have shown that FDI inflows are largely driven by "gravity factors," like market size, income levels, extent of urbanization, geographical and cultural proximity with major source countries, and the quality of infrastructure. Likewise, evidence shows that policy factors, that a multilateral agreement would try to control, play a relatively minor role (Correa and Kumar 2003).

Overall, the multilateral framework under the WTO included many of the provisions that exporters of capital from the developed countries have been demanding. Hence, it was anticipated that in the post-UR era there would be significant increases in the flow of FDI to developing countries. However, investment flows to developing countries have actually declined as a proportion to total FDI since the establishment of the WTO (see Table 6.1). The share of developing countries in the global FDI inflow, however, increased once again in 2001, not because they performed better but because the developed countries were adversely affected by the global slowdown in the aftermath of September 11.

Table 6.1 International FDI flows, 1996–2003 (in US$ billions)

Host region	1996	1997	1998	1999	2000	2001	2002	2003
Developed countries	220 (58.2)	275 (58.2)	481 (70.7)	636 (73.5)	1,005 (82.3)	503 (68.4)	490 (72.2)	367 (65.5)
Developing countries	145 (38.4)	179 (37.8)	179 (26.4)	208 (24.0)	240 (15.9)	205 (27.9)	158 (23.3)	172 (30.7)
Economies in transition	13 (3.4)	19 (4.0)	20 (2.9)	21 (2.5)	25 (1.8)	27 (03.7)	31 (4.5)	21 (3.8)
Total	378 (100)	473 (100)	680 (100)	865 (100)	1271 (100)	735 (100)	679 (100)	560 (100)

Source: *World Investment Report* (various editions), UNCTAD

Note
Figures in parentheses are percentages of total

Developing countries remain unconvinced about the existing investment-related provisions in the WTO and they fear that the proposed agreement on investment will further limit the scope for domestic control of transnational corporations (TNCs) without any balancing measures, particularly in the context of least developed countries (LDCs), whose economic might is much weaker than that of many transnational corporations. The agreement would tie the hands of governments trying to channel investment flows according to their national development strategies. There is also a concern that WTO rules might effectively give foreign investors preferential treatment relative to national investors, if the rules are modeled on the pattern of the investment provisions in the North American Free Trade Agreement (NAFTA).

Developing countries also point out that the UN initiatives to establish standards of behavior for TNCs, particularly the Code of Conduct that should have been adopted, was aborted in 1992 under pressure from developed countries, especially the US. Ironically, developed countries, so inclined to impose trade sanctions on grounds of labor and environmental standards, walk the other way when developing countries demand responsible behavior from their TNCs. Proponents of an investment agreement have shown no inclination to include either investors' behavior or home country obligations in the proposed agreement. This amply shows that the basic objective of an investment agreement is not to promote development but to ensure unrestricted freedom for their TNCs to operate in developing countries without providing any safeguards against misuse of that freedom.

Another counterargument is that while a multilateral agreement on investment deals with mobility of capital, one factor of production, the mood of rich countries to respond equally enthusiastically to another factor of production, i.e. mobility of labor, under Mode 4 of the GATS is absent. Many DC members of the WTO have been demanding a better deal on Mode 4.[2] Moreover, most countries, besides unilaterally liberalizing their policy environment, are going out of their way to provide incentives to foreign investors leading to the "race to bottom" situation. Thus, if there is one reason for going for a multilateral agreement on investment, it is possibly to check the "incentive war." However, it is unlikely that this will be addressed in any WTO agreement.

It is noteworthy in this context that a multilateral agreement on investment (MAI) was attempted at the OECD. It was launched in 1995, somewhat in parallel to discussions at the WTO. One of its goals was to ensure that DCs bring their investment laws in line with the

MAI. However, DCs were not involved in the negotiations, except five countries that sat in on the negotiations as "observers." Discussions on the MAI faltered on the issue of rights to entry and establishment. In the negotiations, France clashed with the US over opening up its territory to the American audio-visual industry on grounds that it would harm France's cultural and linguistic heritage. The negotiations proceeded in quite a tense manner and the agreement died in 1999 when France pulled the plug after four year of negotiations. It is quite strange that when the MAI could not be adopted by OECD members, which are a relatively homogenous group, a similar agreement was attempted at the WTO where membership is much more diverse (Mehta and Nanda 2004). More importantly, it was done at the behest of the EU, of which France is a powerful member.

Competition policy

Competition policy is now widely recognized as a useful instrument to promote development in a market-oriented economy. Moreover, the international dimensions of regulatory challenges are becoming more prominent day by day. As developing countries liberalize their trade and investment regimes, inflow of foreign products and companies creates new challenges. While governments regulate domestic markets through various micro measures including a competition regime, there is hardly any mechanism for regulating the international market. Stronger nations are able tackle this problem to some extent through extra-territorial application of their domestic competition laws, but weaker nations are denied that possibility. Therefore, there are some prima facie arguments to suggest that a multilateral discipline will be beneficial to the weaker nations.

Little wonder that during the UR of negotiations, the demand for multilateral rules on restrictive business practices was first mooted by developing countries. However, it is surprising to note that the developing countries, which once promoted the idea of converting the UNCTAD Set (the Set of Multilaterally Agreed Equitable Principles and Rules for the Control of Restrictive Business Practices) to a binding instrument, are now not so enthusiastic about the idea of a multilateral competition framework within the WTO. Their skepticism is not without reason.

Developing countries have seen the approach of both the EU and Japan on the issue of competition policy at the WTO as a "market access" push only. In response to such criticism, the EU has shifted its focus from market access to hardcore cartels. However, this shift is nothing but a change in rhetoric. There has been no change on the ground and the proposed elements for a competition agreement remain much the same. Their strong emphasis on non-discrimination as one of the core principles clearly shows that there has not been any shift in their market access agenda. In fact, just a few days before the Cancun Ministerial, in an article in the Wall Street Journal, Pascal Lamy, then EU Commissioner for Trade, acknowledged that all the new issues were essential to "give effect to market opening" (Lamy 2003).

Although the proposed WTO agreement is expected to cover only hardcore cartels, the principle of non-discrimination would apply on all other provisions should a country have them. International cartels are indeed quite harmful to developing countries. But this has just been used as a ploy to thrust a competition agreement on them. There is no clarity as to how such an agreement will help developing countries to protect themselves from hardcore cartels. The solution offered in this regard is "voluntary cooperation," which is envisaged to work only on a bilateral basis. However, one may wonder how the WTO could act as a forum for promoting cooperation, given that it has been functioning as a dispute settlement body that adopts an adversarial approach.[3]

It has also been argued that competition per se will not necessarily ensure efficient outcomes, nor is it necessarily the case that competition-reducing agreements between firms are welfare reducing (Hoekman and Mavroidis 2003). It is also very often argued that a maximal degree of competition is not optimal and in an ideal situation there should be a judicial mix of cooperation and competition by firms as has been found by Amsden and Singh (1994), especially in the context of Japanese industrial development.

It is also a matter of concern that a ban on hardcore cartels would mean that import cartels will have to be disbanded while there will be no effective mechanism to deal with export cartels and international cartels, as that would require cooperation and strong action by developed countries. Paradoxically, proponents have tried to sell their proposal as development-friendly by highlighting the harm caused to developing countries by international cartels. Import cartels, on the other hand, may be welfare-enhancing if they are formed primarily to get a better bargain from foreign exporters.

An effective and successful cooperative arrangement can be possible only when there is enough mutual trust and goodwill among the parties involved. However, at the WTO, it appears that one group of countries is adamant on forcing an agreement on another. Moreover, there is not much experience of cooperation on competition, especially among developing countries. Although a few developing countries like Brazil, Chile and South Africa have entered into such agreements recently, there is no evidence that they have gained much from these agreements. Even within the developed world, international cooperation has worked mainly on merger control rather than in tackling cartels. In that too, there have been substantial disagreements. The EU and the US have a cooperation agreement, but their approaches to the same mergers have been quite different, as for example, the GE–Honeywell and the Boeing–McDonnel Douglas merger cases.

It is widely recognized that the issues related to competition policy and law are quite complex so much so that even some of the developed countries do not have adequate capacity in this regard (Mavroidis and Neven 2001). Obviously, developing countries with no or very limited expertise have reasons to be apprehensive about negotiating on this issue in a form like the WTO where the stakes are very high.

However, considering the fact that there are good reasons to have a multilateral framework on competition policy, a brand new organization dedicated solely to competition issues under the auspices of the UN will perhaps be the most suitable. The new agency can combine the principles and structures of WIPO and Interpol and similar multilateral bodies rather than those of the WTO (Mehta *et al.* 2005).

Trade facilitation

It is widely believed that there is considerable merit in trade facilitation measures. The losses that businesses suffer through delays at borders and complicated and unnecessary documentation requirements are estimated to exceed, in many cases, the costs of tariffs. About a decade ago, it was estimated by UNCTAD that trade facilitation measures could save more than $150 billion a year (UNCTAD 1994). In a recent estimate, the benefits of improved trade facilitation on the basis of the assumption that the below-average countries are able to achieve halfway up to the global average in terms of trade facilitation standards will involve an increase in trade among 75 major countries worth about $377 billion (Wilson *et al.* 2004). This, however, is an overestimate as it includes several areas of infrastructure that will not come under any possible agreement on trade facilitation at the WTO.

It may also be the case that developing-country traders are more constrained than their developed-country counterparts because of unnecessary hindrances. Since developing-country traders are relatively small in size and also export or import in smaller consignments, they find the cost of documentation etc. disproportionately high, as such costs are very often fixed and do not vary with the size of the consignment (Nanda 2003).

However, it is also felt that trade facilitation measures would place a substantial financial burden on developing countries much beyond any perceived benefit. Even if benefits outweigh costs, it is widely believed that the development payoff might be greater if those resources were spent elsewhere. For example, to create a custom clearance infrastructure that will be as efficient as that of Singapore, even in small developing countries, the amount of money required may well be in excess of $100 million.[4] In many small countries, this figure is much higher than the money government spends on education. Moreover, considering that the share of developing countries in world trade is just about 30 percent,[5] an overwhelming proportion of the estimated benefits of $150 billion would accrue to developed countries, while developing countries would bear a huge proportion of the costs.

The costs of doing business in developing countries are much higher primarily because of inefficient institutions. However, most developing countries operate on tight budget constraints and a binding commitment on trade facilitation could lead to a disproportionate diversion of limited resources from other vital needs to customs administration. This could create a situation where domestic businesses would incur the costs of compliance, which would arguably be much higher than the costs that their foreign counterparts would bear in similar situations. Thus, trade facilitation may effectively mean that foreign players would get more than national treatment, with adverse consequences for domestic business. Moreover, if trade facilitation measures result from a binding WTO commitment, rather than from a domestic demand, issues of interest to importers (foreign exporters) might take precedence over those of interest to domestic exporters. Once again, foreign players will get more than national treatment (Nanda 2003).

Developed countries expect customs-clearance systems in developing countries to be as efficient as their own. However, considering the huge productivity gaps, this is hardly feasible. Some people have raised another important question. If a party found that its consignment took three days instead of two to get customs clearance in a country, would it drag the country concerned to the WTO? There is no ready answer, but if this happened the WTO Dispute Settlement Mechanism would come under severe strain. It has been proposed that there will be a cut-off clause in relation to dispute settlement on trade facilitation matters, meaning that cases relating to small consignments will not be brought to the dispute settlement panel (Shin 2001). But nobody knows what the cut-off point might be. If the cut-off point is set at a high level, the agreement will benefit only developed-country traders and developing countries may not be eligible to bring their complaints to the WTO owing to their smaller consignments.

Some international organizations are already involved in trade facilitation initiatives. In the context of discussions on trade facilitation at the WTO, the work being done by the World Customs Organization (WCO) seems to be most relevant. WCO's Kyoto Convention provides the regulatory framework for trade facilitation. Proponents of the adoption of the Kyoto Convention at the WTO argue that a multilateral agreement already exists. In reality, there are only ten contracting parties that have ratified or acceded to the Convention and six contracting parties that have signed it as of January 2003 (Lucenti 2003). However, it is also astounding to note that some of the proponents of a trade facilitation agreement at the WTO have shown total disregard for the WCO Kyoto Convention but now argue for adopting the Kyoto-Convention standards at the WTO (Nanda 2003).

The advocates of trade facilitation often argue that customs hindrances affect the exporters as well and hence better trade facilitation will boost exports of developing countries. However, looked at from a broader perspective, bad trade facilitation is just a minor obstacle to growth in exports, compared to several supply-side constraints and market access problems in developed countries (Mendis 2004).

Government procurement

Transparency in government procurement is indeed a requirement for development, and hence no one is opposed to it as such. However, some developing countries believe that the issue is better left with national governments to take appropriate action. It is widely believed that a multilateral agreement may be the first step to push a market access agenda, otherwise why would they be so keen on it when it does not seem to benefit them? That this will help only the developing countries by promoting good governance has raised suspicion about the actual motive. Even though the Doha Declaration emphasized that negotiations should be limited only to transparency aspects and should not restrict the scope for countries to give preferences to domestic goods and suppliers, developing countries remain suspicious.

Their distrust is not without reason. If one looks at the existing plurilateral agreement on government procurement (GPA) at the WTO that came into force on January 1, 1996, one can see that it is not only about transparency; it goes much beyond that. Governments are required to apply the principle of national treatment to goods and services, and suppliers of other parties to the GPA, and to abide by the most-favored-nation (MFN) rule, which prohibits discrimination among goods, services, and suppliers of other parties. In terms of services, of course, GPA takes a GATS-type positive list approach and only those services listed in the annexes are covered by the agreement (Evenett 2002).

Thus if the proponents are to be believed, then the proposed multilateral agreement has to be fundamentally different from the existing plurilateral agreement, as non-discrimination (national treatment and MFN) lies at the core of it. It is not clear what will happen to the existing GPA if a multilateral agreement is signed. Obviously, developing countries suspect that the ultimate aim of the multilateral agreement is to establish a framework similar to the existing plurilateral GPA.

Adhering to an internationally set standard of transparency may become a costly affair for many developing countries. This is because making information on procurement available to a wide range of people will involve substantial costs, especially when small developing countries engage in not-so-big procurements. Transparency itself can have market access implications as well, by making information available to foreign suppliers unless they are barred from the procurement bids (Evenett and Hoekman 2004).

Moreover, as many developing countries have argued, if transparency in government procurement does not have anything to do with market access as claimed by its proponents, then it has no trade implication either. If it has no trade implications, then why should such an agreement be negotiated at the WTO? The WTO is there to promote trade and not to promote good governance in developing countries; there are other intergovernmental organizations devoted to this cause. The question remains unanswered.

Current state of affairs

As the other Singapore issues have been kept out of the Doha Work Program of the WTO, discussions are taking place only on trade facilitation. In terms of trade facilitation, the Singapore and Doha

Ministerials as well as the July Package have mandated that GATT Articles V, VIII, and X be considered for future multilateral negotiations. Annex D of the July Package that deals with trade facilitation states that the negotiations "shall aim to clarify and improve relevant aspects of Articles V, VIII and X of the GATT 1994 with a view to further expediting the movement, release and clearance of goods, including goods in transit."

Article V relates to "freedom of transit" for goods from another member, and states that all charges imposed on goods in transit must be "reasonable." Article VIII covers the fees and formalities connected with the importation and exportation of goods and says that these must be about equal to the cost of the services rendered, so that they do not constitute a form of indirect protection. It also calls for reducing the number and diversity of such fees. Article X relates to the publication and administration of trade regulations, that is, measures to ensure transparency, and requires all trade regulations to be clearly published and fairly administered.

In the post-July negotiations, WTO members have agreed to deal first with the clarification and improvement of the three articles mentioned in the July Package. Prior to the Cancun Ministerial Conference the proposals on trade facilitation were, by and large, made by developed countries. As most developing countries were opposed to negotiations on trade facilitation, they were not keen on discussing the issue at the WTO.

Proposals on Article V were made by three members, namely the European Union, Korea, and Canada. Proposals regarding Article VIII were made by Canada, Colombia, the European Union, Hong Kong, Japan, Korea, and the United States. Members that submitted proposals on Article X include the European Union, Japan, Korea, Canada and the United States. Some of the international organizations mentioned in the July Package mandate have already presented their work and findings on trade facilitation to members.

As expected, since the inconclusive Cancun Ministerial and until the July Package was agreed in 2004, there were no substantive proposals on the issue. However, after the July Package, particularly since the beginning of 2005, there has been a flurry of submissions to the Negotiating Group on Trade Facilitation, many of them coming from developing countries. A closer look at the new submissions, however, reveals that the boundaries of proposals have already been defined by the submissions made before Cancun. The new submissions by and large provide clarifications or share experiences or suggest capacity building and technical assistance measures rather than suggesting rules. Some, of course, have suggested some ideas on special and differential treatment for developing countries.

Meanwhile, even though the EU has been the key driver in bringing the Singapore issues into the WTO arena, the US has been more active in pushing these in the international law arena, particularly through bilateral trade agreements. The FTAs negotiated between Australia and Singapore, Australia and the US, and the US FTAs with Chile, Central American countries, Jordan, Singapore and Australia all have provisions related to Singapore issues in varying measures. Moreover, the US has signed a Trade and Investment Framework Agreement (TIFA) with several countries which also have some related provisions, particularly related to investment. Needless to say, most bilateral investment treaties (BITs) signed between several countries, especially those of US-type have provisions that could be included in the proposed WTO agreement on investment. Citing this experience, the US has argued that developing countries should not have much difficulty in accepting additional obligations under a trade facilitation agreement.

The EU, however, has been pushing hard for including Singapore issues in Economic Partnership Agreements (EPAs) with ACP countries. The ACP group, comprising 77 countries from African, Caribbean and Pacific regions, was more vocal in opposing Singapore issues at the WTO in the Cancun Ministerial. Despite this, the EU has proposed that all four Singapore issues, which they term as "development issues"[6] be included in EPAs on a non-discriminatory basis. There is of course little reason to believe that ACP concerns with WTO negotiations on the Singapore issues are any less apparent in negotiating them with the EU. Thus, it would not be easy for the EU to get these issues included in EPAs, except probably trade facilitation on which negotiations are already underway at the WTO.[7] However, if the EU succeeds, then a large group of developing countries will come under a binding international agreement on Singapore issues, the implications of which could be far reaching.

In lieu of conclusion

As we have seen before, even though many developing countries consider an agreement on trade facilitation as harmless, in reality it may not be so. If the agreement tries to facilitate trade by harmonizing documentation requirements and by avoiding complicated and unnecessary requirements, then developing countries may not object. However, if it is to ensure some standards and make some commitment on faster customs clearance that will require huge investment, then developing countries need to be worried.

As examined before, agreement on the three Singapore issues will impose huge costs for developing countries and the benefits are at best uncertain. The costs of their inability to fulfill their commitment under such potential agreements would also be very high as they may face trade sanctions at any time. In the July Package, of course, the technical assistance and capacity building provisions are going to be more binding in the proposed trade facilitation agreement than they are elsewhere, and if developing and least-developed countries do not receive the additional support and assistance they will not have to fulfill the commitments. However, it is not yet known what will be the benchmark for such assistance, i.e. how much assistance would be considered to be sufficient. Another issue is what would be the mode of assistance (grants or loans) and their effectiveness including the issues of conditionalities.

Most developing countries are not yet prepared to fulfill their commitments already made in the Uruguay Round. For example, the obligations under TRIPS would be difficult to implement as most developing countries do not have the required enforcement mechanisms. They have a limited police force. If they have to spend a lot of energy in protecting intellectual property rights (IPR), they might not be able perform many other duties that they are required to do, and which demand a greater priority. Enforcing IPR in a developed country is not a problem as with their much higher income their people can pay the royalty charged by the IPR holders. However, in developing countries, people find it difficult to pay, which leads to violation of IPR laws.

Developing countries, therefore, should be careful in signing an agreement on trade facilitation. It may, however, be noted that negotiating at the WTO is not like walking on a one-way street. Developing countries may sign an agreement on trade facilitation even if the net benefits are negative, provided the concessions received in other areas, especially in agriculture, far outweigh the expected costs.

This has implications for the future of other Singapore issues as well. Though the other Singapore issues have not been included in the current round of negotiations, they have neither been explicitly dropped from the WTO agenda. Thus, the possibility of their returning to the negotiating table at a future date cannot be ruled out. If the EU makes substantial liberalization of agriculture under the current round of negotiations, then they would lose the bargaining chip of further agricultural trade liberalization to push for the Singapore issues once again, unless something new emerges. The future of the Singapore issues will thus largely depend upon what happens in agriculture in the current round of negotiations. However, inclusion of these issues in several bilateral and regional trade agreements may gradually make these issues more acceptable to developing countries even at the WTO.

Notes

1 Joint Communication from Bangladesh (on behalf of the LDC Group), Botswana, China, Cuba, Egypt, India, Indonesia, Kenya, Malaysia, Nigeria, Philippines, Tanzania, Uganda, Venezuela, Zambia and Zimbabwe, December 12 2003 (WT/GC/W/522).
2 See, for example, 'Proposed Liberalization of Mode 4 Under GATS Negotiations', Communication from Argentina, Bolivia, Chile, The People's Republic of China, Colombia, Dominican Republic, Egypt, Guatemala, India, Mexico, Pakistan, Peru, Philippines and Thailand to the Council for Trade in Services of the WTO, July 3 2003 (TN/S/W/14).
3 A procedural approach, such as in the Anglo-American legal system, involving active and unhindered parties contesting with each other to put forth a case before an independent decision-maker.
4 According to an estimate by Finger and Schuler (2000) the minimum costs of customs reforms alone will be about US$40 million in most developing countries.
5 This includes the share of countries like South Korea, Taiwan and Hong Kong who can now be considered as developed countries.
6 Many termed the Doha Work Program that came out of the Doha Ministerial as the Doha Development Agenda (DDA) due to its inclusion of the issues such as TRIPS and Public Health; WTO rules (anti-dumping and subsidies); agriculture; implementation problems; trade, debt, finance and trade, and transfer of technology, etc. Taking its cue from this, the EU has termed Singapore issues as development issues as well. Critics, however, have been skeptical about the development-friendliness of DDA. For example, see Malhotra (2002).
7 'ACP-EU Ministers Meet To Launch Phase II of EPA Negotiations', *Bridges: Weekly Trade News Digest*, 7 (33), October 8 2003.

References

Amsden, A.H. and Singh, A. (1994) 'The optimal degree of competition and dynamic efficiency in Japan and Korea', *European Economic Review*, 38: 941–51.
Correa, C. and Kumar, N. (2003) *Protecting Foreign Investment: Implications of a WTO Regime and Policy Options*, London and New York: Zed Press.
Evenett, S.J. (2002) 'Multilateral disciplines and government procurement', in B. Hoekman, A. Mattoo and P. English (eds) *Development, Trade and the WTO: A Handbook*, The World Bank.

Evenett, S.J. and Hoekman, B. (2004) 'International disciplines on government procurement: a review of economic analyses and their implications', in CUTS (ed.) *Unpacking Transparency in Government Procurement*, Jaipur, India: CUTS.

Finger, J.M. and Schuler, P. (2000) 'Implementation of Uruguay Round Commitments: the development challenge', *World Economy*, 23 (4): 511–25.

Hoekman, B. and Mavroidis, P.C. (2003) 'Economic development, competition policy and the WTO', *Journal of World Trade*, 37 (1): 1–27.

Jonquières, Guy de (2003) 'Cancun's failure threatens end to Machiavellian games', *Financial Times*, London, 19 September.

Lamy, Pascal (2003) 'It's all about development', *Wall Street Journal*, 17 July.

Lucenti, K. (2003) 'Is there a case for further multilateral rules on trade facilitation?', in SECO and S.J. Evenett (eds) *The Singapore Issues and the World Trading System: The Road to Cancun and Beyond*, Berne: World Trade Institute.

Malhotra K. (2002) 'Doha: is it really a development round?', Carnegie Endowment for International Peace, Trade, Environment and Development, Issue Paper No. 1.

Mavroidis, P.C. and Neven, D. (2001) 'From the White Paper to the proposal for a Council Regulation: how to treat the new kids on the block?', *Legal Issues of Economic Integration*, 28 (2): 151–71.

Mehta, P.S. and Nanda, N. (2004) 'Multilateral framework on investment', in *FOCUS WTO*, VI (3), Sept.–Oct.

Mehta, P.S., Nanda, N. and Pham, A. (2005) *Multilateral Competition Framework: In Need of a Fresh Approach*, Jaipur, India: CUTS.

Mendis, R. (2004) 'Trade facilitation – scope and definition', in CUTS (ed.) *Trade Facilitation: Reducing the Transaction Costs or Burdening the Poor!*, Jaipur, India: CUTS.

Nanda, N. (2003) 'WTO and trade facilitation: some implications', *Economic & Political Weekly*, XXXVIII (26).

Shin, Y.H. (2001) 'New round and trade facilitation – proposing a tentative draft agreement on trade facilitation measures', *Journal of World Trade*, 35 (2): 229–52.

UNCTAD (1994): 'Fact Sheet 5', presented at the United Nations International Symposium on Trade Efficiency, Geneva, 17–21 October.

Wilson, J.S., Mann, C.L. and Otsuki, T. (2004) 'Assessing the Potential Benefit of Trade Facilitation: A Global Perspective', Working Paper No 3224, Washington, DC: World Bank.

WTO (2001) *Doha Ministerial Declaration*. Available at: <http://www.wto.org/english/thewto_e/minist_e/min01_e/mindecl_e.htm>.

WTO (2002) 'Agreement establishing the World Trade Organisation', in *The Legal Texts: The Results of the Uruguay Round of Multilateral Negotiations*, Geneva: WTO.

7 Bilateral negotiations in a multilateral world

Implications for the WTO and global trade policy development

Larry Crump

The WTO Doha Development Agenda has moved from initial hope in Doha Qatar, to fiasco in Cancun Mexico, to postponement in Hong Kong, to indecision in most of 2006, to finally, indefinite suspension. After almost five years of multilateral trade negotiations WTO Director-General Pascal Lamy formally suspended Doha talks on 24 July 2006 by stating: "There are no winners or losers in this assembly. Today there are only losers" (WTO 2006). Readers with a long memory will recall that this is not the first time multilateral talks have been suspended. The Uruguay round was essentially suspended by GATT Director-General Arthur Dunkel in the early 1990s followed by the production of the "Dunkel Draft," which laid the foundation for concluding the GATT Uruguay round in December 1993. It is too soon to say if the Doha round is finished, but media reports immediately after suspension often quoted Indian Trade Minister Kamal Nath who claimed the round is not dead but it is definitely between intensive care and the crematorium. Only time will tell ...

Two themes emerged immediately after Doha's suspension. The US and the EU sought to blame each other for the stalemate and suspension of Doha talks, and there were calls or indications by many nations that they would more vigorously pursue bilateral or regional trade agreements. *The Times* of London and *The Australian* each reported that France called on the EU to switch its efforts to regional trade talks following Doha collapse. *The New York Times* reported that EU Trade Commissioner Peter Mandelson said that Europe now needed to focus on new economic opportunities in Asia. The same report indicated that India was prepared to pursue a bilateral trade agreement with the EU and was close to concluding a deal with Japan. *The Australian* said that Australia would now refocus it trade efforts on free-trade deals with countries such as China, Japan and South Korea. United States Trade Representative Susan C. Schwab told *The*

New York Times that Asia would be a prime target for trade deals. The *International Herald Tribune* recognized that the failure of Doha will encourage the proliferation of regional and bilateral trade deals, while *The Washington Post* cautioned that Doha's failure could weaken the multilateral system that governs global commerce with possibly a splintering into regional blocks.

If the developed world is coming to Asia, what about Africa, South America and other forgotten parts of the world? Unquestionably, multilateral agreements are the most inclusive means for distributing gains created by the global economy – and this should never be forgotten. Unfortunately, if a developing country does not have a large market or an emerging middle-class or something else to exchange and if there are no political or strategic imperatives, then nations in the developed world will likely be too busy to even consider a bilateral trade agreement. These are the new realities that many nations must now consider. However, at this point in time these are only possibilities.

The Doha Development Agenda could just drift away or it may produce some sort of marginal or symbolic agreement but its implications for multilateralism are presently unclear. The WTO Doha round has not destroyed multilateralism but multilateralism will no longer be the centerpiece of global trade policy, as it must now compete with bilateral and regional processes. For example, all but 12 countries, Mongolia and 11 island nations (World Bank 2005), have begun pursuing bilateral and regional trade agreement.[1] As a point of comparison, 124 bilateral and regional trade agreements were concluded in the 48-year GATT regime (1947–94), but 196 bilateral and regional trade agreements have been concluded during the 11 years (1994–2005) of the WTO regime (Crawford and Fiorentino 2005). However, it is not the number of agreements that is important but the amount of world trade managed through these agreements. Bilateral and regional trade agreements now make up nearly 40 percent of total global trade (World Bank 2005: 27). It is clear that many countries have already embraced non-WTO trade negotiations as fundamental to their national trade policy strategy. This development is interesting, significant and controversial.

Complex debates often degenerate into slogans to facilitate public comprehension. Unfortunately, simplification can at times distort that which we seek to understand. In this debate the relevant slogan is stated as follows: do bilateral or regional trade agreements serve as a building block or as a stumbling block to a WTO-sponsored agreement? In recent interviews with several WTO administrators responsible for monitoring bilateral and regional trade agreements, I learned that the WTO seeks to move beyond this dichotomized view, as other views exist. Specifically, there is no official WTO position on non-WTO trade negotiations, but a consensus exists within the WTO that these trade agreements have both a positive and a negative influence on WTO-sponsored negotiations and world trade; thus it is not an either-or question. A useful question to consider is: What are the positive and negative influences that bilateral processes have on WTO-sponsored Doha negotiations and the global economy? In addition, it will be useful to consider the positive and negative influences that bilateral trade negotiations have on nations that are conducting such negotiations. It may be that bilateral trade negotiations and the agreements they produce contain intrinsic value that is separate and independent of any WTO-sponsored process. If so, it will be useful to understand the fundamental nature of bilateral trade negotiations both from the perspective of the WTO and from the perspective of those nations engaged in such negotiations. This may be even more important now that the Doha round is in doubt.

WTO Secretariat staff observe that, for some countries, multilateral and bilateral strategies are equally important parts of their national trade policy, while in many other countries, bilateral and regional trade negotiations have emerged as a higher priority than WTO-sponsored negotiations (Crawford and Fiorentino 2005). The players in this game – both developed and developing countries – have not shifted to another field, but it is clear that these players are now performing on bilateral, regional and multilateral fields.

Bilateral and regional negotiations involving trade in goods have been an accepted part of the multilateral system since the establishment of GATT Article XXIV in 1947, while the Enabling Clause adopted in 1979 provides for the mutual reduction of tariffs on trade in goods among developing countries. Article V of GATS, negotiated during the Uruguay round, covers trade in services for bilateral and regional trade agreements. More recently, with the proliferation of bilateral and regional trade agreements, several trade policy trends can be observed: (1) trade agreements are being negotiated that demonstrate deeper degrees of integration, with treaty provisions containing measures to liberalize, eliminate and harmonize trade-impeding regulatory policies; (2) enlargement and integration of regional trading blocks (e.g. Europe, North America, South America and Asia to some extent) via bilateral and regional trade agreements; (3) trade agreements that link countries from two or more regions; and (4) an increase in trade agreements between developed and developing countries (Jordan–United States FTA of 2000, Chile–EC FTA of 2002, Thailand–Australia FTA of 2004). Of the trade agreements in force, 75 percent are bilateral (Sampson 2003: 3–17; Crawford and Fiorentino 2005). Clearly, the global trading system has become more complex as a result of these developments.

The World Bank (2005: 27) identifies two trends within the international trading system. The first trend created the WTO, which has sought to consolidate an evolving system of rules based on non-discrimination among trading partners within a multilateral system. A second trend, though, is rapidly gaining momentum under a different set of rules, resulting from a sudden increase in the number of nations negotiating bilateral and regional trade agreements. This second trend reduces barriers to trade on a reciprocal and preferential basis for those nations that are a party to such agreements. Some studies see this emerging system as complementary to the multilateral system (Sampson and Woolcock 2003) and other studies articulate deep concerns about the spread of bilateral and regional trade agreements (WTO Consultative Board 2004). Nevertheless, both systems do exist and will co-exist for the foreseeable future. This fact needs to be accepted so that knowledge can be gained from the challenges and opportunities that may be present.

We require greater understanding about this emerging system of bilateral and regional trade negotiations and the agreements they produce. What are the strengths and weaknesses, and opportunities and challenges presented by a trade policy development system that is bilateral and regional in nature? Once we gain this knowledge we will then be in a position to seek understanding about the interaction or linkage between this emerging trade policy system and the WTO-sponsored multilateral system. In so doing, we should focus on establishing methods that will contribute to the development of high-quality international trade policy. "High-quality trade policy" is defined as trade rules between nations that support free market principles and encourage trade liberalization, as compared to the status quo. Rules guiding such liberalization should be as simple and transparent as possible. It is useful to recognize that high-quality trade policy is sometimes achieved all at once (e.g. a "big bang") and sometimes incrementally over decades (e.g. GATT).

In pursuing these objectives, the present study will examine both negotiation process and outcome, as interaction between bilateral and multilateral policy development systems occurs in both dimensions. As such, this chapter intends to move the debate beyond the "building block–stumbling block" view of bilateral–multilateral trade negotiations. It is time to broaden and reframe the current debate to build another lens for viewing this world.

We will begin by examining those arguments that are often presented against bilateral and regional trade negotiation – also called preferential trade negotiations by prominent multilateralists. In considering such arguments we seek understanding about the actual costs and benefits that bilateral and regional negotiations have on the global economy and on WTO-sponsored negotiations. This review is presented in the next section of this chapter. Then we consider the relationship between bilateral negotiations and the development of global trade policy based on data from negotiations that established the Australia–United States Free Trade Agreement of 2004 (AUSFTA), the United States–Singapore Free Trade Agreement of 2003 (USSFTA), and the Singapore–Australia Free Trade Agreement of 2003 (SAFTA). In 2004 I interviewed 86 trade negotiators and trade policy specialists that were involved in AUSFTA, USSFTA and SAFTA. Recommendations for the WTO in more effectively managing a multilateral–bilateral trade policy development system are considered in the final sections of this chapter.

Bilateral trade negotiations and the global economy

Multilateralists present three primary concerns about the negative influence that bilateral and regional trade processes have on the global economy. They argue that (1) bilateral and regional trade agreements create distortions in the international economy, and such distortions make the global economy less efficient, while harming countries that are not a party to the treaty; (2) transaction costs increase for both business and government; and (3) they serve to unravel or undermine the multilateral trade policy system.

Bilateral negotiation and trade distortion

Viner's (1950) seminal work on trade creation and trade diversion in a customs union continues to serve as the foundation for the concern that bilateral and regional trade agreements contribute to distortions in the international economy. Since bilateral trade agreements liberalize trade in a preferential manner, they create new trade between the parties to a treaty, while concurrently the treaty can divert trade from low-cost suppliers who are outside the treaty to high-cost suppliers who are covered by the treaty. Overall, bilateral treaties that create trade are defined as beneficial, and treaties that divert trade are defined as harmful to the global economy. This trade creating–diverting issue has been hotly debated within economics (see Panagariya

1999, Ch. 1, for an excellent overview), although this debate has not been helped by the fact that examination of the trade creation and trade diverting effects for a specific trade treaty are difficult, as the empirical evidence remains ambiguous (WTO Consultative Board 2004; Crawford and Fiorentino 2005).

Aside from the empirical evidence, Viner's argument is intuitively logical. A useful illustrative example is found in the US–Singapore trade agreement concerning textiles and apparel (USSFTA 2003: Ch. 5) – an industry considered "extremely sensitive" in the United States (Ng 2004: 90). Textile and apparel trade negotiators that I interviewed in the US and Singapore talked at length about the "US Yarn Forwarding Rule," which stipulates that raw material (cotton, wool, etc.) can be sourced anywhere in the world, but the yarn from this raw material must be made in either partner country (i.e. Singapore or the US in this case). Such rules of origin may have made economic sense in NAFTA when Canada and Mexico were treaty partners to the US, but such logic stops at the Pacific Ocean, as Singapore does not have a yarn industry. Nevertheless, to gain full tariff preferences on textiles and apparel (total removal of US tariffs that can range from 10 to 33 percent) via USSFTA, Singaporean companies must source yarn locally (generally, none available) or transport yarn from the US to Singapore so that textiles and apparel are "fully processed and assembled in Singapore" (Ng 2004: 85) so that these companies can then transport the finished product back to the US. After substantial objections (this was one of the final issues resolved in USSFTA negotiations), Singapore was forced to recant and accept the US Yarn Forwarding Rule if they wished to conclude their trade treaty with the US.

Obviously, Singaporean textiles that are manufactured for the US market would be less expensive if Singapore could source yarn from China or perhaps even Australia. Are China, Australia and other countries that could sell yarn to Singapore harmed by the USSFTA Chapter on textiles and apparel? Tongzon (2003: 12–19) concludes that the trade diversion effects from the USSFTA should be marginal. How do Tongzon's observations apply to the textiles and apparel covered under USSFTA? Given traditionally high US tariffs, few of the 156 Singaporean textile companies in operation were exporting to the US prior to USSFTA. For example, total tariff savings on Singaporean textiles and apparel due to the USSFTA will be around S$140 million (Ng 2004: 91). Singaporean companies that were previously exporting to the US will likely be diverted from low-cost yarn suppliers to more expensive US suppliers, and so these low-cost yarn suppliers and their countries will be harmed. However, it is expected that overall

Singaporean textile and apparel manufacturers and exporters will create new business opportunities in the US, resulting in new job opportunities in Singapore.

Although highly inefficient, the overall balance will be trade generating rather than trade diverting. Some of Singapore's former yarn suppliers are harmed, while US yarn-makers and Singaporean transport and warehouse companies should benefit. What about companies in countries that never previously supplied yarn to Singapore, but could now supply less expensive yarn? Are they being hurt? I argue that they are not being hurt as being hurt means losing. Rather, such suppliers are not gaining any new business. There is a difference between being harmed and not gaining benefit from someone else's opportunity.[2] Each is a form of discrimination but each (trade-loss and no-trade-gain) is a different type of discrimination that can exist within a trade-creating or trade-diverting treaty. Being damaged through loss is a much more significant form of discrimination than being excluded from someone else's opportunity. Calculations of trade distortion should distinguish between these two forms of discrimination. Moreover, perhaps the WTO should devote more attention to the type of discrimination and the degree of discrimination in any specific bilateral treaty, as a means of recommending acceptable and unacceptable bilateral trade proposals, since the multilateral trading system is based on rules grounded in non-discrimination.

Transaction costs: business

Bilateral and regional trade agreements also increase transaction costs, while some studies observe that transaction costs associated with rules of origin (ROOs) are recognized as being increasingly important as the number of bilateral and regional trade agreements multiply (Garnaut 2002). ROOs assist a country to establish where a product was actually made. If a country decides, via a bilateral trade agreement, to give preferential treatment to the products of another country then both countries must be assured that the products being imported are actually made in the partner country. Studies critical of bilateral and regional trade agreements claim that the administration of differing ROOs is complex, inconsistent and contributes to confusion (WTO Consultative Board 2004). This issue is at the core of the "trade policy spaghetti bowl" (Bhagwati and Panagariya 1996b; Snape 1996) – a negative spin on the issue – or "lattice framework" (Dent 2003; Desker 2004) – a positive spin on the issue – that is often presented in discussions on ROOs in international trade studies. This issue warrants closer examination given the differing views.

I argue that the striking illustrations of the African spaghetti bowl (Schiff and Winters 2003), the spaghetti bowl of the Americas and the Asia–Pacific (Devlin and Estevadeordal 2004), and the Eastern Europe and Central Asia spaghetti bowl (World Bank 2005) are alarmist, as they suggest a degree of complexity that can be derived conceptually, but do not actually exist in the practice of international trade by individual traders and their companies. What is being presented in these illustrations is a visual image of formal trade relationship between nations. However, there is not a multitude of complex ROO systems – just a multitude of trading relationships formalized through bilateral and regional treaties. This concept of a trade policy spaghetti bowl is inadvertently deceiving, as it gives the impression that an international trader must understand hundreds of bilateral ROOs when in fact there are not hundreds but three fundamental forms (Rossman 2004: 61–73). Basically, all bilateral and regional trade agreements that address ROOs can be placed under one of three headings:

- the local value-added ROO system
- the ROO process system
- the change in tariff classification or ROO transformation system.

Each system has its own fundamental logic – so in practice the logic of three systems must be mastered. Briefly, (1) the local value-added ROO system requires that a percentage of the total value of a product (e.g. 50 percent) be added in a partner country if it is to be eligible for tariff benefit in the other partner country; (2) the ROO process system requires that a defined manufacturing process occur in one of the partner countries (often used in manufacturing chemical products); and (3) the ROO transformation system requires that material used in a product experience a change so significant that it achieves a new tariff classification (as per the WTO Harmonized System Nomenclature or HS). For example, water (HS number 11) plus imported malt (HS number 25) plus other imported inputs (HS number 32) are combined to produce beer (HS 2203). In this case the imported malt and other imported input has undergone a change in tariff classification and so are eligible to receive tariff benefits (Rossman 2004: 67). The relationship between the value of the imported products to the overall value of the beer is not an issue in the ROO transformation system, while such a comparison is at the logical core of the ROO local value-added system.

Out of these three systems of logic grow differing tariff schedules and rules in each treaty (not unlike the differing tariff schedules and rules of each nation), but how complicated is this when compared to the GATT/WTO system? Every company interested in exporting to a country where they may gain a tariff advantage must take the time to learn the specific ROO system and the specific tariff schedule and rules that a treaty adopts. Generally, this is no different from the present multilateral system, but rather than looking at the GATT Uruguay round treaty (plus a country's tariff schedule and rules) they must now look at a much smaller bilateral trade treaty that includes the tariff schedule and rules. How complex is this? The fundamental argument is that this complexity inhibits international trade. How can this be when trade concluded via bilateral and regional trade agreements has grown to almost 40 percent? An analogy seems relevant: businesspeople complain that national tax systems are too complex, but do these businesspeople choose to stop making money because of this complexity? When we carefully examine the issue of complexity and increases in business transaction costs we find that it lacks logical coherence, as it can not be demonstrated that the costs inhibit trade.

I am not arguing that this is an ideal system for a business interested in conducting international trade – it is not – but it does not contain the complexity and transaction costs implied by the mythical spaghetti bowl. The scholars that carry out these studies look at the entire world and perceive substantial complexity in the whole, which there is, but an individual trader or company never seeks to understand the whole – they have no need – and they do not search the entire world for every opportunity, rather they examine one single opportunity at a time. On the other hand, a multinational corporation (MNC) may examine hundreds of opportunities a year, but this simply means that the MNC assigns sufficient staff, each of whom is focused on an individual opportunity or group of related opportunities.

Where is the increase in transaction costs for business when we compare the GATT Uruguay system with a system that is based on a bilateral treaty? Business has to learn a new tariff system, but this new system is normally GATT-plus so it is to the economic benefit of a business to learn this new system.

I conducted interviews in 2004 with many trade negotiators who were in regular contact with the business community, as negotiation team–stakeholder relations was a primary theme in my research program. Trade negotiators only reported business community concern when a nation considered adoption of a new ROO system. No trade negotiator reported that the local business community complained that multiple ROOs disrupted their international business plans. A nation that manages multiple ROOs may impose increased costs on business, but these costs are minor relative to the benefits that the business community enjoys.

Transaction costs: government

Customs officers report that it takes longer to process goods covered in a bilateral or regional treaty (World Bank 2005). These individual observations are intuitively logical, but how does it apply at the organizational level? Australia is a case in point. Historically, Australia has used a local value-added ROO system, as its treaties with both New Zealand and Singapore adopt the value-added system. But, as of 1 January 2005 the Australian Customs Service (ACS) was required to administer the transformation ROO system, as Australia's bilateral treaties with Thailand and with the US each adopted this system for implementation on this date. Now the ACS has to administer two ROO systems depending on an imported product's country of origin. Moreover, the ACS has known that they would be implementing both systems since October 2003, when Thailand–Australia treaty negotiations (see: TAFTA 2004) were substantially concluded (AUSFTA negotiations were substantially concluded in February 2004). How has the ACS responded to this apparent workload increase? See Table 7.1.

ACS learned that they would be required to apply both the value-added ROO system and the transformation ROO system in the 2003/04 fiscal period (3a) and began to implement both ROO systems in the 2004/05 fiscal period (3b). Total ACS employee operating expenses for this two-year period is $676,058,000 (3c) (see Table 7.1). If we analyze the difference in employee operating expenses between the second period (2c 2001–02 and 2002–03) with the third period (3c) we find that ACS employee operating expenses increased by 12.8 percent from the second to the third period. It is also useful to look at recent historical differences to provide perspective. If we analyze differences in employee operating expenses between the first period (1c 1999–2000 and 2000–01) and the second period (2c) we find employee operating expenses increased by 17.3 percent when comparing these two periods.

Granted, many unidentified factors contribute to ACS employee operating expenses. However, for our purposes it appears that Australia's adoption of a second ROO system has *not* caused ACS substantial financial distress, as employee operating expenses increased more slowly – from 17.3 percent to 12.8 percent – when comparing the periods under investigation (see Table 7.1). ACS

Table 7.1 Australian Customs Service (ACS)

Fiscal year ending 30 June		*Operating expenses: Employees:	Operating expenses: Employees per 2-year period	
1a	1999/2000	$234,507,000	1c	$487,143,000
1b	2000/01	$252,636,000		(1a + 1b = 1c)
2a	2001/02	$278,825,000	2c	$589,221,000
2b	2002/03	$310,396,000		(2a + 2b = 2c)
3a	2003/04	$320,524,000	3c	$676,058,000
3b	2004/05	$355,534,000		(3a + 3b = 3c)

Note: * ACS Financial Statement 1999/2005, Statement of financial performance

employee costs are continuing to rise but they actually rose more slowly during the period that the ACS was planning, implementing and operating two ROO systems for the first time in Australia's history. How can this be explained?

Some understanding of ACS responsibilities provides perspective about the administration of multiple ROO systems. First, ROOs are not mentioned at all in the ACS "Significant Events in 2003–04" (ACS Annual Report 2004: 8–9) nor are they mentioned in the ACS "Corporate Priorities 2004–05" (ACS Annual Report 2005: 9–10). ROOs also receive no attention in "Outlook for 2004–05" (ACS Annual Report 2004: 10) or in the 2004–05 "Anticipated Results" (ACS Annual Report 2005: 10). Buried on page 85 of the 2005 ACS Annual Report is a discussion on rules of origin related to the implementation of AUSFTA and TAFTA and that training courses for customs staff were conducted as part of the implementation process. Nowhere is it mentioned that the ACS is administering two rules of origin systems for the first time in Australian history, as it appears that the ACS has more important matters to address. For example, early in these annual reports the ACS expresses concern about securing Australia's borders including issues related to terrorism, narcotics and precursor chemicals. The ACS is especially focused on implementing their Cargo Management Re-engineering project (the world's first fully integrated imports and exports system), starting their neutron scanner pilot project, opening a container facility in Western Australia and continuing to reassess emerging threats in the aviation and maritime security environment (ACS Annual Report 2004, 2005). Compared to these concerns the operation of two ROO systems seems to lack real significance for the ACS.

Scholars writing about the "trade policy spaghetti bowl" express substantial concern about the transaction costs to business and government due to the administration of multiple rules of origin. Additional costs undoubtedly exist, but these scholars have overstated their case to the point of being alarmist. I recommend that these scholars depart from presenting theoretical arguments and start to gather data to quantify the problem that they claim exists as a result of the trade policy spaghetti bowl.

An unraveling multilateral system?

Multilateral trade agreements provide a greater degree of economic liberalization and integration, as compared to bilateral trade agreements. Although much easier to achieve, bilateral trade agreements are second-best options (Desker 2004; LeClair 1997). But in addition, are bilateral trade agreements damaging the multilateral system? Critics claim that such trade agreements unravel or undermine the multilateral system (Bhagwati 1991; Bhagwati and Panagariya 1996a: 1–78; Garnaut 2002; Panagariya 1999). We will not jump to this conclusion so quickly, rather we will ask if bilateral and regional trade agreements are unraveling or enhancing the multilateral system? This question is at the heart of the stumbling block–building block question that we hope to move beyond.

Any negative effect that bilateral or regional trade agreements have on the multilateral system is based on two concerns. The first involves the influence of bilateral and regional trade agreements on the multilateral trading system, with their potential for trade diversion and increased transaction costs (see previous sections of this chapter). The second concern focuses on the effect of bilateral and regional trade negotiations on the actual multilateral WTO Doha process. This section is focused on this second concern.

Countries such as the US, Australia and Singapore have each embraced what is known as "competitive liberalization." By pursuing bilateral trade agreements this action is believed to drive or motivate achievement in the multilateral process (Senate Committee Report 2003; Desker 2004; USTR Trade Policy Agenda 2004). From this perspective bilateral trade negotiations will enhance the multilateral system although it is unclear how this actually occurs. For example, how do bilateral negotiations between the US and Singapore or Australia or Chile or Morocco or Bahrain or the regional CAFTA agreement (Central America Free Trade Area) motivate WTO member nations to move Doha forward? The connection is unclear. Some studies conclude that bilateral and regional agreements complement rather than undermine multilateral rules (Woolcock 2003: 330), but complementing is not the same as motivating or driving the multilateral process.

On the other hand we also find observers who claim that bilateral trade negotiations inhibit or stall the WTO Doha process by diverting national negotiation resources. Bhagwati (2003) notes that bureaucratic and political attention is diverted to bilateral negotiations rather than to the WTO Doha round. Australia did require some time to learn how to manage a two-track bilateral–multilateral strategy (the upcoming section on "Trade Policy and Process Management" (p. 190) will address this issue in greater detail). Part of the challenge here is coordinating between bilateral and multilateral processes. For example, one Australian trade lobbyist I interviewed complained bitterly that the Australian Department of Foreign Affairs and Trade scheduled public hearings on Australia–US trade negotiations in Canberra at the same time as the WTO Fifth Ministerial Conference in Cancun (Australia and the US set an unrealistically tight one-year deadline for their bilateral negotiations). This trade lobbyist went to Cancun.

If WTO member countries are going to become engaged in bilateral or regional negotiations they need to add an extra layer of planning to coordinate between these multiple levels. More than one Singaporean negotiator I interviewed indicated that their government's robust pursuit of bilateral trade agreements was difficult to manage, as the workload was onerous. An American financial services negotiator I interviewed advised that two bilateral trade negotiations are the most that can be handled at any one time, as each negotiation requires around one week of travel every 4–6 weeks; so that means that the trade negotiator will be out of the office for about one week of every 2–3 weeks if they are involved in two bilateral negotiations. Doha negotiations do not move as quickly and do not require as much travel, but careful multilateral–bilateral coordination will be required if a specific negotiator is assigned to two bilateral negotiations plus Doha negotiations. Any unraveling or undermining of actual WTO Doha negotiations can be managed by proper resourcing and careful coordination of such resources. Administrators of negotiation teams need to be in regular communication with their political leaders so that these leaders do not over-stretch a nation's capability to effectively participate in bilateral and multilateral trade negotiations.

Bilateral and regional trade agreements have not undermined the WTO Doha process, as the WTO process has succeeded in undermining itself. There is generally broad consensus among the 86 trade negotiators and trade policy specialists that I interviewed. The fundamental nature of global trade negotiation shifted somewhere near the end of the GATT Uruguay round in 1994 and the establishment of the WTO in 1995. First, a flood of nations with experience in multilateral processes gained via the United Nations, but with no prior multilateral trade negotiation experience, sought GATT membership near the conclusion of the Uruguay round in 1994. Although 124 governments signed the Marrakesh agreement that concluded the Uruguay round and established the WTO, many of these nations were new to international trade policy negotiations. A 50 percent increase in new members presented this multilateral forum with challenges that were amplified by a substantially expanded trade agenda. The new global trade agenda would not only incorporate economic sectors that had been previously exempt, such as agriculture and textiles – both considered to be "sensitive sectors" in many powerful countries – but trade in services would also be considered. Trade-related aspects of intellectual property rights (TRIPS) – one of the few WTO successes in its first ten years – and electronic commerce and the so-called "Singapore issues" were also added to the Doha agenda. In total 21 subjects are listed in the Doha Declaration (see the Doha Declaration at: <www.wto.org/>), many of these never before considered or only superficially considered in a multilateral trade forum. A third factor is the recent involvement of representatives of non-governmental organizations (NGOs). NGO participation is generally welcomed, and the WTO is given credit for developing an inclusive culture; however, the addition of more parties – even if observers – increases the complexity that must be managed. Are the WTO and its members up to the task? It seems that political leaders who send representatives to the WTO have generally voted with their feet. One foot clearly remains in the multilateral form but the other foot has gone off in search of bilateral and regional partners. Why is this?

High-level government officials and former high-level WTO officials that I interviewed are not optimistic about the WTO. The general view is that multilateral progress was made in the first and fourth WTO Ministerial Meetings held in Singapore and Doha respectively. The second, third and fifth Ministerial Meetings held in Geneva, Seattle and Cancun were often described as either disasters or fiascos. The sixth Ministerial Meeting in Hong Kong in late 2005 was more sedate, but the assembled trade ministers decided to postpone all the important decisions. A former Chair of the General Council of the WTO observed that trade negotiations were once a technical field but now they have become politicized. Once, customs officers and other specialists exchanged compromises on tariff schedules; such simple days no longer exist. Concluding a GATT/WTO-sponsored trade treaty requires too much time. National governments operate on 3–5 year planning cycles, as this is how long most governments have a guaranteed hold on office. Why should a government devote trade negotiation resources to accomplish a task that will only be finalized after it has retired from office? Given such circumstances it can be said that government leaders are behaving rationally by adopting a two-track trade policy strategy. It is clear that if the WTO is to continue to convene complex multilateral trade negotiations then WTO members must agree on restraining measures in order to limit the size of the agenda and the length of the process so that results can be delivered to national leaders in a more timely manner.

Bilateral negotiations and trade policy development

The observations and conclusions in the second half of this chapter are directly derived from six months of field research into bilateral trade negotiations. As mentioned previously, I interviewed 86 trade negotiators and trade policy specialists in Canberra, Geneva, Singapore and Washington, DC in 2004. Many of these professionals were involved or had once been involved in GATT/WTO trade talks, but most were involved in one or more of the following bilateral trade negotiations: Singapore–Australia (SAFTA: 11/2000–2/2003), United States–Singapore (USSFTA: 11/2000–5/2003), and Australia–United States (AUSFTA: 11/2002–5/2004). Table 7.2 provides an overview of these three trade negotiations by listing the chapter title found in each trade treaty.[3] Data were also gathered from negotiators involved in China–Australia, Japan–Singapore, Thailand–Australia, and United States–Chile bilateral trade negotiations, although these negotiations were not a primary focus of this research program.[4]

In considering bilateral trade negotiations, WTO-sponsored multilateral trade negotiations and global trade policy development, this chapter examines (1) bilateral and multilateral approaches to trade policy development; (2) creating, testing, refining and learning of trade policy solutions; (3) bilateral trade policy and facilitation of domestic reform; and (4) trade policy negotiation and process management.

Bilateral and multilateral approaches

Regardless of bilateral or multilateral processes, trade policy is a product that is manufactured by governmental officials, diplomats

Table 7.2 Bilateral trade negotiation outcomes: SAFTA, USSFTA and AUSFTA

Singapore–Australia (SAFTA) Treaty chapters	*United States–Singapore (USSFTA)* Treaty chapters
Preamble	Preamble
1 Objectives and general definitions	1 Establishment of a free trade area and definitions
2 Trade in goods	2 National treatment and market access for goods
3 Rules of origin	
4 Customs procedures	3 Rules of origin
5 Technical regulations and sanitary and phytosanitary measures	4 Customs administration
	5 Textile and apparel
6 Government procurement	6 Technical barriers to trade
7 Trade in services	7 Safeguards
8 Investment	8 Cross-border trade in services
9 Financial services	9 Telecommunications
10 Telecommunication services	10 Financial services
11 Movement of business persons	11 Temporary entry of business persons
12 Competition policy	12 Anti-competitive business conduct, designated monopolies and government enterprises
13 Intellectual property	
14 Electronic commerce	
15 Education cooperation	13 Government procurement
16 Dispute settlement	14 Electronic commerce
17 Final provisions	15 Investment
	16 Intellectual property rights
	17 Labor
	18 Environment
	19 Transparency
	20 Administration and dispute settlement
	21 General and final provisions

Australia–United States (AUSFTA) Treaty chapters

Preamble	11 Investment
1 Establishment of a free trade area and definitions	12 Telecommunications
	13 Financial services
2 National treatment and market access for goods	14 Competition-related matters
	15 Government procurement
3 Agriculture	16 Electronic commerce
4 Textiles and apparel	17 Intellectual property
5 Rules of origin	18 Labor
6 Customs administration	19 Environment
7 Sanitary and phytosanitary measures	20 Transparency
	21 Institutional arrangements for dispute settlement
8 Technical barriers to trade	22 General provisions and exceptions
9 Safeguards	23 Final provisions
10 Cross-border trade in services	

and political leaders. Although the outcome is the same – a trade treaty concerned with goods and services – bilateral processes or multilateral processes creating such treaties differ inherently from each other. This difference in process provides opportunities and challenges for effective global trade policy development. One significant difference between bilateral and multilateral negotiations is in the degree of complexity because of differences in the number of parties at the negotiation table. For example, around 150 negotiators participated in the two-party AUSFTA negotiations. Compare this to the 148 parties (technically speaking) and the thousands of official negotiators that attended the WTO Fifth Ministerial Conference in Cancun in 2003 or the WTO Sixth Ministerial Conference in Hong Kong in 2005. Responding effectively to this complexity is a substantial challenge for all parties as each lose some control in managing process and securing a desired outcome in multilateral, as compared to bilateral, negotiation (Crump and Zartman 2003; Zartman 2003). Differences in the degree of complexity and in the extent to which a party can exercise control are defining characteristics when bilateral and multilateral negotiations are compared with each other. In multilateral trade negotiations, the degree of complexity negatively influences a party's ability to efficiently achieve the outcomes that it seeks. In bilateral trade negotiations there is a much stronger relationship between input and output, risk and reward, and action and outcome. For example, SAFTA and USSFTA required 24 and 29 months respectively from the first negotiation round to the signing of a treaty, while AUSFTA required only 14 months. Compare this to the GATT Uruguay round, which required seven and a half years from start to finish.

Just as some trade policy problems are best managed or can only be managed on a multilateral basis, other trade policy problems are best managed bilaterally. One WTO staffer who I interviewed observed that:

> Some issues are too complex to deal with at a multilateral level but they can be dealt with in regional [or bilateral] trade negotiations. Other issues, such as the "Singapore Issues" are unacceptable to some WTO members in multilateral settings but can be addressed in regional trade agreements.[5]

For example, trade in services is much more complex than trade in goods, although an international consensus appears to be emerging that a "negative list" is less complex than a "positive list" for trade in services.[6] A negative list is more liberalizing and more transparent because it opens markets by clearly identifying those services that are not tradable within a nation. An international businessperson can review a negative list for a specific nation and quickly determine if a nation has restrictions on a particular service (if it is not listed then it can be assumed that it can be traded when a trade treaty applies). Although a negative list is superior to a positive list, a positive list for trade in services is the approach used by most nations because GATS uses a positive list.

The process of building a positive list rather than a negative list is substantially different for a national government and holds significantly different consequences if errors and oversights are involved. When compared to a negative list, building a list of services that can be traded in a nation (i.e. a positive list) requires much less thought and analysis, much less inter-agency consultation and much less government–business consultation. Forget to add a specific service on a positive list and the only party damaged is a foreign company (domestic consumers may also experience damage but usually domestic consumers are unaware). Forget to add a specific service on a negative list and foreign competition may suddenly bankrupt a domestic business, while it is possible that foreign competition can remove an entire economic sector from a domestic economy. This may be beneficial to domestic consumers but it is not beneficial to the political leaders and trade policy specialists who agreed to such arrangements; hence the reluctance to pursue such trade policy and a willingness to accept a second-best multilateral solution that comes with fewer costs but also produces much lower liberalizing benefits.

In observing Singapore's shift from a positive list to a negative list for trade in services I learned that a nation does not conduct such an analysis once and then apply it to every subsequent bilateral trading partner. Unlike a positive list, a negative list is not a one-size-fits-all solution (e.g. compare Singapore's negative list in SAFTA Ch. 7 and in USSFTA Ch. 8). Shifting from a positive list to a negative list requires substantial government planning including inter-agency and business consultation. Part of this planning needs to be conducted only once, but additional analysis is required each time a national government starts negotiating with a new trading partner over trade in services, as this latter analysis is focused on the economic integration of the services on offer in the two nations negotiating a treaty.

How can this understanding be used at the multilateral level via WTO-sponsored trade negotiations? By its very nature it is less likely that a negative list for trade in services will be adopted in a multilateral setting, since it does not offer a one-size-fits-all solution although it is more liberalizing, while the trade policy is inherently more simple and more transparent when compared to a positive list. If a negative list for trade in services were adopted, it is likely that each WTO member nation's negative list would be so long as to make the exercise meaningless. On the other hand, as nations become more familiar with a negative list for trade in services, through bilateral trade negotiations and then through the actual administration of such trade policy, they will become better able to conduct such analysis in a meaningful manner. Singapore resisted US and Australian arguments to adopt a negative list for trade in services for a year but finally accepted this template in the end. Now the Singaporean government has much greater understanding of the strengths and weaknesses of positive and negative lists through bilateral processes.

On the basis of such observations, WTO members could pursue an intermediate step in facilitating trade liberalization in services. This intermediate step would have the WTO disseminate information to encourage member states to investigate the strengths and weaknesses of positive and negative lists in services by experimenting with negative lists via bilateral and regional processes. In so doing, the WTO will be motivating nations to use a solution that is simpler, more transparent and more effective in liberalizing trade, while encouraging countries to become familiar with both trade policy and trade policy administration for a negative list for trade in services. Via a bilateral trade policy strategy, WTO member nations may then become sufficiently familiar with the planning and management of a negative list for trade in services to be able to negotiate a global services agreement that is based on a negative list – perhaps 20 or 30 years from now. It is doubtful whether the WTO and its members will be able to truly liberalize trade in services until a majority of nations become familiar with the concept and application of a negative list. For the present, the WTO can only hope to facilitate understanding, thereby laying a foundation for future liberalization – perhaps in the round that follows the round that follows Doha. Here is an example of how bilateral and multilateral processes can be combined to improve international trade policy over an extended time period.

In addition to issues of complexity, some national governments are simply unwilling to consider trade policy issues in a multilateral forum but are willing to consider these same issues in a bilateral setting. For example, government procurement is one of four "Singapore issues" that many nations refuse to discuss in multilateral settings. In 1980 a handful of GATT members negotiated the Government Procurement Agreement (GPA) of 1981, and since then almost 40 countries have signed the GPA. Conspicuously, Australia is one of the few developed countries not to have signed the GPA because Australia believes this trade policy is too proscriptive, although it has recently begun to experiment with some GPA ideas via bilateral processes.

After protracted bilateral negotiations between the US and Australia regarding government procurement, Australia agreed to relinquish its system of invited tenders or selective tendering and adopt an open tender process – procedures that are at the foundation of the GPA (AUSFTA Ch. 15). Operationally this means that Australia agreed to announce and set a date to receive expressions of interests via the Internet for all federal and state tenders that are above a defined threshold. In making this compromise, Australia's government procurement policies became consistent with the 1979 US Trade Agreement Act, which will now allow Australian companies to compete for US Federal and State government contracts. In addition to this tangible achievement, this process also provided Australia with an opportunity to re-examine its government procurement process and the trade policy principles underlying this process, which should give the Australian government some insight into this sector. A multilateral government procurement agreement established in 1981 was unable to bring such enlightenment to the Australian government, but bilateral negotiations were successful in this regard.

Some trade policy solutions, such as a negative list for trade in services, may require analysis that is too complicated to conduct in multilateral settings until national governments become familiar with the administration of such transparent and liberalizing trade policy. Party familiarity, acceptance, adoption, implementation and management will neutralize complexity. As suggested in this chapter, the WTO can actively facilitate such learning. In other cases national governments are willing to liberalize trade on a bilateral basis but not on a multilateral basis. However, once bilateral experience is gained it may be possible that these national governments will be willing to liberalize on a multilateral basis. Australia's government procurement trade policy may be worth watching in this regard.

Solution creation, testing and refining

Observations about bilateral and multilateral trade policy negotiations by a senior Singaporean trade official are enlightening. The official I interviewed concluded that:

Free [bilateral] trade negotiations are essentially a laboratory for testing new ideas. This opportunity can provide a new way to frame a typical trade policy problem or provide an opportunity to develop policy solutions that have never been tried anywhere in the world or have never been attempted by the negotiating parties. The process of engaging in a free trade negotiation often prompts countries to consider new approaches and positions. For years, a particular country may have taken a specific position in multilateral negotiations and now has an opportunity to consider arguments in a fresh manner – without all the background noise that accompanies multilateral process and without the large audience that is observing position shifts. Conducting a free trade negotiation allows a country to re-examine its national trade policy and to escape or bypass previously entrenched positions, as internal discussions can acknowledge that a particular position which made perfect sense in a multilateral forum is not now as valid or as desirable in a bilateral setting.

This Singaporean trade official observed that WTO-sponsored negotiations are more limited in their ability to create this type of environment.

Numerous examples illustrate these observations. During the Third WTO Ministerial Conference held in Seattle in 1999, the digital economy received substantial attention although nothing tangible followed within Doha. When the US and Singapore began bilateral trade negotiations in 2000, the US found that Singapore was receptive to considering electronic commerce although electronic commerce had never previously been included in a trade treaty. The Singaporean official responsible for negotiating electronic commerce reported that this chapter (USSFTA, Ch. 14) was painstaking and involved creative ground-breaking work. For example, sidestepping a WTO debate about whether a digital product is a good or service, Singapore and the US created special rules for digital products. Trade negotiators on both sides reported that their basic attitude was to explore every possible opportunity to liberalize trade via electronic commerce, as these two countries extended MFN status and national treatment to each other for all digital products. Since then, we find electronic commerce chapters in the SAFTA, AUSFTA and the Chile–US free trade agreement (CUSFTA). There are also reports that the US took the USSFTA Chapter on electronic commerce to APEC and proposed it be used as model language for APEC trade policy on electronic commerce.

Eventually, WTO-sponsored negotiations will give serious consideration to establishing trade policy on electronic commerce. By then, policy will be better informed because of lessons learned from bilateral negotiations conducted in Australia, Chile, Singapore, the US and other countries. Nations with electronic commerce trade policy can report to the WTO about their experience in administering such policy. When the WTO decides to develop a trade policy on electronic commerce, it is reasonable to assume that it will be developed in a more thoughtful manner because WTO policy in this area will be based on tangible experience of WTO members rather than concepts and speculation about what could be possible. As with any manufacturing process, efficiency and product quality are enhanced when a prototype is first developed and tested in regional markets before going global.

Sometimes a bilateral trade negotiation serves as a venue for less dramatic accomplishments, although such developments are still significant to the nation or nations involved. Australia's experience with rules of origin (ROOs) is illuminating in this regard (see discussion on ROOs in section on "Transaction cost: business" for a description of the three most common ROO types). Australia and New Zealand basically adopted a local value-added ROO system in their 1983 Closer Economic Relationship (CER) trade agreement. At Australia's next bilateral trade negotiation, with Singapore in 2001, Singaporean trade negotiators report that they actively sought to persuade Australia to adopt a change in tariff classification or transformation ROO system. Australia was not persuaded, and so SAFTA contains a value-added ROO system (see SAFTA Ch. 3). However, when preparing to confront the same proposal from the US in AUSFTA negotiations in 2003, Australia recanted its preference for a value-added approach and accepted a transformation ROO approach.[7] Subsequent reports indicate that Australia and New Zealand are now holding talks to modify their 1983 trade treaty to adopt a transformation ROO system for determining product origin (ACS Annual Report 2005), as Australian customs officials report that the transformation approach is straightforward and simple to administer. If so, here is an example of how one nation moved from resistance to acceptance in adopting what may be a more efficient system of customs administration. Bilateral trade negotiations provided parties with an opportunity to experiment with new ideas and methods. Such experience can only benefit the WTO, as Australia now has much greater understanding about the strengths and weaknesses of various ROO systems. It is reasonable to assume that this same kind of experience is built repeatedly via bilateral processes in other countries. It therefore appears that future WTO-sponsored negotiations can only be better informed, resulting in enhanced WTO trade agreements.

In sum, we find that new and creative solutions can be developed via bilateral trade negotiations, which can be tested and refined in regional settings before they are introduced globally. We also find that individual nations can gain greater insight into trade policy alternatives via movement away from long-held positions and toward new trade policies and positions – opportunities that are less likely to occur in multilateral settings.

Facilitation of domestic reform

Bilateral trade policy negotiators seek to establish a foundation for the integration of two economies and the harmonization of their economic institutions. Along the way, bilateral trade negotiations can provide national governments with the power or insight to make domestic reforms that might have been impossible or could be possible but difficult without such action forcing events.[8] An ambassador based in Singapore observed:

> Although people talk about the government as "Singapore Inc.," in fact Singapore has some vested interests that seek to protect arrangements that are not in the best interests of Singapore. These vested interests are resistive to change. Free trade agreements serve as a lever for domestic change. For example, the Singapore government knew that they had to introduce competition policy and AUSFTA and USSFTA helped the government to do this.

When US and Australian trade negotiators began their separate negotiations with Singapore, they found a country without a formal competition policy or law. An Australian trade negotiator responsible for competition policy said that Australia did not want to be seen to be telling Singapore what to do in this area, but Australia wanted a commitment that Singapore would respond to non-competitive practices in a non-discriminatory and transparent manner that provided due process. Both Australia and the US sought a commitment from Singapore to move forward on establishing a comprehensive competition law, and SAFTA Chapter 12 and USSFTA Chapter 12 were negotiated with the understanding that Singapore would quickly take such action. In April 2004, about a year after these two treaties were signed, Singapore sought public comment on draft legislation to regulate anti-competitive practices such as price fixing and other market share agreements, and dominant market players that use their strength to drive out new entrants. The law established a Competition Commission that imposes financial penalties and sanctions, conducts investigations and grants exemptions.

Strengthening its commitment to a free market is not the only domestic reform that Singapore achieved through its program of bilateral trade negotiations, as Singapore has also sought to enhance its commitment to democratic processes.

Leaders of international and foreign chambers of commerce in Singapore and Singaporean trade negotiators observed that Singapore's experience negotiating with the US assisted the Singaporean government in understanding the important role that government–business consultation plays in managing bilateral trade negotiations. Singaporean trade negotiators report that traditionally the Ministry of Trade and Industry (MTI) consulted other governmental agencies only while engaged in trade negotiations. However, the Ministry changed its attitude during USSFTA negotiations. The US has what could be the world's most extensive government–industry trade policy advisory system, including 26 sector and functional committees with a total membership of around 700.[9] More than one Singaporean trade negotiator reported that access to detailed industry knowledge and examples of specific international trade problems, often only obtained from those directly involved in a specific economic sector, is invaluable at the negotiation table. As a result, MTI began to establish formalized consultative processes with business and industry, starting in around 2002. One outgrowth of this effort was the establishment of the Singapore Business Federation in April 2003 – an umbrella body that includes the five major chambers of commerce in Singapore, plus representatives of foreign chambers of commerce based in Singapore, various industrial associations and 15,000 companies based in Singapore. It is too early to determine the success of these government–business consultative systems, but the establishment of these consultative systems demonstrates a move to enhance democratic processes.

Not all domestic reforms inspired by bilateral trade negotiations are trade liberalizing. Bilateral agreements containing provisions on intellectual property, which are said to be TRIPS plus, are more restrictive than those provided under TRIPS (Crawford and Fiorentino 2005: 6). USSFTA Chapter 16 and AUSFTA Chapter 17 on intellectual property offer examples of this. Investors in the pharmaceuticals, computer software, publishing, television, movie and music industries should be pleased with the intellectual property trade policies in USSFTA and AUSFTA, as these chapters are about property rights, not trade liberalization. For example, AUSFTA required Australia to increase its protection of copyright material from 50 to 70 years (70 years beyond the life of an author in published works and 70 years from the point of copyright for film and sound). A Senior Advisor to the Australian Prime Minister reported that this latter issue was sufficiently sensitive to include the judgment of the Prime Minister in the final decision. Australia generally accepted US demand on intellectual property, although it drew the line on weakening the Australian pharmaceutical benefits scheme.

It is apparent that special interest groups are reducing trade liberalization, but this can occur in bilateral and multilateral trade negotiations. Nevertheless, overall bilateral trade agreements appear to enhance trade liberalization and can contribute to positive domestic reform, as we can find examples where a nation's commitment to a free market system and democratic processes were strengthened.

Trade policy and process management

One Australian trade negotiator observed that an active and robust trade negotiation agenda can enhance the skill and ability of a nation's negotiation team. If WTO Doha negotiations slow down and if this is a nation's only trade negotiation, then this delay contributes to the loss of a nation's trade negotiation capacity. Bilateral trade negotiations, conducted concurrently with WTO-sponsored negotiations, maintain a nation's negotiation ability. He felt that this was especially important for developing countries. Moreover, this trade negotiator had observed fundamental differences between WTO and bilateral trade negotiations. A bilateral trade negotiation helps a nation to focus on what negotiating a trade treaty actually means. Experience gained in WTO Doha negotiations may prepare participants to negotiate at the United Nations, but WTO negotiations are less helpful in preparing participants to understand processes relevant to trade negotiations.

Bilateral trade negotiations may be one effective way to prepare a national government to make an effective contribution to WTO-sponsored negotiations. Learning to perform effectively in trade policy negotiations operates at an individual level and at an organizational level. For example, the management of governmental inter-agency relations and government–business relations is especially important for the successful outcome of bilateral trade negotiations. Trade negotiators in Australia, Singapore and the US each observed that engaging in bilateral trade negotiations requires a "whole of government approach." Successful trade negotiators must identify trade issues likely to emerge far into the future, as well as current issues, and then communicate with the relevant agency to gain information or guidance and/or to build a consensus so that a decision can be made on a particular position or issue. In a WTO-sponsored negotiation, this same information is useful, but there is less urgency to gather it because it takes much longer to conduct WTO-sponsored negotiations, while normally the process is compressed in a bilateral trade negotiation. Bilateral trade negotiations can require a high degree of inter-agency communication and coordination within a tight schedule, with a short turnaround time for gathering and analyzing information and then turning this analysis into approved policy that guides development of negotiation positions and compromises. Although substantially enhanced via bilateral processes, improvement of inter-agency relations will be beneficial for bilateral and multilateral negotiation processes.

Government–business relations is another area that a national government must consider in bilateral trade negotiations. Australia found that shifting from a multilateral to a joint bilateral–multilateral trade strategy required careful rethinking about how to manage government–business relations in a bilateral trade negotiation context. One administrator responsible for the Australian Office of Trade Negotiation within the Department of Foreign Affairs and Trade (DFAT) considered the government's experience in seeking external consultation since the establishment of the WTO and concluded that DFAT had engaged in more consultation leading up to the AUSFTA negotiations than in the prior ten-year period. Experience conducting government–business consultation in bilateral trade negotiations should readily transfer to WTO-sponsored negotiations.

Operating a two-track bilateral–multilateral trade strategy offers a national government benefits in enhancing the skills and ability of a nation's negotiation team and in focusing inter-agency relations and government–business relations on trade policy. However, this strategy is not cost-free. A Counselor to the Delegation of the European Commission to Australia and New Zealand asked, "Where was Australia during the WTO Fifth Ministerial Conference in Cancun?" He claimed that the Cairns Group[10] fell asleep when Australia was engaged with the US in negotiating a free trade agreement. He observed that Australia's negotiation resources were diverted and as a result, some Cairns members departed and joined the G-20 in Cancun. Clearly, it can take some time for a nation to move effectively from a multilateral to a bilateral–multilateral trade policy strategy. Errors may be made along the way, but these also represent opportunities for learning. In the final analysis, nations that do not properly resource the administrative units responsible for trade negotiations will have difficulty mounting a two-track bilateral–multilateral strategy. In the case of Australia's management of US bilateral and WTO multilateral negotiations in 2003, the Europeans may dislike the emergence of a new voice for developing countries via the G-20, but not everyone perceives this as undesirable.

In sum, WTO members that divert resources from WTO meetings are not stopping other WTO members from focusing on WTO processes and reaching consensus on trade policy decisions. If anything, the absence of these members could decrease multilateral complexity. This study concludes that bilateral trade negotiation process enhances a government's understanding of both trade policy and negotiation process, and increases its capacity to prepare for multilateral negotiations via internal and external trade policy consultation systems that operate more efficiently and effectively.

Discussion

Damage done to the global economy by a multitude of bilateral trade agreements is not as great as has been claimed. Respected economists allude to the 1930s during US Senate testimony on bilateral trade agreements (Bhagwati 2003), while opposition political leaders warn the Australian government about repeating the mistakes of the 1930s (Senate Committee Report 2003). This is alarmist. Bilateral and regional trade agreements make up nearly 40 percent of total global trade (World Bank 2005: 27). What is the tipping point for world chaos? Will it be at 50 percent, 75 percent? This chapter argues that it will not happen, as there are too many differences between the present and the 1930s to make such comparisons. These scholars should conduct research and analysis and then build arguments to identify the tipping point or they should stop scaring the public with such unsubstantiated statements.

Any process that provides substantial benefits will come with some costs. This is to be expected. Multilateral solutions are preferred, but it must be recognized that some multilateral solutions are of low quality. A positive list for trade in services is a good example of a low-quality trade policy solution derived via multilateral processes. How are WTO member nations going to learn about higher quality solutions if they never have an opportunity to learn? Do we expect that WTO members will learn about negative lists from presentations made at multilateral trade talks? Learning is best achieved when we gain direct and tangible experience. For example, the WTO should encourage its members to learn about negative lists for trade in services. Once a sufficient number of members are familiar with the development and administration of negative lists the WTO may then be able to sponsor a multilateral solution – perhaps 20 or 30 years from now.

Another area where the WTO can provide guidance is in identifying the degree of trade discrimination. Trade creation and trade diversion are analytically sound concepts, but after years of research the application of these two concepts have not been able to provide empirically significant data (WTO Consultative Board 2004; Crawford and Fiorentino 2005). Trade distortion is a useful concept, but the focus should be on degree of discrimination, with a distinction made between the much more damaging "trade-loss" and the far less significant "no-trade-gain." If empirical tools can be developed for these analytical concepts then the WTO could develop guidance about the degree of trade-loss and no-trade-gain discrimination that is acceptable for a specific class of goods that is being traded via a bilateral treaty. The WTO could also encourage members to carefully examine some of the "Singapore Issues." For example, the WTO could encourage all members involved in bilateral trade negotiations to review and consider adopting some of the basic principles found in the Government Procurement Agreement of 1981. Encouraging nations to adopt such trade policy through bilateral negotiations may result in these nations agreeing to something multilateral later. Change often occurs incrementally.

The WTO should also consider the role it could play in coordinating bilateral and multilateral interaction. The WTO should recognize that generally new solutions that are considered in WTO-sponsored negotiations will be of a higher quality if they have been developed and tested in bilateral settings first. The WTO should encourage members to only propose new issues or solutions after prototypes have been carefully examined in bilateral settings. Future WTO-sponsored negotiations can only be better informed, which will result in higher quality multilateral trade treaties. Changes in trade policy may occur more slowly, but the change that does occur will be of a higher quality.

The WTO could also provide guidance about the scheduling of bilateral formal rounds during WTO Ministerial meetings. WTO Ministerial meetings are an ideal setting for key bilateral players to hold discussions, but other bilateral activity should be postponed during WTO

Ministerial meetings, including formal rounds and public hearings. A "bilateral and regional pause or time-out" may take effect from the week prior to a WTO Ministerial meeting to the week after a Ministerial meeting. This is just an initial step, perhaps even a symbolic step, in managing interaction between bilateral and multilateral processes. Eventually, the WTO should sponsor a conference with every national administrator of a trade negotiation unit so that intensive coordination can be conducted between bilateral and multilateral processes. Operating two trade policy development systems comes with additional costs and complexity that can be effectively managed via planning and coordination. In this setting the WTO must conduct such coordination, as no other organization or entity can assume this role.

Initially, the WTO has been focused on the loss of resources that occurs when a nation pursues a two-track trade policy strategy. It is natural to worry about losses, but such losses should also be balanced by a recognition of benefits that are available to the WTO, because bilateral processes can deliver a range of outcomes that cannot be realized in multilateral settings. For example, it is clear that a bilateral trade policy system enhances the skills of a negotiation team, as they actually have an opportunity to conclude agreements involving trade in goods and services – in some nations negotiators have repeatedly had such experiences. Generally, the WTO has not been able to provide this type of experience to trade negotiators since the Uruguay round concluded. We also find that the short-term and intense nature of bilateral trade negotiations, relative to WTO-sponsored negotiations, contributes to enhanced inter-agency coordination and enhanced governmental–business relations. Strengthening the negotiation team, strengthening relations between the team and relevant governmental agencies, and strengthening relations between the team and the business community can only benefit both bilateral and multilateral negotiations.

Bilateral trade negotiations clearly provide national governments with a source of power that they can use to bring about domestic reform. Singapore's decision to enhance government–business communication and to formalize competition policy is an example of such domestic reform. Australia's decision to liberalize government procurement policies also demonstrates how bilateral trade policy can be used to bring about domestic reform. Organizations such as the United Nations, the World Bank, the International Monetary Fund and the OECD are concerned about political, economic and social governance. Here are tools that can help governments effectively implement domestic change. This is an area that requires greater investigation.

The fields of economics, international relations, negotiation and political science have examined the multilateral trade policy development system via GATT and the WTO for many years. Such knowledge is critical to our understanding of the international trading system, but how much do we really know about this new and emerging trade policy development system that reduces barriers to trade on a reciprocal and preferential basis?

Although not exclusively bilateral, the most outstanding structural feature is the bilateral nature of a large majority of the trade agreements that are signed. As with any emerging system, the first step is to describe its fundamental nature. Structural analysis, process analysis and outcome analysis will be most effective in this regard. But this is just the first step, as the real purpose in describing this emerging bilateral trade policy system is to evaluate the interaction between bilateral and multilateral processes. This is where the critical work lies. These two trade policy development systems will continue to exist for the foreseeable future. It will be useful to understand how these two systems naturally interact so that we may be able to design each system and the interaction between them in order to maximize social value. If we are successful in this regard, we can expect higher quality international trade policy, greater national movement toward democratic and free market principles, and negotiation teams that effectively interact within their government and with their stakeholders. All of this is possible if we begin by carefully examining this new and emerging trade policy development system.

Conclusion

For too many years multilateralists have argued that bilateral trade negotiations are a "stumbling block" to the development of a WTO-sponsored trade agreement, political leaders have argued that bilateral trade negotiations are a "building block" toward a WTO-sponsored trade agreement, and the WTO has essentially argued that bilateral trade negotiations are a building block and a stumbling block. I argue that multilateral trade negotiations realize tangible outcomes that are unachievable via bilateral trade negotiations. But this is not the only story, as bilateral trade negotiations serve functions that are not served via multilateral processes. Issues of trade distortion, increased transaction costs and the unraveling of the multilateral system are worries of another era. These were legitimate concerns that existed before bilateral and regional trade agreements became such a prominent part of the global economy. Now it is time to move on. The time has come to examine global trade policy development with a new lens by recognizing that a two-track system exists and that each part of this system has strengths and weaknesses and provides opportunities and challenges. The critical question is how can we design these two systems and the interaction between them to produce higher quality international trade policy than currently exists.

Acknowledgment

The author would like to thank Griffith University and the Griffith Asia Institute for supporting this research project and the book it has produced. The author is also grateful to the Institute of Southeast Asian Studies (ISEAS) for inviting him to serve as a Research Fellow during field research in Singapore in 2004.

Notes

1 Trade negotiations that are not sponsored by GATT/WTO are usually referred to as "regional trade negotiations," "preferential trade negotiations" or "free trade negotiations." This study prefers the term "bilateral trade negotiations" because "bilateral" is a dispassionate, descriptive and structural term. "Global, multilateral, regional and bilateral" is a useful structure for understanding the range of current trade policy negotiations. Most trade policy negotiations in this study are bilateral and will be referred to as such. If an agreement includes a third country (three or more countries) and all countries are in the same geographical region then the treaty is a regional agreement (e.g. Mercosur includes four South American countries). If one country is not in the same geographical region as the other countries then this is a multilateral agreement. "Global" is a better term than "multilateral" for an agreement reached through the WTO, as global distinguishes a WTO-sponsored treaty from smaller multilateral agreements. Unlike many of the terms used in the trade literature, this nomenclature has the benefit of being logically ground in the fundamental meaning of each term.
2 I am not defending the US Yarn Forwarding Rule. The United States is disingenuous to argue for free trade and then force such outrageous trade policies on other countries. The United States government needs to develop a way to counter the political power of the US yarn industry.
3 The Australia–United States Free Trade Agreement (AUSFTA) can be read in full at: <http://www.dfat.gov.au/> or <http://www.ustr.gov/>. The Singapore–United States Free Trade Agreement (USSFTA) can be read in full at: <http://www.mti.gov.sg/>or <http://www.ustr.gov/>. The Singapore–Australia Free Trade Agreement (SAFTA) can be read in full at: <http://www.mti.gov.sg/> or <http://www.dfat.gov.au/>. Case summaries of these negotiations can be found in Crump (2006) or Crump (in press).
4 In addition to the many trade negotiators that were at the table I also interviewed many high-level governmental appointees including staff in

the Australian Office of the Prime Minister, the Singaporean Office of the Deputy Prime Minister, and the Executive Office of the President of the United States (plus former and current staff in the US National Security Council). I also interviewed Ambassadors and High Commissioners, Deputy Secretaries, Private Secretaries and Under Secretaries. These government officials are political strategists and/or serve as the link between the political strategists and the trade negotiators. Most of my interviews were with staff in the Australian Department of Foreign Affairs and Trade in the Office of Trade Negotiation, staff in the Singapore Ministry of Trade and Industry in Directorate B of the Trade Division, and staff in the Office of the United States Trade Representative (USTR).

5 The "Singapore issues" generally emerged at the First WTO Ministerial Conference in Singapore in December 1996. They include trade facilitation, rules on investment, transparency in government procurement, and competition policy.

6 A negative list for trade in services allows for trade in any service unless it is specifically "excluded" in the trade treaty. A positive list for trade in services allows for trade only if a service is specifically "included" in the trade treaty. As such, a negative list is considered to be more liberal in encouraging international trade than a positive list. Building a negotiation position for a negative list requires much more governmental planning, as compared to a positive list.

7 Australia and Thailand also adopted a transformation ROO approach (this development occurred slightly before AUSFTA negotiations began) in their trade treaty of 2004.

8 This study is not the first to make this important observation. See: Echandi (2001) and Jackson (2005).

9 In addition to US interview data, see: USTR, 'Trade Policy Advisory Committee System'. Available at: <http://www.ustr.gov/ outreach/advise>.

10 The Cairns Group is a coalition of 17 agricultural exporting countries (led by Australia) from Latin America, Africa and the Asia–Pacific region that has sought to reform international agricultural trade policy since 1986.

References

ACS Annual Report (1999–2005) Canberra: Australian Customs Service, Commonwealth of Australia.

ACS Financial Statement (1999–2005) Canberra: Australian Customs Service, Commonwealth of Australia.

AUSFTA: Australia–United States free trade agreement 2004. Available at: <http://www.dfat.gov.au/> or see: <http://www.ustr.gov/>.

Bhagwati, Jagdish (1991) *The World Trading System at Risk*, Princeton, NJ: Princeton University Press.

Bhagwati, Jagdish (2003) 'Testimony on US–Chile and US–Singapore free trade agreements before US House of Representatives', Committee on Financial Services, Subcommittee on Domestic and International Monetary Policy, Trade and Technology, 1 April.

Bhagwati, Jagdish and Panagariya, Arvind (1996a) 'Preferential trading areas and multilateralism: Strangers, friends or foes?' in J. Bhagwati and A. Panagariya (eds) *The Economics of Preferential Trade Agreements*, Washington, DC: American Enterprise Institute Press.

Bhagwati, Jagdish and Panagariya, Arvind (1996b) 'The theory of preferential trade agreements: Historical evolution and current trends', *American Economic Review* (May), 86: 82–7.

Crawford, Jo-Ann and Fiorentino, Roberto V. (2005) 'The changing landscape of regional trade agreements: WTO Discussion Paper No 8', Geneva: WTO Publications.

Crump, Larry (2006) 'Global trade policy development in a two-track system', *Journal of International Economic Law*, 9 (2): 487–510.

Crump, Larry (in press) 'Concurrently linked negotiations and negotiation theory: an examination of bilateral trade negotiations in Australia, Singapore and the United States', *International Negotiation*.

Crump, Larry and Zartman, I. William (2003) 'Multilateral negotiation and the management of complexity', *International Negotiation*, 8 (1): 1–5.

Dent, Christopher M. (2003) 'Networking the region? The emergence and impact of Asia–Pacific bilateral free trade agreement projects', *The Pacific Review*, 16 (1): 1–28.

Desker, Barry (2004) 'In defence of FTAs: From purity to pragmatism in East Asia', *The Pacific Review*, 17 (1): 3–26.

Devlin, Robert and Estevadeordal, Astoni (2004) 'Trade and cooperation: A regional public good approach', in A. Estevadeordal, B. Frantz, and T.R. Nguyen (eds) *Regional Public Goods: From Theory to Practice*, Washington, DC: Inter-American Development Bank.

Echandi, Roberto (2001) 'Regional trade integration in the Americas during the 1990s: reflection on some trends and their implications for the multilateral trade system', *Journal of International Economic Law*, 4 (2): 367–410.

Garnaut, Ross (2002) 'An Australian–United States free trade agreement', *Australian Journal of International Affairs*, 56 (1): 123–41.

Jackson, John H. (2005) 'Part I: The state of international economic law', *Journal of International Economic Law*, 8 (1): 3–15.

LeClair, Mark S. (1997) *Regional Integration and Global Free Trade: Addressing the Fundamental Conflict*, Aldershot UK: Avebury-Ashgate Publishing.

Ng, Kim Neo (2004) 'Textiles and apparel', in T. Koh and C.L. Lin (eds) *The United States–Singapore Free Trade Agreement: Highlights and Insights*, Singapore: Institute of Policy Studies and World Scientific Publishing Co.

Panagariya, Arvind (1999) *Regionalism in Trade Policy: Essays on Preferential Trading*, Singapore: World Scientific Publishing Co.

Rossman, Ithnain (2004) 'The goods package', in T. Koh and C.L. Lin (eds) *The United States–Singapore Free Trade Agreement: Highlights and Insights*, Singapore: Institute of Policy Studies and World Scientific Publishing Co.

SAFTA: Singapore–Australia free trade agreement (2003). Available at: <http://www.mti.gov.sg/> or: <http://www.dfat.gov.au/>.

Sampson, Gary P. (2003) 'Introduction', in G.P. Sampson and S. Woolcock (eds) *Regionalism, Multilateralism, and Economic Integration: The Recent Experience,* Tokyo: The United Nations University Press.

Sampson, Gary P. and Woolcock, Stephen (2003) *Regionalism, Multilateralism, and Economic Integration: The Recent Experience,* Tokyo: The United Nations University Press.

Schiff, Maurice, and Winters, L. Alan (2003) *Regional Integration and Development,* Washington, DC: The International Bank for Reconstruction and Development.

Senate Committee Report (2003) *Australia's Foreign Affairs and Trade Policy: Advancing the National Interest,* Canberra: Senate Printing Unit, Commonwealth of Australia.

Snape, Richard (1996) 'Trade discrimination – yesterday's problem?', *Economic Record,* 72 (219): 381–96.

TAFTA: Thailand–Australia free trade agreement (2004). Available at: <http://www.thaigov.go.th/> or: <http://www.dfat.gov.au/>.

Tongzon, Jose (2003) 'US–Singapore FTA: Economic implications for Singapore and the ASEAN region', in C.K. Wah and T.M. Than (eds) *US–Singapore FTA: Implications and Prospects,* Singapore: Institute of Southeast Asian Studies.

Trade Policy Advisory Committee System (2006) Washington, DC: USTR. Available at: <www.ustr.gov/outreach/advise/>.

USSFTA: United States–Singapore free trade agreement (2003). Available at: <http://www.ustr.gov/> or see: http://www.mti.gov.sg/>.

USTR Trade Policy Agenda of the President of the United States (2004) Washington, DC: Office of the United States Trade Representative, Executive Office of the President.

Viner, Joseph (1950) *The Customs Union Issue,* New York: The Carnegie Endowment for International Peace.

Woolcock, Stephen (2003) 'Conclusions', in G.P. Sampson and S. Woolcock (eds) *Regionalism, Multilateralism, and Economic Integration: The Recent Experience,* Tokyo: The United Nations University Press.

World Bank (2005) *Global Economic Prospects: Trade, Regionalism and Development,* Washington, DC: The International Bank for Reconstruction and Development.

WTO Consultative Board (2004) *The Future of the WTO: Addressing Institutional Challenges in the New Millennium,* Geneva: World Trade Organization.

WTO: World Trade Organization (2006). Available at: <www.wto.org/>.

Zartman, I. William (2003) 'Conclusion: Managing complexity', *International Negotiation,* 8 (1): 179–86.

Index